# STRENGTH *for* SERVICE

# STRENGTH *for* SERVICE

## TO GOD AND COMMUNITY

### DAILY DEVOTIONAL MESSAGES *for* THOSE IN THE SERVICE OF OTHERS

Eight
Eleven
Press

Southlake, Texas
www.811press.com

*Senior Editor:* J. Richard Peck

*Contributing Editors:* Larry W. Coppock, Martha L. Davis, Gilbert C. Hanke, Nancy Grissom Self, Greg Arnold

First Edition 2013

10 9 8 7 6 5 4 3 2 1

Printed in the United States of America

Published by Eight Eleven Press—www.811Press.com

Design and layout by LandMarc Design—www.landmarcdesign.com

ISBN-13 978-0-615-74062-1

Library of Congress Catalog Card Number: 2013931544

Scripture quotations are from the New Revised Stand Version Bible, copyright 1989, Division of Christian Education of the National Council of Churches of Christ in the United States. Used by permission. All rights reserved.

For additional information, ordering, volume and bulk sales, and to make a donation, visit www.strengthforservice.org

The genesis for this book is the 1942 publication of *Strength for Service to God and Country*, a book of daily devotions written by 365 leaders of several denominations. The book was especially written for military troops disembarking for previously unknown areas such as Anzio, Dunkirk, Bastogne, and Corregidor.

My grandfather, Eugene Hunsberger, was a sailor who carried the pocket-size book throughout World War II and the Korean War. He treasured the book so much that he had it on his bedside 60 years later.

As an Eagle Scout project, I led an effort to republish the book. In 2000, I worked with my Boy Scout troop to scan copy and I added devotions from contemporary religious leaders. With the support of the General Commission on United Methodist Men, this modest beginning resulted in giving free copies of the updated book to 500,000 members of the armed services.

The next chapter in this historic effort began after groups presented the book to community-service employees. While these fire fighters, police officers, volunteers, and other first responders were grateful, the devotions were clearly addressed to the military.

Some asked for a book that would address their situations and needs.

Whether you pull victims from fires, resuscitate heart attack victims, or patrol dangerous streets, this book is written for you. It is a small token of our appreciation for your service in spite of inadequate pay, dangerous working conditions, and too-frequent criticisms.

Thank you for your service and I pray that just as my grandfather cherished his copy of *Strength for Service to God and Country*, you will cherish this copy of *Strength for Service to God and Community*.

—*Evan Hunsberger*

# NEW BEGINNINGS

*Surely goodness and mercy shall follow me all the days of my life, and I shall dwell in the house of the Lord my whole life long.* —PSALM 23:6

If you and a friend walk out into a field, each with a rifle, and one of you said, "I bet I'm a better shot than you. Let's start shooting and see who can hit something." Of course, that would be ridiculous, but don't we often approach life exactly like that?

Now, if you said to your friend, "I think I'm a better shot than you." Then, put up a target with a bulls-eye on a tree 15 to 20 yards away, then you both will soon have no doubt who is the better shot. Why?—because, you now have the means to measure results.

When was the last time you sat down in the quiet and asked God what He wants for your life? What if you handed Him "the steering wheel"? What would happen? What could happen?

As you stand at the brink of a new year, what do you think God would want to happen in your life this year? What would you need to do to cooperate with Him? What might need to change? Who would help you achieve it? Who might keep you from it?

Take a few minutes now to write out some reasonable goals you have for the coming year. Writing things down helps make them real and not just conceptual.

This could be the best year of your life. Your choices will be a major part of determining that reality.

Write down your goals, hand them over to God, and look to Him this year like never before.

ALMIGHTY GOD, *I want to give You this year. I don't know what's ahead, but You do. So guide me. Lead me. I surrender my goals to You, as You help me through each day.*

# PLUGGING INTO THE POWER SOURCE

*For this I toil and struggle with all the energy that he powerfully inspires within me.* —COLOSSIANS 1:29

Regardless of anyone's religious beliefs, even a brief study of the life of the Apostle Paul reveals a dedicated and tireless servant.

While on the way to persecute Christians, the Lord Jesus Christ manifested Himself to Paul on the road to Damascus. That event forever changed the course of Paul's life. It seemed to also give Paul a supernatural strength and drive that pushed and propelled him through beatings, imprisonment, and disaster after disaster. But, as a human, we know Paul had many frustrations and days where he wanted to give up. But thank God, he didn't. He knew many people were depending on him to keep serving the Lord and the Church.

As a servant yourself, like Paul, you have amazing days where you can take on any challenge your job brings your way, but also days of struggle and disillusionment. You get tired and weary, therefore encouragement and inspiration are necessities for survival. And, like Paul, you have countless people depending on you to soldier on.

In today's verse, Paul revealed the secret for his passion: he labors not with his own energy, but with God's. Paul confessed his source of power was not his own, but literally the power of God—the same power that Jesus relied on to endure the cross for humankind.

The next time you have a rough day, a day that tempts you to quit, remember that the power available to Paul is also available to you. God's strength and energy are just a prayer away. Call on Him and He will answer. Let God's power work in and through you!

MIGHTY GOD, *help me on the days that I feel I can take on the world to realize that is Your mercy and grace, while on the days I am ready to quit, grant me Your power and strength to carry on and serve, just as You would.*

# A HERO'S HOMECOMING

*Death has been swallowed up in victory. Where, O death, is your victory? Where, O death, is your sting? The sting of death is sin, and the power of sin is the law. But thanks be to God, who gives us the victory through our Lord Jesus Christ. Therefore, my beloved, be steadfast, immovable, always excelling in the work of the Lord, because you know that in the Lord your labour is not in vain.*
—1 CORINTHIANS 15:54B-58

Just four months into the war in Iraq, a Humvee was leading a convoy of soldiers between Ar Ramadi and Fallujah when an improvised explosive device exploded as the vehicle rolled over it.

As the blast blew through the armor, Captain Josh Byers, 29, called out, "Sergeant, we've hit an IED. Keep moving forward!" The sergeant hit the gas, the vehicle rolled on, but soon came to a stop from the damage. Investigators said by not stopping at the moment of the blast, at least two lives were saved. Ironically, as the smoke cleared, the other soldiers realized Captain Byers was dead.

No one is certain how he was able to calmly give the order to "keep moving forward," when he was mortally wounded. He was known by all who worked with him to be a strong man of God who was very open about his faith in Jesus Christ. General Charles ("Hondo") Campbell said of Captain Byers, "As a soldier and a leader, Josh was others-focused, a servant-leader, and a Christian soldier."

Captain Byers' life was marked and changed by Christ, so death had no victory. The testimony of his life will forever be his legacy and far outlive him.

What about you? What legacy are you forming for your death by the life you're living today? The good news is if you're reading this, you're still breathing, so you have time to change. Keep moving forward. Stand firm in Christ.

CARING PHYSICIAN, *thank You for the breath in my lungs and another day to serve You. Help me to truly live and may my life save others by my service, just like Captain Byers. Give me the strength, regardless of what I face, to keep moving forward.*

# WANTED: WARRIOR—EXPERIENCE A MUST

*Benaiah son of Jehoiada was a valiant man of Kabzeel, a doer of great deeds; he struck down two sons of Ariel of Moab. He also went down and killed a lion in a pit on a day when snow had fallen. And he killed an Egyptian, a man of great stature, five cubits tall. The Egyptian had in his hand a spear like a weaver's beam; but Benaiah went against him with a staff, snatched the spear out of the Egyptian's hand, and killed him with his own spear.* —1 CHRONICLES 11:22-23

Later in this chapter, we read where King David made Benaiah the captain of his guard, so these Scripture passages are like Benaiah's resume´ for a mighty warrior and soldier.

When Benaiah struck down the two sons of Ariel, killed a lion down in a pit on a snowy day, and killed a huge Egyptian with a club and the man's own spear, do you think he was just trying to build his resume´ for King David? Of course not.

So many people, events, and circumstances have shaped our lives. All things can be used for the preparation and molding of our lives—good and bad. Your place of service today, like Benaiah, is a result of hundreds of little moments and a handful of major events to make you who you are and get you where you are.

Think through the people who shaped you into who you are today. Likely, for most of them, you are grateful for how they poured into you, but maybe there would be a few that rubbed against you like sandpaper and knocked off a few of your own rough edges. Both are necessary.

Lastly, think through who has been placed in your life for you to pour into and mentor. Whose resume´ are you helping to build right now? It is vital as we serve that we are also supporting those coming up behind us, to teach them the value and blessing of service as well. Be thankful for those who shaped you, but stay mindful of those you are shaping.

GREAT SHEPHERD, *thank You for the way You have led me throughout my life, for leading me now, and where You may take me in the future. Thank You for those who poured into me. Bless them. Make me mindful of those You want me to invest in as well. May I follow You, as I lead them.*

# IMPOSSIBLE POSSIBILITIES

*Jesus looked at them and said, 'For mortals it is impossible, but not for God; for God all things are possible.' —MARK 10:27*

Andy Perkins was a salesman for a printing company in Texas. He attended church and read his Bible, but had never been involved in any on-going ministry or service. Andy was invited on a mission trip to Liberia. He decided to go and that single week changed his life forever.

Andy wasn't wealthy or privy to any special abilities, but his heart was broken over the things that break the heart of God. Starving and disease-ravaged children, orphaned and abandoned by a horrible Civil War, motivated Andy to try to bring change.

He returned home, left his job, formed a non-profit company, began to raise money, and poured his time, energy, heart, and soul into Liberia. The result? In just a few short years,

he began running a program that feeds over 500 children a day and a medical clinic is under construction in a rural area where most babies never see their first birthday. He also employs two local men to oversee the day-to-day activity of the programs.

Do you think Andy believes anyone who tells him that one man can't make a difference? No, he would just laugh and say that God can do anything with one willing heart.

Do you sometimes feel your efforts are futile? It is easy to feel that way, looking at the needs of the world. Know and be encouraged that God can use you—even in the little things—to make a huge difference in the lives of those you serve. You may never know, on this side of Heaven, what a difference you have made.

MY KING, *remind me when I feel insignificant or small that You are big enough to do anything. Would You do mighty things with my life by Your power? Let me see people the way You see them and give me the strength to make a true difference.*

# BEYOND ALL OTHER

*We know love by this, that he laid down his life for us—and we ought to lay down our lives for one another.* —I JOHN 3:16

Asbury Park, N.J., firefighter Jason Fazio, was part of a team dispatched to a fire. The day happened to be his birthday.

As Jason was conducting a search and rescue for potentially trapped residents, he was overcome with a flashover that completely covered him with flames. He was forced to jump from a second story window and sustained fractured ribs, a fractured hip, and third degree burns over fifty percent of his body.

He spent months in critical condition, then more time in extensive physical therapy. At his first public appearance after being released from the hospital, Fazio was asked to speak.

Dressed in his uniform and wearing an American flag bandana and gloves from his injuries, he shared, "Firefighting takes dedication. Uptown, downtown, city, suburb, volunteer, or career, if you ain't got pride, courage, don't even think of getting on that truck. It's a brotherhood beyond all other."

This is one of the reasons that few answer the call to this level of service. What motivates anyone to walk into certain danger for total strangers? Oftentimes for people who would not return the favor to them if the tables were turned. Service is a mindset. It's a lifestyle. It's a calling.

Someone once said, "If your job was easy, anyone could do it." There is something to be said for doing a job that few would consider—and potentially laying down your life—day after day.

MY PROTECTOR, *my life is in Your hands. You have appointed the day I was born and the day I will die. I trust You with each day in between. Protect me, carry me, keep me safe in You. Help me to be motivated by Your love for mankind, as I offer myself to You.*

# 47 SECONDS

*Do not lie in wait like an outlaw against the home of the righteous; do no violence to the place where the righteous live; for though they fall seven times, they will rise again; but the wicked are overthrown by calamity.*
—PROVERBS 24:15-16

Deputy Jennifer Fulford-Salvano of the Orange County, Fla., Sheriff's office responded as backup on a call regarding intruders at a home in a neighborhood known for heavy crime.

An 8-year-old boy had made the 9-1-1 call. She and another deputy arrived to find two officers already in the front yard of the home.

The officers soon realized that three children were in a vehicle in an open garage. Deputy Fulford-Salvano crept in, spotting the children, just as two gunmen came out of the house and began shooting at her. She exchanged fire, mortally wounding both men.

All three children were unharmed.

The deputy had been shot ten times—seven in her body and three in her vest. None of the bullet wounds were life-threatening or caused permanent damage. She returned to duty 38 days later after receiving a number of honors for her bravery, including the U.S. Medal of Valor.

All of Deputy Fulford-Salvano's training came into play in just 47 seconds of gunfire. Her senses worked together in both offensive and defensive tactics to do what she was meant to do. Her proper use of that training saved the lives of the innocent that day. That is exactly why "the righteous rose and the wicked stumbled."

In your own service, you also know your training is crucial. Stay current on procedures. Keep practicing what you've practiced a thousand times. Keep your soul righteous and ready.

You never know when you'll need everything you've learned in a single moment in time.

STRONG TOWER, *I run to You where I am safe and secure. When I must walk in the valley of the shadow of death, help me to not fear, but to have faith that You are with me. Keep me ever-righteous and ever-ready, sharp and focused on what You call me to do.*

# FROM FAILURE TO FAITHFUL

*We love because he first loved us.* —1 John 4:19

As humans, we can be steady and solid in our behavior at times—while in others be erratic and unpredictable. Our emotions and moods can get the best of us—sometimes at the exact moment we don't want them to.

Simon Peter was a great example of this paradox of humanity. In Matthew 14, we see Peter walking on the water with Jesus, but then sinking.

In Matthew 16, he actually pulls Jesus aside to rebuke Him, but then quickly gets rebuked himself.

In Matthew 17, Peter asks Jesus if they can stay on the mountain and build some tabernacles.

In John 18, we see Peter cutting off a man's ear to defend Jesus and Jesus having to heal the man.

In Matthew 26, we see Peter denying Jesus three times.

Yet, this same man, Peter, is told by Jesus in Matthew 16 that he is "the rock" on which He will build His Church. In Mark 8, Peter confesses that Jesus is the Christ. And, finally, in Acts 2, we see Peter preaching and leading great numbers to faith in Christ.

How could Jesus look on this faithless, temperamental, and unpredictable fisherman and see a man of faith, who would stand against Hell to defend the Church, and go against tradition to take the Gospel everywhere?

God sees you with those same eyes. He sees every gift, talent, skill, and quality that leads you to serve others today. Always know that God views you with eyes of love, grace, and mercy. He believes in you. Put your belief in Him.

CREATOR, *thank You for my life and the opportunity to give back, every day. Thank You that You value me and the gifts You have given me. May I value You, my life, and the lives of my fellow man today and always.*

# LEGACY OF LOVE

*What good is it, my brothers and sisters, if you say you have faith but do not have works? Can faith save you? If a brother or sister is naked and lacks daily food, and one of you said to them, 'Go in peace; keep warm and eat your fill', and yet you do not supply their bodily needs, what is the good of that? So faith by itself, if it has no works, is dead. —JAMES 2:14-17*

---

*This country will not be a good place for any of us to live in unless we make it a good place for all of us to live in.*
— THEODORE ROOSEVELT, U.S. PRESIDENT (1858-1919)

*Provision for others is the fundamental responsibility of human life.*
— WOODROW WILSON, 28TH U.S. PRESIDENT (1856-1924)

*I am only one, but still, I am one. I cannot do everything, but I can do something. And, because I cannot do everything, I will not refuse to do what I can.*
— EDWARD EVERETT HALE, AMERICAN CLERGYMAN AND WRITER (1822-1909)

*We may have all come on different ships, but we're in the same boat now.*
— MARTIN LUTHER KING JR., AMERICAN CIVIL RIGHTS LEADER (1929-1968)

*This country will not be a good place for any of us to live in unless we make it a good place for all of us to live in.*
— THEODORE ROOSEVELT, U.S. PRESIDENT (1858-1919)

---

Great men tend to *say* great things, but also great men tend to *do* great things. Each of the men quoted above took their place in history to do great things. Greatness is truly born, not out of words, but from actions. Hurting, hungry, or hostaged people don't want eloquent words spoken about them, but engaged action on their behalf.

Your service to humankind is a thread in a beautiful and longstanding tapestry woven throughout history. You serve today in and among a legacy of greatness, as others serve beside the greatness in you.

GREAT GOD, *all good things come from You. The good in me, and the service I live out, is from You and through You. Help me to always take action on behalf of the hurting, while speaking my heart to the hopeless.*

# OUT OF THE SHADOWS

*I have come as light into the world, so that everyone who believes in me should not remain in the darkness.* —JOHN 12:46

The village near Nairobi where Evans Wadongo grew up had no electricity. He had to do his school work by the light from a kerosene lantern. He and his schoolmates suffered from poor grades compared to classmates who had electricity. Evans also saw the health hazards from the fumes and smoke of the kerosene as his own eyesight was weakened from years of strain. Many of his friends dropped out of school, only to continue in poverty. The cost of kerosene for lighting and cooking also cut severely into the village families' money for food.

While attending a university in Kenya, Wodango began to experiment with solar-powered LED lighting. He knew that a lantern powered and charged by the sun's rays would change the life of his village. With the support of family, friends, and a non-profit agency, his prototype was completed and named MwangaBora, which is Swahili for "good light." He named his endeavor, "Use Solar, Save Lives."

Wadongo buys scrap pieces of solar panels in bulk and, with the help of volunteers, hammers out the metal needed for their MwangaBoras. They have distributed over 10,000 lanterns. "I want to reach out to as many rural communities as possible. The impact is saving lives," Wadongo shared.

Children can study. Villagers can buy food with the money saved by not buying kerosene, thereby reducing poverty and hunger. One villager said, "I am so grateful for the lights. My children have light to read and no more sickness brought on by smoke."

Once again, we see the power of one person literally changing the world.

LIGHT OF THE WORLD, *help me today to take my own light into the darkness to shine. Help me to always look for ways that I can offer my heart and mind to be a world-changer. Help me to watch for and take advantage of any opportunity to be Your light.*

# TESTIMONY TO THE HUMAN SPIRIT

*Blessed is anyone who endures temptation. Such a one has stood the test and will
receive the crown of life that the Lord has promised to those who love him.*
—*JAMES 1:12*

A devastating tornado hit Joplin, Missouri, killing at least 16 people. One of the buildings in the twister's path was the St. John's Regional Medical Center. Five patients and one visitor were killed. Hospital walls were knocked as far as ten feet out of place. Rooms were strewn with broken glass, ceiling tiles, and pieces of concrete. X-rays and medical records were sucked out and found as far as two counties away.

Emergency room physician Dr. Jim Riscoe was at home when the tornado struck. He received a text from his team saying that the emergency room was gone.

He arrived on the scene to witness the mass evacuation of 180 patients.

"It looked like a nuclear disaster. Cars had been thrown like playing cards. Power lines were sparking," Riscoe said. The staff set up a triage center in the parking lot among crushed cars and a smashed helicopter.

Dr. Riscoe praised the St. John staff, "They're the kind of people that you just can't knock down. I had staff show up that were hurt, but they worked all night long. It's a testimony to the human spirit."

We can turn on the news and see the worst side of people and the evil in the world every day, but we must pay attention to the selflessness and sacrifice that so many make daily that never reach the headlines.

ALMIGHTY GOD, *although natural disasters are difficult for us to understand, we often see the best in people during those tragic times. Thank You for the strength we gain from seeing the bravery and sacrifice of others. Help me in those moments of my life to rise to the occasion and be an inspiration to others.*

# SECRET SACRIFICE

*No one has greater love than this, to lay down one's life for one's friends.*
—JOHN 15:13

Tim McCarthy had the day off from his job as a Secret Service agent for President Ronald Reagan. A request came through for an additional agent to help on a detail. McCarthy and another agent flipped a coin to see who would go. McCarthy lost.

The president was going across town to speak and would only be exposed for about 30 feet between the limo and the building's entrance, so the decision was made for him to not wear his usual body armor.

Following the speech, as the press gathered outside, John Hinckley Jr. had crossed into the press line with a 22 caliber semi-automatic pistol with the intention of assassinating Reagan. As the president approached the limo door, Hinckley fired six shots in just three seconds. The Secret Service immediately entered into their protocols. Agent Jerry Parr threw Reagan into the vehicle, shielding him with his own body, while McCarthy stepped into the line of fire, spreading his arms as wide as possible to shield the car door. He was hit in the abdomen. Press Secretary James Brady was struck in the head, suffering partial paralysis. Officer Thomas Delahanty's left arm had permanent nerve damage. No one was killed.

President Reagan wrote a letter to McCarthy that stated, "There will always be the special gratitude I feel for your extraordinary heroism on that one cold day in March. It is a gratitude words could never convey."

To step in front of a madman firing a gun; there is something deep inside that has to trigger that kind of greatness in us.

MY SHIELD, *I know there will be many times that You and your angels will protect me and my loved ones at times when I will see it and at times when I won't. Thank You for Your protection and care. In turn, help me to always be willing to go into action to help my fellow man, whether a president or a pauper.*

# LET'S ROLL

*It is my eager expectation and hope that I will not be put to shame in any way, but that by my speaking with all boldness, Christ will be exalted now as always in my body, whether by life or by death.* —PHILIPPIANS 1:20

Todd Beamer was your average young businessman on that September morning in the airport. The married father of three was an account manager who lived in Cranbury, N.J. He taught Sunday school with his wife at their local church for the past six years.

But Todd's life took a tragic, yet heroic turn, as he took his seat on Flight 93. As the hijacking began to unfold and word passed through the plane that a passenger had been killed and the crew forced from the cockpit, Beamer made a call from a phone on a seat back.

Todd told the operator what had happened and that they had learned that the World Trade Center and Pentagon had been attacked.

He said that some of the passengers were planning to stop the hijackers by diverting the plane from the planned target. Beamer recited The Lord's Prayer over the phone and then his last words were. "Are you guys ready? Okay, let's roll!" The plane crashed minutes later outside Shanksville, Pa., killing everyone on board.

No one knows how many lives were saved that day by a handful of ordinary people becoming extraordinary heroes in the face of evil. And they gave their lives to save others.

Scottish writer Sir Walter Scott once said, "Real valor consists not in being insensible to danger; but in being prompt to confront and disarm it."

That is exactly what the passengers of Flight 93 did—confronted and disarmed danger, showing amazing valor. Todd's final words of "Let's Roll!" have been used thousands of times to motivate others to action.

HOLY GOD, *You have always been prompt to confront and disarm danger in the spiritual realm for us and you have empowered countless humans with Your strength and bravery in every scenario imaginable. Thank You that we know the end of the story and that good will triumph over evil. Help me to always be on the side of good and fight evil as I trust You.*

# THE SMALL THINGS

*Whoever is faithful in a very little is faithful also in much.* —LUKE 16:10A

Robert Weaver has been known as "The Ice Cream Man" in Talladega, Ala., for over 30 of his 83 years. Weaver began volunteering at the Alabama Institute for Deaf and Blind and soon started bringing along ice cream for the kids. The Institute estimates Weaver made 12,000 visits to the campus.

He has also done everything from teaching kids to ride tricycles to helping raise more than $200,000 for the construction of the institute's center for prayer and spiritual counseling.

The state of Alabama and the city of Talledega honored Weaver for his years of volunteer service by naming a street Robert Weaver Way. The Institute's director stated, "Robert Weaver is an icon in this city. He grew up here. He has continued to give back to this community for all of his 83 years. Robert has committed more than half of his life to these blind and deaf students. That's astounding."

When asked to respond to the accolades, Weaver said, "I have often said that I don't hit home runs, I just do little things. It is the little things that matter so much in people's lives. As I look back over my life, working with the children here has been part of my calling—it is why I was put on this earth. People think I'm a volunteer, but actually I'm the highest paid person here. I get my pay by direct deposit—direct to my heart."

Whether we have 26 years or 86 years, investing in the lives of people is the greatest exchange we can ever make.

GRACIOUS LORD, *it seems the people who focus on doing consistent small things end up making more of an impact on the world over a lifetime than those who attempt the grandiose. Guide me in the "Weaver Way" to do the little things that make so much difference and help me to stay focused on what You have called me to do.*

# PUBLIC SACRIFICE

*Satisfy us in the morning with your steadfast love, so that we may rejoice and be glad all our days.* —PSALM 90:14

Jared Lee Loughner walked into a crowd gathered at a Tuscon, Ariz., grocery store where Democratic Representative Gabrielle Giffords was holding a "Congress-on-Your-Corner" event. Loughner opened fire, hitting Gifford and 13 others. Giffords was shot in the head and suffered a serious brain injury. Two people were killed. Giffords was the first victim of an assassination attempt on a member of the U.S. House of Representatives.

Giffords endured a medically-induced coma and two operations. Within a few weeks, she was transferred to a rehabilitation facility, after being downgraded from serious condition to good. Her speech began to return. Months later, she began to stand on her own and walk a few steps. Her left side was in full function and she started being left-hand dominant. After more operations and much rehabilitation, Giffords made the decision to resign her House seat, leaving room for the possibility that she may run for public office again one day.

In her 2012 farewell speech, she said, "I don't remember much from that horrible day, but I will never forget the trust you placed in me to be your voice. Thank you for your prayers and for giving me time to recover. I will return and we will work together for this great country."

Giffords likely never suspected that her decision to serve in public office would be the reason someone would want to end her life. She valiantly fought back and even her neurosurgeon called her recovery, "near-miraculous." Ironically, she may well be remembered more for her remarkable recovery, along with the strength and bravery she displayed, than any vote she placed on Capitol Hill.

DIVINE HEALER, *we are so strong and yet, at the same time, so fragile. A microscopic virus can kill us, but a metal bullet in our body may not. You know the number of our days and the hairs on our heads. Please help me to rest in that fact that You have taken care of both life and death, so I may trust You with both.*

# JUST ANOTHER DAY

*But exhort one another every day, as long as it is called "today," so that none of you may be hardened by the deceitfulness of sin. For we have become partners of Christ, if only we hold our first confidence firm to the end.* —HEBREWS 3:13-14

Sergeant Joshua Laughery received the Silver Star for courage under fire. His platoon came under fire while going through an underground cellar complex in Afghanistan.

An insurgent stormed the soldiers, firing his AK-47, while also detonating a grenade in a suicide attack.

The platoon sergeant, the senior team leader, the section sergeant, and the medic were all wounded. Laughery, realizing all leaders were down, began an evacuation effort, while leading a team into enemy fire. The team managed to kill the remaining insurgents and evacuate the wounded.

Laughery's platoon sergeant said that it was moving to watch a young [then] corporal go from being a senior gunner to a platoon leader in an instant, executing his job flawlessly.

The chief of staff who presented Laughery with the Silver Star said, "He stepped up when we needed him, he stepped up under fire, he stepped up under chaos, during incredibly difficult times. That takes courage, that takes leadership, that takes something special inside— someone that we don't know that we have until we're actually involved in a situation like that."

Laughery stated, "Seeing my guys down motivated me and the rest of my platoon to do what we needed to do to get everyone home safe. It was a group effort to bring everyone home safely. It was just another day."

We don't know what we are made of until we are presented with the challenge to find out. The mystery is that we never know when those moments will come. Meanwhile, it is "just another day." Or is it?

MY STRENGTH, MY SHIELD, *I pray I am taking in what I need each day for the moments I will have in life to step up as Sergeant Laughery did. I pray I will be faithful to see my moment and seize the day. Prepare me today for my challenges tomorrow.*

# EVEN IN THE FACE OF EVIL

*But the Lord sits enthroned forever, he has established his throne for judgment. He judges the world with righteousness; he judges the peoples with equity.*
—PSALM 9:7-8

One of the toughest public service jobs is being a correctional officer.

Pelican Bay State Prison in California incarcerates some of the worst criminals on the planet. In an interview, a guard at Pelican Bay tells about guarding the worst-of-the-worst.

"The job is more clear-cut than at lower-security prisons. You know who you're dealing with. Every guy is a murderer or a rapist."

He tells the interviewer about the time nine inmates jumped him, punching and kicking, while he thought, "This is it." It wasn't. They were stopped and he survived.

"You become pretty cynical. The trick is keeping that inside. And that's been the challenge for a lot of us." The suicide rate for correctional officers is six times the national average.

When asked what is the worst part of his job, he answered, "Seeing one of my partners lying dead. She did end up surviving, but probably in my life that has been the most intense thing I've ever had to deal with."

"A lot of officers will tell you they're just doing it for the money. But you can make good money doing other things. People are here because they love their work. The only job satisfaction we get is knowing we're here to keep these inmates out of the community."

Regardless of the job description, there is a definite calling to public service, even if it's protecting the bad from the good—to serve more than to receive, even in the face of evil.

RIGHTEOUS JUDGE, *it is difficult to understand how all sin looks the same in Your eyes, when here on the earth, it certainly seems to have categories and levels. But You are perfection and we are not, so You see us all the same—a people Who need salvation. Thank You for Your forgiveness and grace—no matter what we do.*

# THE LAST TO LEAVE

*The eyes of the Lord are in every place, keeping watch on the evil and the good.*
—PROVERBS 15:3

When Hurricane Katrina swept through New Orleans and the levees broke, ushering the gulf waters in, the silent heroes of the Coast Guard also swept into the city.

Members of the guard made 24,000 rescues and evacuated 9,000 from hospitals and nursing homes. Helicopters and boats were quickly deployed. These units ran 24 hours a day for a week. Approximately 4,000 were pulled from the rooftops of their submerged homes. Barges were commandeered to load survivors who had been stranded on broken levees.

Coast Guard Lt. Chris Huberty, a chopper pilot on the night shift, reported, "We'd put a rescue swimmer down to determine who needed to be taken away. I'd see three women, all healthy adults, and a guy in a wheelchair who was a diabetic; I'd say he needs insulin, let's get him out of here first. The others might have to wait. As many bad stories as you hear about looting, there were plenty of people sacrificing for others. I can't tell you how many times a man would stay behind an extra day or two on the roof and let his wife and kids go first. It broke my heart. We'd go to an apartment building and you'd see someone in charge, organizing the survivors. We'd tell him, 'We can only take five,' and they'd sort out the worst cases. It happened many times that the guy in charge was the last to leave."

In any tragedy, we can find the worst of human behavior, but we can also find the best of us as well. As you serve, be inspired that you are representing our best.

GOOD SHEPHERD, *help me to believe the best about people, look for the best in people, and expect the best in people. And may people expect—and find—the best from me.*

# SLINGSHOTS & SCEPTERS

*David was thirty years old when he began to reign, and he reigned for forty years.*
—2 SAMUEL 5:4

From his successes to his failures, David was a fascinating and colorful icon of faith.

His preparation for leadership and service started with guarding his family's sheep. When a lion or a bear attacked his herd, David singlehandedly killed the predator. His strong relationship with God gave him the boldness and bravery to fight wild animals and win. This was also training for his many challenges to come.

When David learned that a Philistine was threatening his nation's army, he informed the king that God would give him the victory. As we know, David killed the giant. His life was never the same again. David not only served the Lord, but his nation, for the rest of his life.

As today's Scripture documents, David ultimately became king himself, reigning and serving for 40 years. Each of those early tests was a steppingstone to his ultimate destination.

Are there situations that make you feel like you're staring down a lion or a bear? Are there giants in your life bearing down on you right now? Be encouraged that two things are true.

First, the same God that delivered David, that gave him strength and boldness, is available to you right now.

Second, each challenge you face is preparing you for God's grand plan. Hiding or denying will only delay your blessings down the road. Face the giant today and watch him fall. You can and will overcome whatever is pressing in on you today.

GREAT SHEPHERD, *thank You that you see every giant in my life and have a plan for victory. It doesn't mean I will win every battle, but it does mean You will see me through—no matter what. Give me the strength to carry on and serve in Your name.*

# DIVING IN DEEP

*Do not neglect to do good and to share what you have, for such sacrifices are pleasing to God.* —HEBREWS 13:16

Special Agent Daniel Knapp had joined the FBI and had been assigned to the field office in Puerto Rico for the past five years. On this particular day, he was at Playa Escondida beach in Fajardo. He was approached by a group whose friend was out in the surf alone and in trouble. The weather conditions that day were considered severe by nautical authorities.

Without hesitation, Knapp jumped in and swam out. He was able to assist until the Puerto Rico Maritime Police arrived.

But in saving the swimmer, Knapp himself was overcome by the waves and drowned. He had survived over five years in the FBI, while receiving commendations, yet died serving essentially as a lifeguard.

"Special Agent Knapp exemplified each of the ideals of the FBI, as well as possessing those traits which define a genuinely wonderful person. He died a hero, saving another life. We will miss him greatly," said Joseph S. Campbell, Special Agent in charge of the FBI San Juan Field Office.

Special Agent Knapp was a recipient of the FBI Director's Award for Outstanding Criminal Investigation and the Attorney General's Award for Excellence in Law Enforcement.

There is something instilled in a person trained to serve and protect that doesn't consider job descriptions or personal schedules when a crisis arises. When someone is in trouble, a public servant responds. This cost Agent Knapp his life, while saving another. The world may never have enough Daniel Knapps, but that one struggling swimmer will always be grateful there was at least one that day on the beach in Puerto Rico.

OUR SAVIOR, *thank You that anytime I am sinking in this life, You are there to raise me up and pull me out. Thank You for the inspiration of those in service who will disregard personal safety to risk their lives for others. May I be counted among those who will jump into action in any crisis.*

# AMAZING AND AGGRESSIVE

*Therefore take up the whole armour of God, so that you may be able to withstand on that evil day, and having done everything, to stand firm.*
—*EPHESIANS 6:13*

Sergeant Kimberly Munley, a civilian police officer assigned to Fort Hood in Texas, heard the call come over her radio. Inside a soldier readiness facility, Major Nidal M. Hasan, an Army psychiatrist, had opened fire with two handguns. Hasan was evidently unhappy with his upcoming deployment. The unarmed soldiers inside the facility, who had been waiting for medical appointments, scattered or dropped to the floor. Hasan shouted "Allahu Akhbar!," which means "God is great" in Arabic. He emptied at least six magazines during the rampage.

Kimberly raced toward the scene, trained for just such a crisis. She arrived as Hasan was fleeing the building. Kimberly fired twice at Hasan. He charged at her, firing back, as Munley continued shooting. In the exchange, she was struck in both thighs and one wrist. Hasan was shot four times, none fatal.

Acting alone, he killed thirteen people and wounded at least 30 others. Army officials said credit for stopping the gunman belonged mainly to Kimberly, who was hospitalized in stable condition. Her decisive actions to stop the gunman made her a hero as word swept the nation's media. Lt. Gen. Robert Cone said, "It was an amazing and aggressive performance by this police officer."

It has been said many, many times that police work can be 99% boredom, but 1% terror. The problem is one never knows when the terror may come, which means readiness and preparation are critical. Part of that state of mind is spiritual, being at peace and focused on faith. That's a good place for any us to stay, regardless of our role in service.

RIGHTEOUS ONE, *thank You that You have created spiritual armor that I may choose to wear each day. Armor that guards my heart and mind from distractions and keeps me focused on what truly matters. May I live ready to walk in Your ways.*

# THE GREATEST HIGH IS HELPING SOMEBODY

*Do not lag in zeal, be ardent in spirit, serve the Lord.* —ROMANS 12:11

While fighting a four-alarm fire at a Brooklyn row-house, Timothy Stackpole learned that a woman was trapped inside. Without hesitation, he and two firemen ran into the flames, and the floor collapsed.

"My whole body was trapped up to my neck," Timothy said. "The fire was still roaring all around us. And I remember praying to God: just let me die bravely." Timothy and his colleagues were trapped for almost a half-hour.

Firefighter Michael Brady rode in the ambulance with Timothy, recalling his words, "He was comforting the EMTs and cheering them on: 'Thank you, brother. Thank you for helping me.' His zeal could never be squashed."

With burns over 30 percent of his body, Timothy was near death, but after 66 days, he limped out of the hospital to a hero's welcome, returning to work soon afterward.

Though he could have retired from the department, Timothy chose not to. "It was his life, his calling," said his wife. "He couldn't not do it. This is what he felt he was supposed to do in his life."

Firefighter Timothy Stackpole, then promoted to captain, was one of the hundreds of firemen who answered the call to the World Trade Center, after it was struck, and he was one of the 343 firefighters killed when the twin towers collapsed.

"The greatest high you can get in life is by helping somebody," he said in a public service announcement that was taped before his death. Ten thousand people attended Timothy Stackpole's funeral, including Mayor Rudolph Giuliani, who called him "one of the most exceptional human beings I've ever met."

Allow Timothy's story to inspire you to press on and never quit.

ALMIGHTY HEALER, *suffering—especially when it happens to amazing people—is very hard to understand. Yet out of great tragedy, so often comes incredible triumph. Out of pain comes a renewed passion. Today, may I serve with zeal and enthusiasm.*

# A CONSTANT YEARNING

*For surely, O Lord, you bless the righteous; you surround them with your favor as with a shield.* —PSALM 5:12

Lieutenant Colonel Anthony Henderson of the 1st Battalion, 6th Marine Division was in command of 1,200 Marines in southern Afghanistan. Just two months into his deployment, he was ordered to capture a Taliban stronghold known as Jugroom Fort. It was surrounded by tunnels, machine-gun bunkers, minefields, IEDs, and defended by up to 400 Taliban fighters.

Anthony's battalion eventually moved into the fort to engage directly with the enemy.

"It was the most vicious fighting I had ever seen," he reported. "Grenades and rocket fire were exchanged. The enemy was around everyone and everyone was around the enemy."

When the firefight finally subsided, the Marines retreated to nearby shelter. The next day, intelligence reports indicated that the enemy was leaving and heading toward the Pakistani border.

It became a major victory for the ISAF forces and Anthony's Marines.

"We spent the next two weeks clearing the fort and the surrounding villages where the Taliban had stocked weapons and ammunition," said Anthony. Back in the U.S., Anthony reflected, "It's humbling and fulfilling to lead Marines. I have a constant yearning to be back there and amongst them."

On the Battle for Jugroom Fort, he concluded, "Your preparations for those types of moments span your entire career. After 18 years of education and training, it's what prepared me to listen and learn."

Years of experiences and struggles can culminate into single moments in our lives when we call upon all we have to survive. The challenge is, we may never know that moment until we are upon it. Press on today. Each moment is an investment, not only into your future, but also to those whom you serve.

EVERLASTING GOD, *You waste nothing. Everything counts. Help me to remember that during the mundane days, yet call on all You have taught me when the madness breaks out.*

# IN THE STORM

*He will cover you with his pinions, and under his wings you will find refuge; his faithfulness is a shield and buckler.* —PSALM 91:4

When the Deckers built their dream home, like many families, they allowed their kids to put their initials in the freshly poured concrete, recalling, "We're never going to be leaving here." But, on this particular day their home would be forever changed.

A massive tornado passed right over their home. Mom Stephanie had been able to get herself and her two children, Dominic, 8, and Reese, 5, into the basement and covered with a comforter as it hit.

"I could see the wind. I could see the window blow out and the house burst," Stephanie recalled. She covered her children with her own body, as the house collapsed and debris fell on them. She continued, "I knew my leg was barely attached or it was severed. I didn't know which, but I knew it was bad. If I didn't get help soon, I was going to bleed out."

After the storm passed, Dominic crawled out from under his mom and ran to get help.

Stephanie was determined to keep her kids safe and her actions saved both their lives. But the cost was great. Their home was destroyed and both of her legs had to be amputated—one just below the knee and the other just above the knee.

There is no other love on Earth quite like a mom for her children. It is deep and intense, to the point of sacrifice of life—and limbs. But like the names etched in the concrete in the foundation of their home, this story represents the solid foundation of a family's love.

MIGHTY FORTRESS, *I know there are so many times when You have covered me in protection in ways I may never know. Help me today to love with that kind of relentless love, as a mother for her children.*

# THE LEAST OF THESE

*And the king will answer them, "Truly I tell you, just as you did it to one of the least of these who are members of my family, you did it to me."* —MATTHEW 25:40

When a 7.6 magnitude earthquake hit Pakistan killing over 90,000 people, 13 New York EMTs answered the call for help. They were flown deep into the high valleys of Kashmir.

Combining their street smarts and medical skills, they spent two weeks treating 1,200 people, most of them children. In many instances, the EMTs had only a pocketknife to perform delicate medical procedures. They had to overcome steep, rugged terrain to reach injured people and then deal with language barriers once they began treatment. They rarely had electricity and were continually jolted by aftershocks.

EMT Phil Suarez said they mostly traveled by foot to isolated towns.

"The lack of response there to these injured kids hit me the hardest," he said. From one devastated village they carried an orphaned 13-month-old boy, on the verge of dying from dehydration, three-and-a-half hours by foot to the nearest medical camp, giving him fluids intravenously.

EMT Ruben Flores told of a 16-year-old boy with a brain injury that they carried from the rubble using an old wooden door as a makeshift gurney, getting him onto a helicopter just in time to save him.

Many positions of service are great careers, but taking those skills to "the least of these" and serving those who could never repay can be an incredible blessing and a reminder of why you do what you do.

Giving away our money to worthwhile causes is great, but giving away our skill and talent to those who could never afford it is a powerful way to give back for the blessings that we have received.

GIVER OF ALL THINGS, *remind me daily to give back what I have been blessed with to those who need blessing so badly—whether that's around the world or across town. Teach me to look for ways to share what I have been so freely given by You.*

# I DO IT ANYWAY

*Jesus went throughout Galilee, teaching in their synagogues and proclaiming the good news of the kingdom and curing every disease and every sickness among the people.* —MATTHEW 4:23

Of all the things that God in the flesh could have done, He chose to spend His life serving humankind. He also knew that some of these same people would be calling for His execution; yet, He served anyway, and continued His healing ministry until the crucifixion.

Country singer Martina McBride has a song that was inspired by Mother Teresa's encouragements. Here's an excerpt:

*You can spend your whole life buildin'*
*Somethin' from nothin'*
*One storm can come and blow it all away*
*Build it anyway*
*You can chase a dream*
*That seems so out of reach*
*And you know it might not ever come your way*
*Dream it anyway*
*God is great, but sometimes life ain't good*
*When I pray it doesn't always turn out like I think it should*
*But I do it anyway*
*I do it anyway*

When you have a bad day, when the storm comes, when the dream dies, even when you don't think your prayers are being heard, work, build, dream, and serve. Do it anyway. Just like Jesus did.

LORD JESUS, *thank You that You are the ultimate example of service in spite of the circumstances. You kept on no matter what happened or who opposed You. You had a greater goal, a stronger mission to accomplish. Strengthen me to press on.*

# GETTING THE JOB DONE

*Happy are those who observe justice, who do righteousness at all times.*
—PSALM 106:3

One of the stories to come out of 9-11 was the plight of fighter pilot Heather "Lucky" Penney. She and her commanding officer were ordered to stop United Airlines Flight 93 from hitting its target in the nation's capital. But they didn't have any missiles or even ammunition loaded onto the planes. So Colonel Marc Sasseville decided they would use their own planes to bring it down.

"He planned to strike the plane's cockpit. I opted to go for its tail," Heather said. "I was prepared to die for my country. I didn't have time to feel fear. We had a mission and there was a sense of urgency," she said. Heather was in her jet, hand on the throttle, awaiting orders to take off.

Heather and Marc didn't know it at the time, but the plane had already crashed in a field in Pennsylvania, due to the heroism of the flight's passengers. Her mission was soon changed to escorting Air Force One, with then-President George W. Bush aboard, to Andrews Air Force Base. "I really didn't have much emotion or time to reflect that day, because I was focused on getting the job done," Heather recalled.

Heather, a single mother, also served two tours in Iraq. She now flies a C-38 as a traditional Air Guard member. "We saw so much of the best of ourselves come out that day, with strangers helping strangers and many courageous acts," she said. "We remembered something more important than ourselves and that was the community to which we belonged."

Today, whether you will risk your life or not, serve the community well to which you belong.

RIGHTEOUS ONE, *may I be so focused on accomplishing my goal and doing my job that I don't stop to fear, question, or worry. Help me to stay focused on the community at large and serve for the greater good. Help me to take action when I know the right thing to do.*

# RIGHT PLACE AT THE RIGHT TIME

*To do righteousness and justice is more acceptable to the Lord than sacrifice.* —
PROVERBS 21:3

Lucas McKinney was a new medic in the National Guard and also an employee at a Lowe's Home Improvement Store. Store employees were alerted that a customer had collapsed in the Garden Center and was lying unconscious. Immediately Lucas rushed to the man and applied his medic training.

"I checked to see if he was breathing and checked his pulse. He wasn't breathing, he had no pulse, so I went ahead and started CPR immediately," he reported. Lucas was able to revive the man and keep him calm until the paramedics arrived.

Lucas said as a medic in the National Guard, he was just doing what he was trained to do. He states, "If it would have happened back in combat, I would have done the same thing. Whether it is civilian life or military life, it is the same thing for me."

Lowe's manager Charles Morris said, "He absolutely is [a hero] to me."

"Anybody that saves somebody's life and does it as a matter-of-fact kind of thing, that is what makes a hero." Lucas responded, "I honestly don't think I am a hero. Anyone that had CPR training would have done the same thing if they were in that situation."

Be it calling or career, the training we receive that can make a difference in a life or death situation also brings a great responsibility to act. With the training, comes the expectation that it will be used whenever needed.

Our world would be a better place if the expectation to help or heal were placed onto everyone—no matter the situation.

SAVIOR, You *came into this world to save it, and once we know You and Your message of grace and mercy, we are commissioned to also share. Whether it be a medical emergency or a spiritual crisis, may I be available to You and surrender my ability to help.*

# A DAILY CHOICE

*But you, take courage! Do not let your hands be weak, for your work shall be rewarded.* —2 CHRONICLES 15:7

Paul Frontiero had been an EMT for two years and the following week he was going on his second mission trip with his church to the Dominican Republic to set up medical clinics. Around 10:30 on a Sunday night, Paul had just gotten into bed when he heard a commotion outside.

Two female friends were walking down the street when one of them shouted a silly remark at a car driving by. A passenger jumped out, shouting, and waving a knife.

The man grabbed one of the girls and held the knife to her neck. That's when Paul came running from his apartment to help. He tackled the assailant to stop him, but in the fight, Paul suffered several stab wounds to the chest with one fatal blow to his heart. He was transported to a local medical center, and he died shortly thereafter. His attacker was charged with second-degree murder.

One of the victims said through her tears, "Paul was there, protecting us. He did absolutely nothing to deserve this. There was no reason for this to happen, but if it was going to happen, Paul was going to be there trying to help," she said. "He was one of the best people I've ever known."

"If you did know Paul, you were blessed to have him in your life," added another friend.

There are senseless acts committed in our world every day. Then there are heroic acts that take place as well. Whether you ever have to risk your life as Frontiero did, you can give your life every day. That is true heroism.

DEAR LORD, *anytime I hear of someone giving up their own life for the saving of another, I am reminded of Your sacrifice on the cross for me and all mankind. You burst out of Heaven to save us and suffered mortal wounds in the process. But thank You that You rose again and live today. Thank You that I may serve You to battle the evil in this world.*

# PUT MYSELF IN THEIR SHOES

*But those who wait for the Lord shall renew their strength, they shall mount up with wings like eagles, they shall run and not be weary, they shall walk and not faint.*
—ISAIAH 40:31

The American Federation of Teachers annually recognizes "Everyday Heroes" from six different segments of the workforce. One of the winners in the Public Employee segment was Michael Morris. Morris and the other five heroes were honored at the annual AFT convention.

Here is a list of Michael's accomplishments: —Three tours in Iraq and one at Guantanamo Bay, Cuba —Volunteer medic and fire fighter —Sergeant in the Maryland National Guard —Vice president of the Baltimore County Federation of Public Employees —Correctional officer at the Baltimore County Detention Center in Towson

"The first time I ever saved a life, I knew I was going to be in public service," said Michael.

When he was 16 years old, a house across the street caught on fire. He followed his uncle, a fire captain, into the burning house and they led everyone out of the home to safety. Michael also earned a director's commendation by stopping an inmate from hanging himself. During his last tour in Iraq, he saved the life of a fellow soldier after their vehicle was hit by a roadside bomb.

On a typical day, Michael spends the morning volunteering at the firehouse, then he's off to work for the 3 p.m. to 11 p.m. shift at the detention center. At the detention center, "I always try to put myself in their shoes. Sometimes just asking how they are makes the biggest difference in the world.

"I gotta feel like I'm doing something," Michael said. "If you can make one positive change in someone's life or have one positive influence, you've done your job."

That's Job One for today—one positive change or influence in just one life.

MY STRENGTH, *I understand that drive to feel like I'm doing something good, to make positive changes in a negative world. Hold me up today as I seek to serve, so I can say. "I have done my job."*

# THEY BROUGHT ME THROUGH

*O Lord my God, I cried to you for help, and you have healed me.*
—*PSALM 30:2*

John Meyer contracted a deadly German strain of the e-coli virus and spent an entire month in the Milford Regional Intensive Care Unit in Massachusetts. He and his wife, Loreen, recalled the support offered by intensive care nurses that stayed by their side and helped save John's life.

"I think they are the unsung heroes. We wouldn't be sitting here today if it wasn't for those nurses," said Loreen. "The nurses were able to detect subtle differences in his health and react immediately. That's a savvy group of people."

John recalls their constant presence. "When I was awake, they were always talking to me," he said. Loreen continues, "They were so good at engaging him in conversations and really pushing him to get out of bed," she said. "The minute that they recognized he could put his legs over the side of the bed, they got him moving as quickly as possible. They never lost patience."

Looking back on the experience, John remembers the ICU nurses more than his own pain and suffering.

"All the really bad stuff, I just don't think about that," he stated. "What the ICU nursing staff did for me—I think about that a lot. The ICU team stands out as being exemplary. They brought me through the worst experience I've ever had. They really are the gold standard."

Someone who is passionate at what they do is a wonder to behold. The qualities that nurses exhibit on a day-to-day basis, such as patience, care, and inspiration are ones that we all should aspire to today and every day.

OVERCOMER, *there have been so many days and nights when You have watched over me when I was in "critical condition," sometimes in a condition that no one could visibly see. Thank You for caring for me and for Your patience.*

# DIFFERENT MISSION, SAME GOAL

*Do not let loyalty and faithfulness forsake you; bind them round your neck, write them on the tablet of your heart. So you will find favour and good repute in the sight of God and of people. —Proverbs 3:3-4*

Major Mark Thompson, deployed with the 11th Military Police Brigade in Iraq, spent a good deal of his time at a most unlikely place—a playground.

U.S. soldiers had previously built a children's playground right outside of the detainee facility. While serving as commander for security of the facility, Iraqi children, visiting their loved ones detained there, would come play on the seesaws and swings. The playground provided the opportunity to reach out and connect to the Iraqi children.

"Once I see kids playing, I want to play too," laughed Major Thompson, father of a 12-year old son. "I'm the biggest kid."

He, and the other soldiers under his command, often kicked soccer balls and played with the kids there. They also collected toys and school supplies for the children. "We were changing the negative stereotypes some were led to believe about Americans," reported Mark, who received the Bronze Star for his leadership in Iraq.

"There are a lot of civilians paying prices as well there," said Mark of the non-military serving abroad. "I appreciate all of the sacrifices they make. They truly support us."

After Major Thompson came back to duty in the U.S., he was yet again responsible for ensuring soldiers' safety and morale, just set against a different backdrop. "The mission is different, but the goal is the same," explained Mark. "Taking care of people."

Regardless of the responsibilities you have, be sure you engage and focus on the people around you. The end result of service is always about people and meeting their needs.

HEAVENLY AUTHOR, *draw me to the hearts of the people around me—no matter the size or the age. May I love people as You did and meet needs as You would.*

# LIVES ON THE LINE

*For God is not unjust; he will not overlook your work and the love that you showed for his sake in serving the saints, as you still do.* —Hebrews 6:10

Cook County in Illinois, which includes the city of Chicago, recognizes outstanding law enforcement officers in an annual ceremony. One particular year, two of the men honored were involved in shootings.

Chicago Police Officer Nathaniel Taylor was a narcotics officer who went to serve a search warrant at a known drug house. He was gunned down there by drug dealers.

Another police officer, Timothy Gramins, responded to a call and encountered a suspected bank robber. In the shoot-out, the assailant fired 22 rounds at Gramins. The officer ended up killing the suspect.

"You do not have time to be scared. You go out, you do the job you were trained to do," said Timothy.

"One minute you see a car and the next minute it's on fire and people are inside and you have to react. You don't even think, you just think about getting the people out of the car," said Gregory Strelczyk, a Chicago police officer.

It is difficult to understand why on one day, a good man is gone, while in another, he survives to serve and protect another day.

We must trust that two things are true: First, we are all going to die. It's only a matter of how and when. And, second, promoting good and battling evil will always be the right thing to do. These two truths together tell us that we must make every day count. No time to waste. Make a difference with this day you've been given.

CREATOR GOD, *You told us that Your rain falls on the just and the unjust, so we know life won't always be fair. Help me to make a difference in someone's life today.*

# WHAT'S IN A NAME?

*Honest balances and scales are the Lord's; all the weights in the bag are his work.
It is an abomination to kings to do evil, for the throne is established by righteousness.*
— Proverbs 16:11-12

It is common knowledge that Abraham Lincoln's nickname was "Honest Abe." But how did he get such a reputation for honesty? What major event took place to cause the public to espouse such virtue to his very name?

Early in his adult life, Lincoln ran a small country store. As he was getting ready to close up one evening, he was balancing his money from the day. He realized that he had unknowingly taken too much money from a customer. He put the amount in his pocket, locked up the store, and walked all the way to the customer's house. He knocked on the door, explained what had happened, and returned the money.

On another occasion, he realized the next morning that the afternoon before he had inaccurately weighed out some tea on the store scales for a lady customer. The woman didn't receive the amount she had actually paid for. Lincoln carefully weighed out the amount needed and delivered the difference to the lady's home.

Taken alone, none of these stories seem noteworthy; however, the sum total is indicative of a lifestyle to which Lincoln adhered.

Honesty and integrity were important to him, regardless of the amount of the discrepancy. He knew small added up to big. This is what made him one of the greatest presidents in the history of the United States and also allowed him to carry the people through one of the greatest crises in its short life.

TRUTH, *help me to remember that You don't just know truth, but that You are the embodiment of Truth. Qualities such as honesty and integrity come directly from You. May I be known for truth and righteousness in my words and actions.*

# LIFE IN REVERSE

*But this one thing I do: forgetting what lies behind and straining forward to what lies ahead, I press on towards the goal for the prize of the heavenly call of God in Christ Jesus.* —Philippians 3:13b-14

David Depallo regularly volunteers at the Salvation Army. His passion is working with at-risk youth. Depallo is a former gang member and drug addict who spent 18 years of his life in prison. Growing up in a poor household with an alcoholic, abusive mother and a father involved in the Mafia, David spent time in and out of foster care, and soon got involved in gangs, drugs and crime at an early age.

"The only out for me was the streets," he said. "I thought the way the gang was teaching me was the right way to live."

At 16, David began to sell drugs. Shortly afterwards, he began using drugs himself. "That's when the nightmare opened up," he said. He was repeatedly arrested on charges of drug abuse and burglary. "I learned the hard way over and over again," he said.

At 36, sitting in a jail cell, David thought, "What if I reversed this? What if I used my energy to help another human being?" He realized that he had had no adult mentors to help him make the right choices. David decided to become the role model he never had.

David has now been drug and crime free for many years. Along with handling a full time job, David is studying to become a drug counselor for youth. "The Salvation Army saved my life," said David. "They gave me a bed when no one else did. That's why I volunteer there. I got through it. If I could do it, anyone can do it."

And applying David's words for today—you can do it too!

REDEEMER, *stories of people's lives turning around for good never get old and give us hope in a dark world. Thank You for always being at work to offer hearts another path. Thank You that we can leave the past and head towards a bright future in You.*

# ANYTHING, EVERYTHING

*Give, and it will be given to you. A good measure, pressed down, shaken together, running over, will be put into your lap; for the measure you give will be the measure you get back.* —Luke 6:38

If you ask Rebecca McKim what she does at Graham Elementary School in Talladega, Ala., she'll likely answer you with one word: "Everything." Rebecca said she decided to volunteer where her daughters started to school.

"I was a stay-at-home mom and I got bored," she said. "I started volunteering one or two days a week and it blossomed into every day." Rebecca has now logged four years as a parent volunteer at the school. She continued, "I'm there to do whatever a teacher needs done. I'll even clean out cabinets and vacuum the floors if they need me to," she said.

Graham's principal said volunteers like Rebecca are vital to schools. "They do for us what teachers and administration often don't have time to do, because our attention needs to be focused on the students. They help school wide. We never have to worry if the jobs are being done right. They always take care of everything for us and do a great job."

Rebecca said she has organized school picture days and fundraisers, made goody bags for students, and arranged special rewards luncheons, among many other tasks.

"I love it," Rebecca said. "I don't think I would enjoy it as much if I were getting paid."

There can be a vast difference between making a dollar and making a difference. Today, may you be able, by God's grace and provision, to do both.

GIVER OF GOOD GIFTS, *when You came to Earth, You never asked anything in return for healing, teaching, or even saving the world. You simply gave. May I respond by giving back to You, as well as daily to my fellow man.*

# LAST ONES OUT

*He will give you a message by which you and your entire household will be saved.*
*—Acts 11:14*

In the final hours of the Vietnam War, 11 Marine Corps Security Guards directed the evacuation of American soldiers and other personnel from Saigon as 150,000 North Vietnamese and Viet Cong soldiers marched toward the city.

When a C130 campaign was no longer possible due to the shelling of Saigon Airport, Operation Frequent Wind was engaged. In about 20 hours, American helicopters raced back and forth between the capital city and the 7th Fleet parked in the ocean.

Throughout those last hours, the Marine Guards' orders were to allow only American personnel, allied third-country citizens, Vietnamese officials, and civilians with the proper documents into the American Embassy compound. The Marines also had to determine whether any paperwork was forged, while literally thousands of frightened people pressed against the gates.

People were offering bribes of all kinds. Mothers were throwing their babies over the gates into the arms of the guards, trying desperately to save them before the North Vietnamese soldiers converged. Anyone left outside those gates would be executed or imprisoned and the Marine Guards knew it, but both their resources and time were limited.

The 11 Guards were the last ones to be pulled out—rescued from the roof onto helicopters, just before they would be captured.

In war, there is always the necessity of taking lives to defeat an enemy, but there are also horrible instances, such as this in 1975, when a handful of brave men stood against unimaginable circumstances to save so many. May the valiant story of these men encourage you today to help those who may be perishing around you.

SAVIOR, *thank You that You desire for all people of every nation to receive You. You made provision for everyone, leaving no one behind. You give us freedom to make our choice about You, but thank You that You chose to save us.*

# SOMETHING FROM NOTHING

*When they were satisfied, he told his disciples, "Gather up the fragments left over, so that nothing may be lost." —John 6:12*

A young boy was going out to explore one day. As he looked through the family food supply, he grabbed some bread and a couple of fish. He stuck them into his pouch and ran off for adventure.

In the distance, he could hear a great crowd. As he topped a hill, there before him were thousands of people. As he worked his way through the crowd, he came upon a group of men who seemed very concerned. He heard one protest, "How can we possibly feed all these people with no food?" Another said, "It would take months of wages to pay for this much food."

The boy walked over to one of the men and said, "I'll be glad to share my food with you," as he opened up his pouch. The man announced to the leader, "This boy has five barley loaves and two small fish. He's the only one here with food."

The leader told the people to sit down as a hush fell over the crowd. He held the boy's lunch and began to pray, then told his helpers to pass the bread and fish out to the people. Just then, the boy saw the most amazing thing he had ever seen in his life. As the men began to hand out the food, five loaves became thousands. Two fish became an all-you-can-eat buffet.

The boy ate until he was stuffed. The man who performed the miracle walked over and said, "Thank you for offering your lunch today. I hope you got plenty to eat." The boy smiled and said, "Master, I was filled today with much more than bread and fish. Thank You!"

Remember—God can make something from nothing and anything out of everything.

PROVIDER, *I recognize that all I have comes from You. Because You are the Creator, You are also Provider. May I be a good steward of all You have given me and I pray You multiply my efforts to reach thousands, like the boy and his lunch.*

# HE CHOSE THEM

*Now my head is lifted up above my enemies all around me, and I will offer in his tent sacrifices with shouts of joy. —Psalm 27:6*

The United States Department of Defense posthumously awarded Navy SEAL Michael Monsoor the Medal of Honor from then-President George W. Bush.

Michael was part of a sniper overwatch security position in eastern Ramadi, Iraq, with three other SEALs and eight Iraqi soldiers while forces were conducting missions in the area. An insurgency fighter managed to throw a grenade into the overwatch position where it hit Michael in the chest before falling in front of him. He yelled, "Grenade!" and dropped on top of the device. Michael's body shielded the others from the brunt of the blast and two other SEALs were only wounded.

A 28-year-old Lieutenant, who sustained shrapnel wounds to both legs that day, said of Michael, "He never took his eye off the grenade. His only movement was down toward it. He undoubtedly saved mine and the other SEALs' lives, and we owe him."

A writer for the Chicago Tribune summarized the tribute, "The men who were with Monsoor on the day he died said they could see the options flicker across his face: save himself or save the men he had long considered brothers. He chose them."

During Michael's burial ceremony in San Diego, as his coffin was being carried, every SEAL who attended removed his gold Trident from his uniform, slapped it down, embedding it into the wooden coffin. The slaps were audible from across the cemetery; by the time the coffin arrived graveside, it looked as though it had a gold inlay from all the Tridents pinned to it. This was a fitting send-off for a warrior hero.

Our days of life write the legacy that we leave. Today—write well!

OUR SAVIOR, *anytime I hear of the sacrifice of one human for others, I am reminded of Your great sacrifice that has inspired so many to also lay down their lives when the time came. May I live for You, while always being willing to die for others.*

# THAT'S WHAT IT'S ALL ABOUT

*In my distress I called upon the Lord; to my God I cried for help. From his temple*
*he heard my voice, and my cry to him reached his ears.* —Psalm 18:6

Captain Kim Campbell was a veteran pilot in the A-10 Fighter Squadron that had already sped through a dust storm before they burst down upon enemy positions, firing each Warthog's 30mm, seven-barrel Gatling gun and anti-tank missiles, working to assist ground troops in Baghdad.

Just after Kim turned her Warthog toward home base, she heard a large explosion in the back of the aircraft. The A-10 had been struck by a surface-to-air missile. Hundreds of shrapnel holes were in the fuselage and tail. The jet immediately began pulling toward the ground. As caution lights flashed all around, she realized the hydraulic system was out.

"When you lose hydraulics, you don't have brakes and steering," she explained. Kim had to instantly switch to "manual inversion," using a system of cranks and cables, to fly the aircraft. Fortunately, the A-10 responded and climbed up and out.

"The trip back to Kuwait was one of the longest hours of my life," she said. As a seasoned pilot, Kim knew that few had ever attempted, and fewer still had survived, a manual landing of such a severely damaged Warthog; however, she executed a nearly perfect landing, employing emergency braking techniques to bring the damaged A-10 to a stop.

Among the letters she received about the flight was a thank-you note, written on a napkin and addressed to her and her fellow Warthog pilots by the ground troops in Iraq. "When you get a note from somebody saying, 'If you'd been a few minutes late, I wouldn't be here now,' that's what it's all about," she said.

It is a privilege anytime we are allowed to see the fruit of our lives. We will never know, on this side of Heaven, how many lives we have touched, but today, sow seeds for that great day.

STRONG TOWER, *there have been so many times in my life where the circumstances looked grim and I wasn't sure I would make it, but You came through every time and gave me the strength to stand. May I grow in those long hours of my own life to trust You more.*

# ALWAYS READY

*For God so loved the world that he gave his only Son, so that everyone who believes in him may not perish but may have eternal life. Indeed, God did not send the Son into the world to condemn the world, but in order that the world might be saved through him. —John 3:16-17*

The Coast Guard's motto has long been "Always Ready" from the Latin phrase "Semper Paratus."

In the movie The Guardian with Kevin Costner and Ashton Kutcher, Costner plays a seasoned veteran Coast Guard rescuer they call "Senior" and Kutcher plays the young, arrogant trainee, "Jay."

Throughout the movie, the recruits have tried to find out the Senior's "number," meaning the number of people he had rescued in his career. There were only rumors of how high his number was, because he would never tell anyone.

Near the end of the movie, Jay asks his trainer before he leaves to retire, "Senior, before you go, I gotta know one thing. What's your real number?"

Senior hesitated and then said, "22."

Jay looks surprised and disappointed, then said, "22. That's not bad. It's not 200, but ..." Senior interrupts and said, "22 is the number of people I lost, Jay. It's the only number I kept track of."

In the business of serving humankind, it is easy to focus on the failures, because there is such an understanding of the great cost to others. But take heart, regardless of the type of service you provide to the world, you are always working to be a part of the solution and not the problem. That is the role of leadership and being a leader will always be costly. Always ready!

SAVIOR, *thank You that You want all people to be saved. Thank You for allowing me the privilege of joining You in Your work. May I be faithful today to my mission.*

# SO HELP ME, GOD

*Obey your leaders and submit to them, for they are keeping watch over your souls and will give an account. Let them do this with joy and not with sighing—for that would be harmful to you.* —Hebrews 13:17

Harold "Hal" Moore, Jr. was the Lieutenant Colonel in command of the First Battalion, 7th Calvary Regiment at the Battle of la Drang in 1965 during the Vietnam War.

This was the first major battle between American troops and the North Vietnamese army and lasted about five days in a strategic effort known as Operation Silver Bayonet. Moore's book, We Were Soldiers Once . . . and Young was made into a movie entitled We Were Soldiers with Mel Gibson cast to play Lt. Colonel Moore.

Before his battalion left for Vietnam, Hal Moore told his men: "I can't promise you that I will bring you all home alive. But this I swear, before you and before Almighty God, that when we go into battle, I will be the first to set foot on the field, and I will be the last to step off, and I will leave no one behind. Dead or alive, we will all come home together. So help me, God."

Little did Hal Moore know that his men would be involved in the worst ambush of American troops in the entire Vietnam war, with most of the casualties coming in one battle that lasted over 16 hours. Lt. Colonel Moore kept his word that he made to his men and their families.

It takes a special kind of leader to call others into sacrifice and danger. It takes a special person to lead any group to sacrifice and serve humankind. Regardless of the service you are engaged in, if you have a trustworthy, honorable leader, be sure to thank him/her for their service and watchcare over you.

*LORD OF ALL, help me to lead with honor anytime I am called to do so and help me to follow with loyalty anytime I am called to do so. Help me to always be an encouragement to everyone I encounter in any role I am in.*

# $1 + 1 = 3$

*Two are better than one, because they have a good reward for their toil. For if they fall, one will lift up the other; but woe to one who is alone and falls and does not have another to help.* —Ecclesiastes 4:9-10

The Calgary Stampede has been known for many years as one of the premier rodeos in the world. One of their most exciting, action-packed events is the Heavy Horse Pull. Teams of two horses are harnessed together to pull up to five times their own body weight over a distance of 14 feet.

On one particular year, the story is told of a horse that pulled 9,000 pounds, while another pulled 8,000 pounds. Working together you would expect them to pull 17,000 pounds, right? No! When teamed together, they pulled 30,000 pounds! But how?

The principle is called synergism. The definition is the combined action of two things being greater than the sum of their efforts working alone.

So oddly enough, like saying $1 + 1 = 3$. Much more can be done in a team effort than can be accomplished solo.

Think about the people you "yoke up with" to serve. Even though you may "pull more weight" with one person than another, the synergy principle is always true with everyone with whom you work.

Two heads are better than one, four arms are better than two, and one can reach out to the other when one stumbles.

Keeping those relationships strong and growing are important to the work you are involved in. Maintain those connections just as carefully as any equipment you rely upon. The people around you will always be your most valuable resource.

ALMIGHTY GOD, *no other relationship upholds me and sustains me like Yours. You are my Strength, but thank You for all those I "yoke up with" every day to serve. Bless and keep them all as we continue to serve and work together.*

# GROWING AN ARMY

*Very truly, I tell you, the one who believes in me will also do the works that I do and, in fact, will do greater works than these, because I am going to the Father.*
—*John 14:12*

On July 2, 1865, William Booth preached at a series of meetings for the poor and destitute in London's East End. This led to the beginning of The Christian Mission and they quickly began to feed the hungry and homeless there, all the while preaching the Gospel. It is estimated, at that time, there were about 500 charitable organizations ministering in that area of London.

William Booth, his wife, and army of volunteers pressed on and by 1878, the Salvation Army was born. In his lifetime, Booth established the Salvation Army in 58 countries.

On the day of William Booth's burial, 10,000 uniformed "Salvationists" marched behind his casket. His vision and legacy lives on today as the Army serves in over 120 nations. At Christmastime in the United States, over 25,000 volunteers become "bell ringers" in front of stores to raise money, standing beside the iconic kettle with the classic red shield logo to hold people's offerings.

From the 1900 Galveston Hurricane to the tsunami of 2004 to Hurricane Katrina, the Salvation Army has been present at natural disasters around the world to help those in need.

It is safe to say that most of the 500 ministries in late 1800s London are long since disbanded, but what makes a start-up like the Salvation Army spread and grow internationally—even outliving its own leader? It must be a strong sense of belonging and commitment, inspired and encouraged by the leaders, coupled with a simple, single purpose to care for people. A century ago or today, taking care of people is a timeless need and message.

GRANTOR OF VISION, *You alone allow men and women to see things much higher and grander than anything we can see on our own. Then You grant us the power and strength to accomplish what You call us to. May our vision grow and our service increase.*

# THE FIRST VALENTINE

*If then there is any encouragement in Christ, any consolation from love, any sharing in the Spirit, any compassion and sympathy, make my joy complete: be of the same mind, having the same love, being in full accord and of one mind. Do nothing from selfish ambition or conceit, but in humility regard others as better than your-selves.* —Philippians 2:1-3

Most people don't know that Valentine's Day began with a prison ministry. In the year A.D. 320, the early church set aside February 14 to remember the heroic death of a man named Valentine, who was beheaded on a pagan altar, because he refused to renounce Jesus Christ.

According to historic tradition, Valentine was born into a wealthy Roman family and converted to Christianity as a young man, sometime around the year A.D. 240. It was an era when the church was being severely persecuted by the Roman emperor Claudius II. Thousands of Christians were imprisoned in the dark, tomb-like jails of Rome.

Wealthy Romans considered it entertainment to visit the prisons and watch as Christians were tortured and put to death. Valentine took ad-vantage of his family connections to visit the prisons too—but made it his mission to smuggle in small gifts of food to those facing martyrdom, always with a short note expressing love and encouragement.

Valentine, devout and strong-hearted, was eventually arrested and martyred in Rome about A.D. 270.

Though the roots of the traditions are largely forgotten, his ministry of love and caring is still commemorated today, centuries later.

In what ways can you put others' needs in front of your own? Is there someone you know who could use a word of encouragement today? If so, why not call that person or write him or her a note? It is easy to love those who are just like us, but true love sees others through Christ's eyes.

AUTHOR OF LOVE, *grow my capacity to love. Not just those in my family, even though I want to love them more, but also to love the unloved.*

# WALK IN MY PATH

*I will instruct you and teach you the way you should go; I will counsel you with my eye upon you.* —Psalm 32:8

Long ago, a very wealthy man lived in a spacious castle near a small village. He had vaults full of gold and silver and his estate stretched on for many miles.

One day the man came into the village and announced that he had built a giant maze on his property. The walls were very high and it stretched out over several hundred acres. He had placed all of his gold and silver in the center of the maze and any man who could get to it could have everything.

Since the village was very poor, many men said goodbye to their families and set out to find the treasure. After several weeks, a few men began to emerge from the maze. They told of some dying and others going insane from being hopelessly lost.

One day a young man stood at the entrance, contemplating his own journey, when he heard a voice behind him ask, "Are you going in alone?" Startled, the young man turned and saw an elderly gentleman behind him. "No, I am afraid of what might happen to me in there," said the young man.

The old man said, "My son, I built that maze and I have the map. I know every corner and turn. You can follow me and I will lead you straight to the treasure. Now stay close and walk in my path."

The young man would have the benefit of walking through the maze with its creator.

We have the benefit every day of following the maker and creator of all through life's twists and turns. We have the choice.

CREATOR GOD, *even though I understand that You know every twist and turn in life, I still struggle with fear from time to time. Let today's story remind me that You want to walk with me every day, to navigate me through every mile in life.*

# I'M GOING TO GIVE MY LIFE

*He called the crowd with his disciples, and said to them, "If any want to become my followers, let them deny themselves and take up their cross and follow me. For those who want to save their life will lose it, and those who lose their life for my sake, and for the sake of the gospel, will save it." —Mark 8:34-35*

William "Bill" Borden was heir to the Borden Dairy estate and millions of dollars. For a high school graduation gift, his parents sent him on a trip around the world. As he traveled throughout Asia, the Middle East, and Europe, he began to sense a growing burden for people of other nations.

Bill wrote home, "I'm going to give my life to prepare for the mission field."

During his years at Yale University he wrote in his journal, "Say 'no' to self and 'yes' to Jesus every time." Bill began a Bible study on campus that by the time he was a senior, saw 1,000 of the 1,300 students involved. He founded the Yale Hope Mission where he brought alcoholics off the streets to help them.

Bill Borden went on to Princeton Seminary in New Jersey and upon graduation, he set sail for China to begin his missionary career. He stopped in Egypt to reach out to Muslims and learn Arabic. While there, he contracted spinal meningitis and within the month, 25-year-old William Borden, a multi-millionaire, was dead.

Found written in Bill's Bible were these three phrases: "No Reserves," "No Retreats," "No Regrets."

In his biography, author Mary Taylor wrote, "Borden not only gave away his wealth, but himself, in a way so joyous and natural that it seemed a privilege rather than a sacrifice."

Regardless of where you are in life, with Christ you can know and understand Borden's motto: "No Reserves, No Retreats, No Regrets."

GREAT SHEPHERD, *Thank You for this great example of someone who "had it all," yet chose to sacrifice and serve. Remind me when I am tempted to walk away, or I am distracted by things, to simply repeat: No Reserves, No Retreats, No Regrets.*

# MY DAUGHTER'S TEACHER IS MY HERO

*. . . . they shall not hunger or thirst, neither scorching wind nor sun shall strike them down, for he who has pity on them will lead them, and by springs of water will guide them —Isaiah 49:10*

Not every first responder is a firefighter, police officer or healthcare worker. Sometimes average citizens are forced into situations where they become first responders.

As a gunman's terror gripped a Connecticut elementary school, killing 27 people, 20 of them children, several teachers on the scene acted with heroism.

Maryrose Kristopik, a music teacher for all grade levels, most likely saved an entire class by quickly ushering students into a closet.

"[The teachers] will be applauded for their efforts," an ABC newscaster said during the station's live video report in December 2012. "There was no screaming, which indicates just how carefully these teachers carried this out this afternoon."

Harrowing images recorded outside Sandy Hook Elementary School show children exiting the building in single-file lines, guided by their teachers.

"My daughter's teacher is my hero," said Brenda Lebinski, mother of an eight-year-old student. "She locked all the kids in a closet and that saved their lives."

With large musical instruments blocking one door, Maryrose tightly held shut the other door as the gunman, attempting to enter, banged loudly.

"We stayed quiet, we held hands, we hugged," said Maryrose. "I tried to talk to them calmly."

At the suggestion of a student, the group said a prayer. They remained safely in the closet until exiting the school together a short time later.

"I did what any other teacher would have done," said Maryrose.

GREAT COMFORTER, *we cannot imagine the trauma experienced by Sandy Hook teachers and children. There is no explanation for the evil that visited that Connecticut town. We can only trust these children and adults to your loving care.*

# PUT YOUR HAND IN HIS HAND

*And I heard a loud voice from the throne saying, "See, the home of God is among mortals. He will dwell with them; they will be his peoples, and God himself will be with them; he will wipe every tear from their eyes. Death will be no more; mourning and crying and pain will be no more, for the first things have passed away." —Revelation 21:3-4*

Mother Teresa died at the age of 87 after many years of sacrifice and service to the poorest of the poor in Calcutta. Although we know much of her life's work and her simple, outspoken messages, her beginning is just as fitting for her unique life.

She was born Agnes Gonxha Bojaxhiu to devout Catholic parents in Macedonia. Her father died when she was only nine. As early as 12, Agnes felt called to religious life.

Although her mother was initially against the idea of her beloved daughter leaving home to become a nun, she eventually understood the call and gave Agnes this piece of prophetic advice, "Put your hand in His hand and walk all alone with Him."

This charge would mark Mother Teresa's life for the rest of her days.

Her work eventually established the Order of Missionaries of Charity and work in over 130 countries worldwide including a network of over 600 homeless shelters, orphanages, AIDS hospices, leprosy clinics, and homes for single mothers.

A Gallup Poll survey reflecting on the 20th Century named her first on the list of "The Most Widely Admired People of the Century." This tiny woman with a huge vision from God was never wealthy or powerful by the world's standards, but no one can deny she used her life to change the world.

Let Mother Teresa's life inspire you to greatness and let her mother's words become your advice of how to live: "Put your hand in His hand and walk all alone with Him."

LOVING CREATOR, *today may I put my hand in Yours and walk with You, even if I walk alone.*

# SOLDIER'S SACRIFICE

*But he was wounded for our transgressions, crushed for our iniquities; upon him
was the punishment that made us whole, and by his bruises we are healed.*
—Isaiah 53:5

As a group of veterans and their friends in Roanoke, Va., began to see permanently wounded and disabled soldiers coming home from Afghanistan and Iraq, they decided to take action to help.

They began to distribute backpacks and totes full of personal items helpful to someone staying in the hospital. Over time, the needs they saw gave birth to more programs and the Wounded Warrior Project (WWP) was born.

The three-fold purpose of the project is to:

1—Raise awareness and enlist the public's aid for the needs of injured service members.

2—Help injured service members aid and assist each other.

3—Provide unique, direct programs and services to meet the needs of injured service members.

Besides the distribution of backpacks, their programs include combat stress recovery, family support retreats, technology and job training, rehabilitation and adaptive sports training, and peer mentoring.

For every U.S. soldier killed, seven are wounded, so the need is great. It is estimated that approximately 400,000 soldiers live with some form of post-traumatic stress disorder, an unseen wound that can be as debilitating as any physical injury.

The WWP motto is: "The greatest casualty is being forgotten." WWP volunteers work daily to be sure our wounded veterans are not forgotten; they are found and fostered.

So many great movements have come from one simple, single need to which someone responded. Be inspired to keep meeting needs and stay in the movement.

GREAT PHYSICIAN, *I pray today for all those who have been wounded for our freedom. Bless them, keep, them. and heal them. Thank You for their sacrifice. Thank You also for Your sacrifice on the cross that has made our ultimate healing possible.*

# JUST DOING MY JOB

*But let all who take refuge in you rejoice; let them ever sing for joy. Spread your protection over them, so that those who love your name may exult in you.*
—Psalm 5:11

School security officer Mike Jones was on vacation, but chose to attend the school board meeting to answer questions they would have on a security-related issue.

During the meeting, a gunman walked in, angry over his wife's dismissal as a teacher. At point-blank range, he fired at the superintendent, who dropped behind the desk as did all the school board members.

Jones then entered the room firing, and he hit the assailant three times. The gunman fell as he fired back, but he then turned the gun on himself and fired.

Miraculously, all the school board members and the superintendent came out from behind their desks unharmed. Jones was never hit.

Jones was already well-known in his Florida community as the "Salvage Santa," who fixed up broken bikes and toys and gave them to underprivileged children at Christmas. His yuletide service had even landed him on the Oprah television show.

After the gun battle, the media labeled him a hero. Jones simply said, "I'm not a hero, folks. I was just doing my job." He then added, "I didn't see the shots being fired. I didn't see the bullets. I saw the superintendent and the others coming out from behind that desk and I knew it was OK."

At the press conference, Jones introduced his son, who had just graduated from the police academy.

The role of defending and protecting innocent lives, the lives of his co-workers and friends, gave Jones the courage and focus to risk his own life, even while on vacation from his job of security at the school. That attitude of 24/7 duty is what separates the great from the good.

Today—be great!

SAVIOR, *whether on-duty or off, help me to always stay ready to, not only do my job, but to serve selflessly to those around me. May I be alert and prepared for anything today and every day.*

# IN ORDER TO PROTECT

*For God did not give us a spirit of cowardice, but rather a spirit of power and of love and of self-discipline.* —2 Timothy 1:7

The thermometer hovered around 20 degrees at 4 a.m., when the emergency dispatch call went out in Dingman Township near Milford, Pa.

A vehicle accident had occurred on Route 6, north of the Interstate. The car was on fire and a young man was trapped inside.

Emergency crews on call with the fire department began responding. Fire Department Lieutenant Eric "Jacko" Jakubowski decided that going to the station first might take too long to save the man, so he drove his own car straight to the scene. As he pulled up, he saw the car engulfed in flames.

Jacko grabbed a shovel from his trunk and smashed the window. He then dragged the victim away from the burning vehicle, covered him with his coat, and began administering first aid. Within a few minutes, other firemen arrived to put the fire out and assist. The young man was soon airlifted to a Burn Center in Allentown. He survived due to Jacko's decisive actions.

Kyle Wright, fire chief of Station 33 expressed his appreciation and pride in Jacko, "The volunteers of the fire and ambulance departments go through extensive training and spend a lot of time away from their families in order to protect our community—Just another fine example by the Milford Fire Department."

It would have been absolutely acceptable for Jacko to follow procedure and go to the station to meet the rescue vehicle and other personnel, but as with many volunteer responders, the priority of saving a life overrode all else. So many lives are saved because of quick and pro-active thinking.

DELIVERER, *You came to our rescue when we were in danger of the fires as well. You put everything aside to save us. May I think in such a way to serve and save others with my own life.*

# AS LONG AS THERE'S ANOTHER CHILD

*Let the little children come to me; do not stop them; for it is to such as these that the kingdom of God belongs.* —Mark 10:14b

Colonel Craig Lambrecht, MD, FACEP, an emergency physician stationed in southern Iraq on his second tour of duty, was walking outside of the military base when he walked inside a metal building to find 30 children awaiting medical attention.

Medics inside were treating burns that children had received, mostly from kerosene and diesel oil fire burns, often from cooking on open fires.

"I saw these soldiers volunteering their off-duty time to help Iraqi kids and realized I needed to be involved," Dr. Lambrecht stated.

The medics were surprised to see an Army colonel walk in, especially one trained in emergency medicine.

"I was profoundly impacted that we were doing procedures like surgical tissue removal and redressing, which are extraordinarily painful, and had no pain medication," said Dr. Lambrecht.

He contacted everyone he knew back home. Local newspapers picked up the story and money started pouring in.

Patients began to come from as far as Iran and Syria to get American health care.

"Iraqi physicians would bring children by ambulance from another hospital, even though they knew we were an outpatient facility," Dr. Lambrecht reported.

After completing his second tour, the doctor went back to work as an emergency physician back home, yet halfway around the globe, his desire to help the children of Iraq is unstoppable.

"As long as my medics keep saying there's another child we have to help and we need supplies," he said, "I'm going to continue to be there for my fellow soldiers and those kids."

Job descriptions and distance rarely stop true passion.

DEAR GOD, *thank You for children and how they remind us of the gift of life and the simplicity of love. Help me to always pay attention to the smallest of Your sons and daughters and care for them as my own.*

# WE JUST KNEW

*Seek the Lord and his strength, seek his presence continually.*
—*1 Chronicles 16:11*

Dominic Deroberts had just gotten out of his grandfather's car to walk toward his elementary school when he tripped and fell.

A driver didn't see him and struck Dominic, pinning him under the engine. His grandfather thought he was dead, but when the boy began to scream, they knew they had to act quickly. As local police arrived, they knew there was only one way to save the boy.

"We didn't have to communicate," Officer Mike Daly of the Boca Raton Police Department said. "We just knew, we had to try to lift this and hopefully somebody else would grab him and try to pull him out."

"He was like Hercules," Matthew Deroberts, Dominic's dad, stated. "He picked up the whole car—him and his partners. It was unbeliev-able." Four police and two men lifted the car off the boy.

In intense, life-threatening circumstances where time is of the essence, we often hear of people exhibiting super-human strength. In many cases it is actually the synergy of several people that brings about a happy ending. A group of people, even total strangers, who commit to a common goal, no matter how incredible it may seem at the time, can do amazing things together by committing their total focus at once.

Do you serve on a team? Or maybe you lead a team? Do you need some inspiration or motivation to continue to do amazing things together? Stay unified and focused on your goal. Encourage your teammates to stay strong and stand together in service to your community and to each other.

ALMIGHTY GOD, *help me, strengthen me, to stay a catalyst for inspiration and motivation among my team. May we stay focused on the fact that we are so much stronger together than we ever could ever be alone.*

# RIGHT PLACE AT THE RIGHT TIME

*The salvation of the righteous is from the Lord; he is their refuge in the time of trouble. —Psalm 37:39*

Brenda McCallister is an EMT in Atlanta, Ga. She was off-duty and attending her son's t-ball game.

Six-year-old Ethan Vose was playing ball on a nearby field when he was struck in the chest with a bat and was knocked out cold. Bystanders saw no movement and began screaming for help.

Brenda ran to Ethan and began to administer CPR. After two minutes, the boy revived. Paramedics soon arrived and transported Ethan to a hospital, still in critical condition, but alive.

A local journalist said Brenda was "the right person in the right place at the right time."

But what if Brenda had never received her EMT training? How might Ethan's story be different? What if she had left just minutes before the accident? What if she had been on-duty and waiting at the station for the call? Would it have been too late?

We hear many instances where someone with the right training was at the right place just when he/she was needed to save a life. Whether that may be an EMT, police officer, fireman, or doctor, every day, highly trained people who are "off duty" save the lives of others.

Thank God the same kind of person who will be trained to save lives never decides to be unavailable when needed. If that were the case, Ethan's life might not have been saved. And the same is true with thousands of survivors, saved by trained personnel.

Whatever your expertise, being on duty 24/7 can be a burden, but it is also one to which you are owed a great debt of gratitude by society.

MERCIFUL GOD, *though we will never understand why some lives are saved, while others are lost, we know You produce miracles every day, using every day people just like myself. Thank You that You are always on-duty and never sleep. You are always watching over us.*

# CONTRIBUTE TO THE COMMUNITY

*For how can I bear to see the calamity that is coming on my people? Or how can I bear to see the destruction of my kindred? —Esther 8:6*

Sara Hooker grew up in Swaziland, Africa, which has been devastated by HIV/AIDS for many years. One in four adults there are living with HIV. Life expectancy is at 32 years with the highest infection rate in the world.

During high school, Sara volunteered to teach English to children orphaned by HIV and AIDS. This gave her the chance to use her education and experience to help others. She shared, "For the first time, I started to seriously think about volunteering and using my time to give back."

Volunteering has influenced Sara's future plans in studying economics where she hopes to someday help the homeland of her childhood. While going to college in the U.S., Sara sees her new community through the eyes of a volunteer. "I find the most honest approach to understanding a place is to contribute in some way to its community. The organizations I have met here are probably the most generous with their volunteers. It has definitely built my confidence and communication skills. I'm looking forward to meeting the next set of new people." Sara said.

So what advice would she give to volunteers?

1—Pick projects carefully.

2—Maintain a constant communication with your supervisor to make sure you are contributing to the level they expect.

3—Have clear objectives to guide what you want as a volunteer and review these objectives.

4—Take time to find out about the organization's mission statement and how you fit in.

MAN OF SORROWS, *You see the great pain and devastation all over the world and it grieves You; yet at the same time, You provide Your servants with both gifts to share and opportunities to serve to change the outcome. Give me wisdom in every situation to find where I can make the most difference.*

# I'LL NEVER FORGET YOU

*For I was hungry and you gave me food, I was thirsty and you gave me something to drink, I was a stranger and you welcomed me, I was naked and you gave me clothing, I was sick and you took care of me, I was in prison and you visited me.*
—Matthew 25:35-36

In the 1970s, Chuck Colson was known only as a ruthless politician, known as the "hatchet man" for President Richard M. Nixon. In the Watergate scandal, he voluntarily pleaded guilty to obstruction of justice and ended up in prison in Alabama. During this personal crisis, Colson placed his faith in Jesus Christ. The media reported, "If Mr. Colson can repent of his sins, there just has to be hope for everybody."

While in prison, he was deeply moved by the hopelessness he saw there. One day near the end of his sentence, an inmate named Archie said, "Hey Colson. You'll be out of here soon. What are you going to do for us?" Colson answered, "I'll help in some way. I'll never forget you guys or this stinking place."

"Bull!" Archie responded. "You all say that. You big shots come and go. There ain't nobody who cares about us—nobody!"

For over 35 years now, Chuck Colson and an army of thousands of volunteers visit prisons daily, mentoring, helping prisoners' families, and sharing their faith. Prison Fellowship is the world's largest prison outreach in the world with ministries in 113 countries. It all began with a man no one thought could be reached and a question from an inmate that thought no one would care.

Do you have a situation that you feel is hopeless? A person you think can't be reached?—a burden that seems unbearable? Remember—God is still in the business of miracles every day. Today just might be yours! Live as if it is; act as if it is done.

MY ADVOCATE, *help me to see everyone as reachable. Help me to take advantage of any and every opportunity to make a difference—even in places where it seems hopeless. Help me to see You everywhere I go.*

# SOMETHING SPECIAL

*Be strong, and let your heart take courage, all you who wait for the Lord.*
—Psalm 31:24

The poem below, simply titled "To Our Town from the EMTs," was shared by a retired EMT at a service banquet in Wisconsin. The author is unknown.

*We're sorry if we wake you in the middle of the night,*
*But someone in your neighborhood is fighting for their life.*
*We're sorry if we block the road and make you turn around,*
*But there's been a bad wreck, people dying on the ground.*
*When you see us coming, we hope you understand,*
*Let us have the right of way, someone needs a helping hand.*
*Sometimes a person is choking, sometimes a broken leg,*
*Sometimes a heart stops beating, when we get there, it's too late.*
*So if you see us crying, when we think we are alone,*
*You'll know we've had a "bad one," and we're feeling mighty down.*
*You ask us why we do it, "How can you watch them die?"*
*It's never very easy, but we'll try to tell you why.*
*Somewhere deep within us, our souls are crying out,*
*"We're here to help our neighbors in their hour of pain and doubt."*
*God gave us something special to help us see you through.*
*We do it 'cause we love you and we care about you too.*

There will always be those people in this world who feel they are too good to serve others and complain about their own inconvenience when others must be helped. That is exactly what provides the contrast against those who serve and makes their lives even more special.

MY COMFORTER, *thank You for that "something special" that I feel in me to help my fellow man. Help me to keep Your perspective by displaying courage, while also feeling compassion as I serve.*

# INSIDE THE PERIMETER

*For the righteous will never be moved; they will be remembered for ever.*
—Psalm 112:6

Dick Morgan's name is included on the 9/11 Memorial at Ground Zero for first responders. The unique thing about Dick is that he is the only civilian listed there. The others are police, firemen, or paramedics.

Dick Morgan, 66, was a former executive turned consultant for Con Edison, a gas, steam, and electric company. He had started a biological weapons response team for the company.

Cathy Morgan, Dick's daughter, explains, "He was quite good at staying calm when under pressure during gas and steam explosions and water main breaks."

After the first tower was hit, Dick set up a ground-level command center in the South Tower. When that tower collapsed, he and others ran into an outdoor atrium near the North Tower to assemble another command post. When the North Tower fell, he died trying to escape.

Dick Morgan's name was initially grouped with people who died while visiting the center that day. His family went to work, correcting the mistake by meeting with U.S. Representatives.

"Clearly, my father had met all the criteria of a first-responder, even though he was not a police officer, fireman or paramedic. He died there, had a career in responding to emergencies, and was there that day doing the same. He kept people out until you assess the danger and then brought in your emergency people. That's why he was killed. He was inside the perimeter," Cathy Morgan explained.

First responders, and any service personnel where danger is involved, are often inside a perimeter of risk, attempting to protect untrained, innocent lives. Dick Morgan may have died as a civilian, but like all first responders, he knew risk was a part of the job.

EMMANUEL, *as much as I pray for safety, I know there will be a day when I, too, will not be able to escape death. Help me to live in such a way each day that my life will speak for itself when I'm gone.*

# I CARE FOR HEROES EVERY DAY

*The Lord answer you in the day of trouble! The name of the God of Jacob protect you! May he send you help from the sanctuary, and give you support from Zion.*
—Psalm 20:1-2

Debra Watkins, RN, MSN, was driving to work early one morning when, on the bridge ahead of her, two trucks collided head-on. She pulled over and ran to the truck that was burning. A female passenger wasn't breathing and had sustained severe trauma.

"She had no heart rhythm and was bleeding profusely. Two male volunteers were trusting and did anything I asked," Debra reported.

A student nurse arrived and assisted with CPR after the victim's pulse was lost.

After both victims were pulled from the truck, it was engulfed in flames. Rescue crews began to arrive, as did the local media. Debra told the student nurse to go on TV, so her professors could know she had a valid reason for being late to class.

Nineteen years earlier, Debra was trained as a paramedic and ran emergency squads for a year before becoming a nurse manager of an ICU at the Dayton, Ohio VA Medical Center.

"I never forgot those skills and they got me in the ICU," she said.

In order to award unknown rescuers, police asked the VA which nurse had been late that day.

"It was hard to accept recognition at the expense of someone's trauma," said Debra. "I accepted, so I could see the others. We came together in tragedy, but the feelings they gave me, I'll never forget. I care for heroes every day. The other rescuers may say I'm the hero they couldn't do without, but they're heroes because I couldn't have done it without them."

Volunteerism, service, and even heroism is always experienced best inside a community of people, rather than as a solo performance.

*MIGHTY GOD, thank You for all the people around me daily who assist me and help me to live my life. Thank You for every hero I have around me that I can't do without and life wouldn't be the same if they were not in it.*

# FOR THE LORD HAS GIVEN

*His armor-bearer said to him, "Do all that your mind inclines to. I am with you;
as your mind is, so is mine." —1 Samuel 14:7*

In 1 Samuel, we read an account of Jonathan, the son of King Saul, and his armor-bearer. An armor-bearer was like a military personal assistant, literally carrying the shield and weaponry of the leader. Jonathan decides to single-handedly engage a Philistine outpost, obviously a very risky, dangerous act.

Jonathan said, "Now we will cross over to those men and will show ourselves to them. If they say to us, 'Wait until we come to you,' then we will stand still in our place, and we will not go up to them. But if they say, 'Come up to us,' then we will go up; for the Lord has given them into our hand. That will be the sign for us."

Both of them came out of hiding and showed themselves to the garrison of the Philistines. The men of the garrison hailed Jonathan and his armor-bearer, saying, "Come up to us, and we will teach you a lesson." Jonathan said to his armor-bearer, "Come up after me; for the Lord has given them into the hand of Israel."

Then Jonathan and his armor-bearer killed 20 Philistines.

In life, we tend to be either Jonathans or armor-bearers—the leader or the support to the leader. Oftentimes, we are a Jonathan in one setting and an armor-bearer in another. Both roles are critical; one is not more important than the other.

MIGHTY KING, *whether I am a Jonathan or an armor-bearer, may I have this attitude of service and like-mindedness for the greater good. When I lead, may I lead with servant-leadership and when I support, may I say, "I am with you!"*

# THE SAME MIND

*Let each of you look not to your own interests, but to the interests of others. Let the same mind be in you that was in Christ Jesus.* —Philippians 2:4-5

Many expected the Messiah to arrive on a white horse, slay the oppressive enemies, and free the people. A military deliverance was a great prayer of the day.

Obviously, Jesus did not arrive that way or set up His Kingdom in this manner. He chose something far more difficult to do—conquer one heart at a time. Not rule the people, but redeem their hearts.

To create this movement and mindset, He served. Look at the action verbs associated with Jesus in the New Testament.

Preached, called, healed, delivered, taught, loved, reached out his hand, went to a home, touched her hand, spoke in authority, calmed the storm, cast out, had dinner with sinners, addressed the crowd, touched their eyes, went through the towns and villages, had compassion, sent out the 12, gave authority, taught in the synagogue, multiplied food, walked on water, prayed for children, healed blindness, drove out the moneychangers, challenged the Pharisees, and finally, gave up His life, then rose from the grave.

Jesus' life was marked daily by active, tireless service to people and continual glory to God.

Our lives can find no greater purpose and have no greater goal. An active life of service without faith in God can lead to burn-out and bitterness toward those we serve.

A life of faith that has no active service is, according to the Bible, dead works. That is why it is crucial we balance our lives as Christ modeled for us, giving our work to people and our hearts to God.

FAITHFUL AND TRUE, *thank You that You came here for our hearts and not after power, fame, or anything that the world deems great. May my faith be active and my life produce glory for You always.*

# TO IRAQ AND BACK

*Now to him who by the power at work within us is able to accomplish abundantly far more than all we can ask or imagine… —Ephesians 3:20*

Bob Woodruff, co-anchor of ABC's World News Tonight, one of the most sought-after spots in journalism, was embedded with troops from the 4th Infantry Division. He was reporting on U.S. and Iraqi security forces, riding in an armored vehicle, when they were struck by an IED near Taji, Iraq.

Woodruff survived, but had to undergo brain surgery and was kept in a medically induced coma for 36 days. Over the next year, Woodruff struggled back from this traumatic brain injury, finally returning on-air a year later to report on his ordeal. He also returned to Iraq to visit the troops he was with when the incident occurred.

As he dealt with his own painstaking recovery, he realized the plight of thousands of service members returning from Iraq and Afghanistan with similar injuries. He has contin-ued to cover traumatic brain injury stories and was honored with a Peabody Award in 2008 for his reporting on the subject.

The Woodruff family has also established the Bob Woodruff Foundation to help heal the physical and hidden wounds of war by providing resources and support to injured service members, veterans, and their families.

Bob Woodruff could have easily returned to his safe news anchor desk, never returned to the horrors of his ordeal, and no one would blame him. Yet he decided to use his own experiences and tragedy to shed light on a mostly-ignored area of soldier injury and to help victims such as himself to deal with their circumstances. One of the great responses to tragedy is to find ways to turn it into triumph to help others—exactly what Bob Woodruff did.

ALMIGHTY HEALER, *I recognize today how You can, not only heal, but redeem. You can take a horrible circumstance, and with some determination and hope, bring about something that didn't exist before.*

# DOCTOR IN THE HOUSE

*As God's chosen ones, holy and beloved, clothe yourselves with compassion, kindness, humility, meekness, and patience. —Colossians 3:12*

An often-used phrase is "art imitates life," but in this case "life imitated art."

Seventeen-year-old Weston Masset was driving his Ford Mustang through the curvy streets of a Malibu, Calif., neighborhood when he lost control of the car; it flipped over, injuring the young man, and trapping him inside.

Actor Patrick Dempsey, who has played a doctor on a popular TV show for several years, lived nearby and heard the crash. He grabbed a fire extinguisher and a crow bar and ran to the car.

By this time, Weston was barely conscious. Patrick pried the car door open with the crow bar and began to drag Weston out of the vehicle.

As the actor was pulling the boy from the car, the boy asked, "Are you famous?" Patrick responded, "Yeah, I'm a doctor."

The actor then called 9-1-1 and paramedics soon arrived. Patrick located the boy's cell phone and called his mother.

"He had a certain authority in his voice," said Mary Beth Masset. "I asked if he was a paramedic and he said, 'No, this is Patrick Dempsey.' I'm just super-grateful and can't wait to thank him."

Weston said, "I was scared for my life. I was upside down. " Patrick Dempsey stayed with the boy until he was put into the ambulance and then called the family that evening to check on him.

In our culture, it is easy to think that all celebrities are self-centered and isolated, but it's good to know that there are some who will sacrifice and serve when called upon. They're in good company.

BRIGHT AND MORNING STAR, *whether it's a car crash or a homeless beggar on the street, help me to pay attention to life outside my door and be ready to help. May my life imitate Yours.*

# TRADE UP & GIVE AWAY

*They are to do good, to be rich in good works, generous, and ready to share, thus storing up for themselves the treasure of a good foundation for the future, so that they may take hold of the life that really is life.* —1 Timothy 6:18-19

On a Memorial Day, 9-year-old Brendan Haas walked up to the front door of a Duxbury, Mass., home and surprised the family of Timothy Steele, a soldier killed in Afghanistan, with a family trip to Disney World.

The young boy had heard that many of our fallen soldiers leave behind young children and he wanted to do something to help, so Brendan and his mom set up a Facebook page they called "A Soldier for a Soldier."

He was inspired by the story of a man who traded a paper clip up to a house. He wanted to trade a toy soldier eventually up to a Disney World trip to give to a soldier's family.

Brendan not only acquired the trip, but airfare as well. Once he completed his trades and secured his goal, he announced his intention for the trip. People submitted names of families through Facebook and email.

Brendan drew the name of Liberty Hope Steele, a deceased soldier's two-year-old daughter.

When the media asked the boy why he would donate his trip, he answered, "I think it would make them a lot happier."

Stories like this prove, not only that children can do amazingly unselfish things, but that great acts of service can start small and grow. We should never assume we can't make a difference or that our efforts are too small, as Brendan's story reminds us once again.

BREATH OF LIFE, *may I see no opportunity too small or too big to make a difference or change a life. No matter what life brings today, help me to trade up.*

# IN THE FACE OF DANGER

*Incline your ear to me; rescue me speedily. Be a rock of refuge for me, a strong fortress to save me.* —Psalm 31:2

When hikers, mountain climbers, rock climbers, and thrill-seekers get into trouble in the mountains of a national park, U.S. Park Rangers are called upon.

One such instance was the largest rescue operation ever attempted in the Grand Teton National Park. A severe lightning storm moved in, while 17 people were on a mountain. Three groups were scattered between 13,000 feet and the summit of 13,770 feet.

Three rangers spent the night on the mountain and rescue teams saved 16 of the 17 climbers via helicopter.

All the victims suffered various burns or neurological issues, such as paralysis and numbness, from lightning strikes. Rangers gathered up the climbers one by one, suspended on ropes from the helicopters. One climber had fallen to his death and the search went on to retrieve his body. "It's vertical terrain," one Ranger stated.

One of the climbers spoke with the media after the rescue, "There was no noise, just a blinding flash of white light. Your body just feels like it has turned into boiling soup. And then the dread of waiting for the next strike."

One ranger commented, "We were pretty much at the mercy of the weather. We had clouds from the word 'go.' And there's not a lot of air to work with up there."

Another added, "It just seemed like any other rescue, just really long." Seven rangers received Department of Interior's Valor Awards for "demonstrating unusual courage involving a high degree of personal risk in the face of danger."

So often those who serve and save must overcome almost insurmountable odds and dangers, yet the goal of a saved life is always at the forefront.

SAVIOR, *thank You for all my brothers and sisters out there in so many roles of service who risk their lives every day for others. Bless them all and keep them close.*

# BE PREPARED

*Let no one despise your youth, but set the believers an example in speech and conduct, in love, in faith, in purity.* —1 Timothy 4:12

Alexander Beaumont, a Boy Scout, was working on his Eagle Scout project in his hometown of Queen Anne, Wash. Two years prior, Alexander and his dad had brainstormed about potential projects with the chairman of the emergency preparedness committee of the local council. The chairman told Alexander how he needed volunteers to run emergency radio communication in Queen Anne and surrounding communities in the event of a disaster.

If cell towers, landlines, Internet, and traditional communication were ever disrupted, there had to be a plan to connect first responders.

Alexander engaged his entire troop to train in ham radio communication and created an instructional video for local residents. He also worked with the Seattle Office of Emergency Management in four citywide drills to practice communications during simulated disaster scenarios.

Alexander set up booths at community events, dispensing information to the community. He also set up a Facebook page dedicated to helping area residents know their disaster plans and how to communicate during such an event.

His dad commented, "Alexander has signed up to be the first responder for the first responders." The American Red Cross gave Alexander a Youth Service in Action Hero award—recognizing his work in the community that could most definitely save lives one day.

In this world, there have always been pioneers and settlers—those who blaze the trail and those who follow to join them. The world needs both, yet someone always has to decide to blaze the trail that has yet to be traveled.

MERCIFUL GOD, *communication is such a vital aspect of service. Teach me to open my mouth when I should and listen when I should. Help me to respond as I should, as You would have me.*

# A SENSE OF FAMILY

*So then, whenever we have an opportunity, let us work for the good of all, and especially for those of the family of faith.* —Galatians 6:10

There are over 100 stars carved into the CIA Memorial Wall at the Agency headquarters in Langley, Va., honoring those who died in service. Some names are listed, while others cannot be made public, even in death, due to on-going operations.

One star on the Memorial Wall belongs to James Rawlings. Having just graduated from college in 1955, Jim joined the CIA, still in its formative years.

His son, James, Jr., who is now also an agent, said of his father, "It was the mission and what the agency was responsible for. It was a way to do something important."

Speaking of his and his father's roles, he said, "As support officers, both he and I work hard to support our co-workers. Not all of us are analysts or collectors. A support officer's job is to do whatever you can to be sure that the other people you're working with can accomplish their jobs."

In 1975, James, Jr. was 16 years old when his father was aboard a cargo plane that crashed over Vietnam. Because his body was not found, the agency issued a "presumptive determination of death."

In the early 1990s his body was discovered and positively identified—bringing closure for the family after more than 15 years. In 1994, his remains were finally buried by the family.

James concluded, "My father had a real sense of family, in that if other folks needed help, he would always be there, especially overseas."

Family legacies are crucial for future generations. A life of service and commitment to humankind is a gift to those who follow after.

HEAVENLY FATHER, *thank You for my own mission and knowing I, too, am accomplishing an important role for my community and country. May I have that same sense of family with all I come in contact with and need my help.*

# THEY PUT THEIR LIFE ON THE LINE

*The Lord has made himself known, he has executed judgment; the wicked are snared in the work of their own hands.* —Psalm 9:16

Shervin Lalezary is a reserve deputy for the Los Angeles County Sheriff's Department. His salary is $1 per year. Normally only part-time, Shervin, a native of Tehran, Iran, had been working full-time for four days, due to a crime spree of 50 arson fires.

"You just got the sense that everyone in the city was on edge, rightfully so, because of what was happening," Shervin said.

In a late-night traffic stop, the 30-year-old real estate attorney by day pulled over Harry Burkhart, a German national, a white male adult with a short ponytail and a receding hairline.

The deputy shined his spotlight into the van and realized Burkhart matched the description of the arson suspect taken from surveillance cameras where a fire had been set. Two L.A. police officers had also stopped to assist.

They made the arrest and the suspicious fires around Los Angeles stopped. Sheriff Lee Baca called Harry Burkhart "perhaps the most dangerous arsonist in the county that I can recall."

Shervin's action put a brief spotlight on the over 800 reserve volunteers who provide over 175,000 hours of service to the sheriff's department each year. The $1 a year salary doesn't diminish the dangers these reservists can face.

"That's a tremendous resource for our department," the sheriff said. "They're a huge part of what we do. These are people that really step forward and literally at times put their life on the line for a dollar a year."

When the public finds out a criminal who threatens their community is off the streets, they do not care if the hero is a $50,000 a year employee or a $1 a year volunteer. They are just grateful the job has been done.

PRINCE OF PEACE, *it is so encouraging to know that there are people serving in so many ways to make the world a better place. I pray others will see the great benefits of service and join us.*

# A CHAIN OF GIVING

*And now faith, hope, and love abide, these three; and the greatest of these is love.*
—1 Corinthians 13:13

Nadia Ben-Youssef is a teenager in Montana. She has been singing and performing poetry since she was 6 years old and volunteering since she was 8. Nadia has published three books of poetry and songs. A fourth is in production. She donates all of the profits from the books to children's charities.

Money from her first book went to a school for deaf and blind children in Great Falls, Montana. Money from the second book went to Home on the Range, a shelter for abused children and to the Feed The Children fund for orphans in Bosnia.

Nadia also visits the elderly at a local nursing home. She fixes the women's hair, paints their nails, and sings for all the residents on Sundays.

"I also sing for homebound hospice patients," she said. "I visit them and talk and sing for them. I guess that's what's really fulfilling to me, when I sing to someone who is dying, someone who is really sick, and who isn't aware of what's happening, but when I'm done, there's a smile on that person's face."

Nadia concluded, "Making someone happy makes you happy, and they go on and make others happy, and it's like a chain. Love is a chain of giving. You change when you get older, but love is ageless. Love is the same whether you are 7, 13, or 102."

One of the strongest themes throughout the New Testament is love. It is clear that love is a God-created and God-ordained action, not simply a feeling.

Today, allow love to be the greatest force in your life.

LORD OF *LOVE*, help me to grow in my ability to express and receive love—for You and from You, for others and from others, and even for myself.

# CAN'T WAIT FOR NEXT WEEK

*It is by your holding fast to the word of life that I can boast on the day of Christ that I did not run in vain or labour in vain.* —Philippians 2:16

Achilles International is a non-profit organization with chapters and members throughout the United States and abroad. Every day, in parks, gyms, and tracks all over the world, Achilles provides athletes with disabilities with a community of support. Able-bodied volunteers and disabled runners come together to train in an environment of support and community.

Runners gain measurable physical strength and build confidence through their sense of accomplishment, which often transfers to other parts of their lives.

Keith Michaels is a substance-abuse counselor in Santa Monica, Calif., who volunteers with Achilles. "This organization is not about how fast you are or how many races you've won," he said. "It's just people who love to run. And obviously if you're blind, you can't run by yourself. Running has done so much for me in my life, so I just decided that guiding a blind runner might be a nice way to give a little back to something that's given so much to me. I learned to guide by listening and watching one of the other sighted guides. Learning how to keep as little tension as possible on the tether, which is the equipment we use to stay connected while running."

Keith concluded, "I suppose there's a lot of truth to the saying that 'the best things in life are free,' because I go home after showing up at Achilles—on the days when I want to and on the days when I don't want to, when I really don't feel like running seven miles, always feeling like I can't wait for next week—every time."

There will likely be more days that you don't feel like serving than those you do. But, as Keith shared, press on and you will always be glad you did.

MIGHTY GOD, *in this race of life, help me to always see and hear those who need my help in running their race. May I pace myself to run hard in all that I do and develop endurance to finish strong in all things.*

# THEIR EYES LIGHT UP

*The precepts of the Lord are right, rejoicing the heart; the commandment of the Lord is clear, enlightening the eyes.* —Psalm 19:8

Katherine Pener, 84, is a breast cancer survivor in Miami Beach who has volunteered for the Reach to Recovery program for 22 years.

Reach to Recovery is a program that helps women through the trauma of breast cancer and surgery. One of the reasons for its success is that all the women who volunteer have been in the same spot themselves. There is immediate empathy and understanding.

"A patient's eyes light up when I say it's been 29 years since I had my operation," said Katherine.

Reach to Recovery was founded in 1952 by Therese Lasa who is also a breast cancer survivor. Like others before her, she had no one to turn to during her ordeal.

"I read about the program in the New York Post," said Katherine. "I asked my doctor, 'Shouldn't I have one of these visitors?' The doctor said, 'What do you need them for?' That feeling of being alone I will never forget. I felt hopeless."

When asked about her love for volunteering, Katherine adds, "I guarantee anyone who volunteers will feel better emotionally, physically, and psychologically. I don't care who you are or what you do. The people I know who volunteer have smiles on their faces. The hours they give are worth more to them than any money they could ever receive."

Nothing connects us as people more than a common experience. Sharing those with others helps our struggles make sense and our lives have purpose.

LIGHT OF THE WORLD, *help me to watch for the opportunities that come my way to share anything that I have been through, to empathize with people in struggles that I have experienced.*

# ALWAYS DOING GOOD

*Now in Joppa there was a disciple whose name was Tabitha, which in Greek is Dorcas. She was devoted to good works and acts of charity.* — Acts 9:36

Throughout the Bible, there are people we are introduced to for just brief passages, sometimes only a few verses. To be mentioned in the Bible at all, especially for a noble reason, would be amazing.

In the Book of Acts, one such person is Tabitha (or Dorcas, depending on your version). Oddly, when we are first introduced to her, she is dead.

Peter is summoned to an upstairs room where she is being prepared for burial. He falls to his knees, prays, and proclaims as he saw Jesus do so many times, "Tabitha, get up."

She opens her eyes, looks at Peter, and stands up. Resurrected from the dead!

In this brief story, we also learn a lot about the character of Tabitha. She has become a disciple of Jesus. We see her life has been changed, because verse 36 states she was always doing good and helping the poor.

When Peter came into the room, the women there began showing him all the garments that Tabitha had made for them. There was deep sadness, because the community there loved her and would miss her kindness. Thanks to Peter's obedience and faith, coupled with God's power, Tabitha would continue in her life and now become a living testimony to the reality of Christ.

In today's world, as in the days of Peter, kindness and goodness are qualities that are noticed, because they are far too rare. Don't miss your chance today to simply be kind to anyone in your path.

SERVANT OF ALL, *thank You for the life changing power that You make available to us all. I pray I will continue to grow, so that when I am gone, there will be a legacy of kindness and goodness to follow after me as well.*

# I WANTED TO DO SOMETHING

*For God will save Zion and rebuild the cities of Judah; and his servants shall live there and possess it. —Psalm 69:35*

Leah Bromley was at her home in New York when she received a text message from her mother in her hometown of Tuscaloosa, Ala., that simply said, "I'm in the basement. I love you."

Later that day, Tuscaloosa was the hardest hit city by one of the deadliest tornadoes in U.S. history. The severe weather tore a path through the Midwest and South, killing 327 people.

In Tuscaloosa, more than 5,000 homes were destroyed. Leah said, "I felt helpless and I knew I wanted to do something."

Leah started a "Rebuild Tuscaloosa" Facebook page. "It just became very apparent that it was necessary to provide a credible source of information for volunteers and for the people that were affected," she said.

The page became a hub for connecting people in need with the supplies and organizations that could help them.

A year later, the mission of Rebuild Tuscaloosa still had an active Facebook community that works to identify ongoing needs and fulfill them. Leah and other volunteers regularly deliver donated furniture and household items to families trying to rebuild.

"I just really want people to remember us and to understand that there is still a really great need," she said. "We have barely scraped the surface of rebuilding and there are still a lot of people who need a lot of help."

Today's technology provides us with amazing ways to connect the world in a positive way. Consider a new way today that you could use a social media tool to connect your service to the lives of others in a broader scope.

ALPHA & OMEGA, *You never promised us that bad things wouldn't happen to us, but it is also true that You have been in the re-building business for a long time. Bless those who join You and may I take every opportunity to bless those who rebuild what has been destroyed.*

# 100 ROUNDS

*He leads me beside still waters; he restores my soul. He leads me in right paths for his name's sake. Even though I walk through the darkest valley, I fear no evil; for you are with me.* —Psalm 23:2b-4a

Joey Ramos and his buddy decided to go fishing from their kayaks on the Nueces River. Paddling down the river as the sun began to set, they saw four men on the banks, drinking beer. They later commented to each other how strange and unfriendly the group seemed.

The two men found their spot and stood up in their kayaks to begin casting. It was now dark, but the moon was bright. Suddenly the crack of a high-powered rifle broke the silence. They immediately began to paddle away. Just then, more shots rang out. They heard the bullets whizzing past, hitting the water. "We beached on the bank and hid behind the kayaks," Joey recalled. The pair clung to their boats, cold, muddy, and terrified, while gunfire continued.

"I called 911 and tried to get them to get the coordinates off our cell phones," Joey said. A dispatcher suggested they contact Texas Parks & Wildlife game Warden Kevin Mitchell. Joey called Kevin. "He knew exactly where we were and he said he was on his way." Gunshots went on for the next half-hour, while they waited.

Kevin told Joey to shine a flashlight into the sky when he heard his pickup approach. They floated across the river when Kevin arrived and jumped into his truck, as they heard two final shots. Joey estimates 100 rounds were fired at them. Thanks to the game warden's intimate knowledge of the river and the area, both men were rescued without harm.

Active service, coupled with experience and expertise, is invaluable to serving and saving lives.

SAVIOR, *in this world today, evil is all around, in so many forms. Help me to be wise and discerning when I am in its presence, but help me also to stand strong in boldness and strength by Your power.*

# STOP WATCHING

*For we are what he has made us, created in Christ Jesus for good works, which God prepared beforehand to be our way of life.* —Ephesians 2:10

Youth communicator E. J. Swanson speaks before tens of thousands of teenagers every year.

As a committed partner with Compassion International, he knew many of the teens that he speaks before can't—or won't—afford the monthly commitment to sponsor a child. He was determined to find a way to connect these teens to biblical action. And anyone will tell you that deciding to raise money among teens in the American culture today is a challenging undertaking.

Knowing that fashion watches are popular among teens, E. J. Swanson launched his "Stop Watching, Start Doing" campaign. Each timepiece has "I Won't Watch" imprinted on the face to remind the student to take action toward helping the impoverished children of the world. All of the profits go to specific Compassion International projects.

In less than a year, over $50,000 has been given to Third World countries for projects such as drilling for clean water, providing educational resources, building shelters for homeless families, offering health care, malaria prevention in Africa, and efforts to stop child prostitution in India.

E. J. said, "The average person glances at his or her watch 20 times a day. We see watches as a first entrance into a lifetime of combating and advocating for those who suffer from poverty. We believe people are looking for a way to make significant changes in the lives of the hurting."

Where there's a will, there's a way. Where there's a need and a desire, an answer can be found. Whatever your need today, God has a door open just for you.

ALMIGHTY GOD, *remind me as I look at my watch today to be about action and not just watching or wishing that something could be done. Help me to make a difference today to the people around me and also around the world.*

# PERFECT TIMING

*You will not fear the terror of the night, or the arrow that flies by day, or the pestilence that stalks in darkness, or the destruction that wastes at noonday.*
—Psalm 91:5-6

It was a quiet late afternoon at the mobile home park with kids playing in the streets. 24-year-old mechanic, husband, and father of two, Diaz Chacon, had gotten off work early to spend time with his family.

Diaz's wife tells the story, "We heard a man going, 'Hey, let her go! Let her go!' A man comes running to us and said, 'Men in a blue van just stole a little girl.'"

Diaz jumped in his black pickup and gave chase. After he caught up with the van, the driver crashed, and ran away. Diaz went to the van, picked up the 6-year-old girl cowering in the floorboard, and told her he would take her back home. Later when the assailant returned to the van, police arrested him for kidnapping, child abuse, and tampering with evidence.

Police Sergeant Tricia Hoffman said, "We can only guess what would have happened to this child. Throughout the county, we see situations like this and they do not typically end well."

Diaz said he thought of his own two girls—7 years old and 5 months—and how he would want someone to do the same for him. Martha Diaz said she was grateful that a parent's worst nightmare did not happen that day.

"Everything just worked out," she said, referring to the perfect timing of that afternoon. "Even now we say, 'What if we hadn't been there? What if he would have been two minutes earlier.'" But thanks to every-day heroes like Diaz Chacon, that question doesn't have to be answered.

Always remember—God only asks us to be available. Timing and results are best left up to Him.

MERCIFUL GOD, *miracles and "perfect timing" happen every day. Thank You that You can give everyday people the strength and ability to do heroic things. Guide me today as I walk in this world to watch out for others.*

# THE DAWN OF LIFE

*Truly I tell you, unless you change and become like children, you will never enter the kingdom of heaven.* —Matthew 18:3

Bravery and heroism comes in many shapes, sizes, and in all ages. Leah is just 4-years-old. Born with Down's syndrome, she was a blonde-haired, cute-as-a-button, giggly little girl.

But just two years earlier, her parents feared the worst when she began to have mouth pain, run a high fever, and didn't want to walk. Her pediatrician referred the family to St. Jude's Children's Research Hospital in Memphis. Tests revealed Leah had ALL or acute lymphoblastic leukemia. She began a two-and-a-half year chemotherapy treatment program. St. Jude's breakthroughs in children's cancer treatment have increased ALL patients from a 4 percent survival rate to an amazing 94 percent rate today.

Leah has braved so much sickness in her brief, little life, but her bravery and contagious spirit are seen by all who know her. And through it all she's never stopped being a little girl—playing with her dolls, going to the playground, playing hide-and-seek with her brother, and hugging her mom.

For over 50 years, St. Jude's has been a leader in treating children's cancer. The hospital was born from a prayer offered by the late entertainer Danny Thomas. He dreamed of a day when disease would be conquered and he believed that "no child should die in the dawn of life." Many of the patients from St. Jude's early days now have children of their own.

So many great endeavors begin with a dream and a prayer. What is yours? Dream today. Pray right now.

OUR FATHER, *there are so many areas of my life where I need to re-engage and re-ignite a child-like faith—to trust You as my guide.*

# THE BIGGEST SACRIFICE

*Wealth hastily gained will dwindle, but those who gather little by little will increase it. —Proverbs 13:11*

The horror stories of executives who hold onto their million dollar paydays, while accepting government bail-outs and laying off employees have been widespread over the past few years.

Rob Katz, chief executive officer of Vail Resorts in Vail, Colo., isn't on that list. The resort operates five ski and snowboard slopes in Colorado and Nevada. When the economic downturn hit the ski slopes, Katz said, "If I was going to ask someone making $8 an hour to take a pay cut, they needed to know I was doing something that would really affect me. No one wants to see their salary reduced, but at least in this case those at the top were making the biggest sacrifice."

To prevent layoffs, Katz decided to take the biggest cut himself, so he reduced his $840,000 annual salary down to $0 for one year.

Seasonal employees were asked to take a 2.5% pay cut and the other executives agreed to a 10% reduction. The company's board of directors agreed to reduce their annual cash retainer by 20%. The total saved to avoid lay-offs: over $10 million.

"I'm making changes, but you can't compare the challenges I go through to some of our folks," he explained. "I've saved money, because I've made more over my time. They need to find a way to put food on the table. People here would rather take a pay cut than see their colleagues lose their jobs," he added. "Everyone at this company is a hero."

True leadership is from the top down, with the level of sacrifice directly related to level of responsibility. For this reason, servant leaders breed loyalty and commitment from their team.

PROVIDER, *please grant me the wisdom to deal with my own money. To give as I should, share what I have, and to save all I can.*

# A HERO'S IMAGE

*Keep alert, stand firm in your faith, be courageous, be strong.*
—1 Corinthians 16:13

Off-duty Kentucky State Police trooper Rick Conn was returning home when he turned into his subdivision. He noticed what appeared to be a mist and assumed it was a water leak. As he passed one home, a fiery blast suddenly blew through his driver's side window. "I was on fire," Rick said. "Everything inside the vehicle was on fire." With his hair, eyebrows, and eyelashes burned away and his sweatshirt in flames, Rick dove out the broken window and rolled around on the ground to put out the fire. When he stood up, he heard Jeannie Newsome screaming from her home.

With his hands badly burned, Rick ran to Jeannie. She tossed her two-year-old daughter, Alexis, through a blown-out window in her burning home into Rick's arms. The blast, which turned out to be from a natural gas pipe leak, destroyed five homes and injured nine people.

When called a hero by local media, Rick said, "One of the biggest heroes in my mind was Jeannie Newsome, the mother who wouldn't leave her child. She placed herself between the fire and her little girl. She's the hero in this. She didn't get the credit I got, but she's the one who saved the baby."

Rick was recovering from second and third degree burns on his face, neck, and hands and in rehab twice a week. "He is definitely a picture, an image, of what a state trooper ought to be," Trooper Scott Hopkins of Pikeville said.

So many sworn to serve and protect put their own lives in danger regularly—even risking their ability to do their own job long-term. That's the ultimate service to the public.

MY REFUGE, *I have no idea what today holds and we certainly never know when tragedy may strike, so please remind me to live every moment and be grateful for the life You give.*

# BLOOD IN THE WATER

*For he will command his angels concerning you to guard you in all your ways.*
*On their hands they will bear you up, so that you will not dash your foot against a*
*stone. —Psalm 91:11-12*

Florida Lifeguard Dan Lund noticed a kite surfer bobbing in the water about a quarter-mile out from Stuart Beach. He assumed an equipment malfunction had caused him to be down in the water. So Dan paddled his rescue surfboard out through heavy waves and rough waters to help the surfer.

Dan recalled, "I get to him, I'm probably within 20 yards or so from him, and there's a lot of blood in the water." The surfer yells, "I got hit. I got hit by a shark."

Dan then spotted the sharks circling the man. He paddled in, grabbed the man, and pulled him onto his rescue board and began paddling back for shore.

Martin County Marine Safety Captain Ray Szefinski reported, "He got to the surfer, reassured him, and then he had to hold him physically on the board. The sharks, all that time, were swimming around them and Dan had to have his hand in the water, just paddling with one hand." The captain said that if the lifeguards had known it was a shark attack, they would have called for a boat rescue. But that would have taken too long. He added, "Dan Lund went probably over 500 yards out in the ocean in real rough conditions with sharks swimming all around. It is almost like a miracle that he didn't get hit."

This scene is the stuff of nightmares, yet ocean lifeguards must face this, and other such dangers, in order to be in the business of saving lives; ironically, in a setting where people are only there for fun and recreation.

Whatever the level of risk in your service, no greater gift can ever be given than an effort to preserve life in whatever way you have at your means.

SAVIOR, *help me to grow in faith and calm my fears as I serve You and others today.*

# BROUGHT BACK TO LIFE

*And you will have confidence, because there is hope; you will be protected and take your rest in safety. You will lie down, and no one will make you afraid.*
*—Job 11:18-19a*

Sometimes the work of a police officer is saving people from themselves.

Natalia was distraught over losing her job and her boyfriend breaking up with her.

She went onto the roof of her Manhattan apartment building. She walked along the four-story lip of the roof and passersby called 911. As police units began to show up, Natalia began to yell down to them, "Everything has gone bad at once. I'm sorry. Tell my friends I'm sorry. Tell my mother I'm sorry." She also apologized to the police for wasting the taxpayer's money on the response to her.

She finally sat down on the ledge, beginning to take deep breaths, which is a telltale sign of readying to jump. Emergency Service Unit Detective Brian Glacken and Detective Madelyn McTague had worked their way onto the roof near Natalia.

Just as the young lady flung herself off the ledge, Brian reached out and grabbed her in mid-air as Detective McTague rushed in and the two pulled her to safety. The large crowd that had gathered on the street burst into applause. The half-hour ordeal ended without tragedy, thanks to a strong and quick-thinking New York police officer.

With these tough economic times and isolation from community being at an all-time high, people can be deluded into thinking that ending their own lives is the only solution. The pain becomes so unbearable that the victim doesn't stop to think of all the people who will be devastated and haunted by the "what if's" that suicide brings to the family and friends left behind.

Today, you never know how your kind word, smile, or gentle gesture might just make someone think that the world isn't such a bad place after all.

MY HOPE, *help me pay attention today to those I come into contact with. May I be Your representative as I move throughout life and show others that life is indeed worth living to the full.*

# COMPLACENCY IS AN ENEMY

*For you shall not go out in haste, and you shall not go in flight; for the Lord will go before you, and the God of Israel will be your rearguard. See, my servant shall prosper; he shall be exalted and lifted up, and shall be very high.* —Isaiah 52:12-13

Every day 1.8 million people board an airplane on some 30,000 flights. Prior to 9-11, the U.S. had 33 air marshals on duty. Today there are thousands. The exact number is classified, because this program is America's most secretive federal force.

To become a federal air marshal, recruits must be able to run up evacuation slides, out-score other federal agents on gun ranges, and learn to react in life-or-death circumstances on crowded airplanes with no back-up. Recruits spend 120 hours training with weapons and learn a mix of martial arts and mental exercises.

When it comes to finding new marshals, the TSA is looking for "someone who doesn't live in a black-and-white world, because at 35,000 feet we don't give them black-and-white answers," said Joseph D'Angelillio, head of Air Marshal training.

Air Marshal Kimberley Thompson flew for eight years before moving to headquarters. She said air marshals are taught to continually scan for potential threats. "We are looking continually at the passengers around us, the passengers that are getting up and going into the restrooms, or moving about the cabin for any given reason to determine why that person is getting out of their seat," Kimberley said.

Over the past decade, they've made few arrests, and have never fired a weapon in flight. But air marshals can never let down their guard, because aviation still remains the top target of terrorists. Since threats can emerge without warning, complacency is an enemy.

No matter your own area of service, complacency is also your enemy. Staying fresh and inspired will keep you at the top of your game and doing all you can for those who depend on you.

REFINER'S FIRE, *keep me current with You, in my work, and in the condition of my mind and heart. Guard me from complacency. Replace it with contentment. Fill me with compassion.*

# YOU GIVE IT EVERYTHING

*Teach me to do your will, for you are my God. Let your good spirit lead me on a level path. —Psalm 143:10*

"In this job, you find out what you're made of; if you can hack it or not," stated Major Marci Hodge.

She spent ten years in the Army—five years on active duty and another five in the Reserve. Her last deployment was Camp Victory in Iraq.

"My job is to create stability and win hearts and minds," explained Marci, a logistician and civil affairs officer. "I can move anything," she said. She moved thousands of fourth and fifth grade books for school children that the Department of State had failed to move from Jordan to Iraq for the last few years.

In Iskandiyah, her battalion worked on a project with local government to get a completely staffed plant of 1,000 employees back to fully functioning capacity following the war. Her team even helped establish organizational practices and human resources, bringing in corporate mentors from the United States. They worked to ensure that the plant would be able to operate without U.S. assistance in the future. Local Iraqi truck drivers were also employed to transport refurbished equipment.

"It put folks back to work," said Major Hodge. "People matter, regardless of where they are." She was awarded the Bronze Star for her meritorious service in Iraq. She also credits troops that overcame continual obstacles and disappointments with unity and hard work.

"It's your duty to give back," concluded the major. "You give it everything you've got."

Passion and drive, coupled with the proper resources, are virtually unstoppable. Regardless of your resources, be contagiously passionate today about your own duty, just like Major Marci Hodge.

ALMIGHTY GOD, *I know attitude affects everything. It can turn things around or turn things down. Help me today to have a contagious and positive attitude to "give it everything I've got."*

# MY TEAM EARNED THIS

*For where two or three are gathered in my name, I am there among them.*
*—Matthew 18:20*

It might be a surprise to those unfamiliar with our current armed forces deployments to learn that many sailors are serving, not on the ocean, but on very hot, dry land in Afghanistan.

Petty Officer First Class Lee Chandler, a reservist from Naval Reserve Center Minneapolis, was part of the Provincial Reconstruction Team in Afghanistan's Kunar province, helping with security, reconstruction, and development.

This northeast corner of Afghanistan, bordering Pakistan, has rugged mountains to sweltering desert valleys with extreme heat. For a mechanic, this harsh terrain and climate pose a major challenge and can take its toll on vehicles. Additionally, Kunar is the most militarily active province.

During a vehicle recovery mission Lee's team came under rocket attack from insurgent forces. Under enemy fire, he ensured the safe evacuation of coalition forces and equipment without injury to personnel or damage to equipment.

"Petty Officer First Class Chandler's personal courage and commitment to mission accomplishment in a combat zone, under the most extreme of circumstances, greatly contributed to the success of Operation Enduring Freedom," read the citation from U.S. Army Major General Jeffrey J. Schloesser.

"I was just doing my job," Lee insisted. "My team earned this. I just get the privilege of wearing it."

A common theme among public servants recognized as heroes is to turn the focus onto the team and away from the individual. That is exactly what makes those teams so effective—a strong sense of unity and synergy. Consider anything you need to do today to strengthen your own team from re-grouping to recognition.

MY FOUNDATION, *I am a link in so many human chains. Strengthen me as I lead, as I follow, as I support, and link up with many to accomplish greater things than I ever could alone.*

# HE DIDN'T LET GO

*Our hope for you is unshaken; for we know that as you share in our sufferings, so also you share in our consolation.* —2 Corinthians 1:7

There are times when a police officer isn't called on to enforce the law, but simply to express compassion. That was the case when West Valley City, Utah, police officer Kevin Peck came around the corner just after a city bus had struck a 24-year-old woman in a crosswalk, pinning her underneath, and severely crushing both of her legs. The driver didn't see her in time to stop.

When Kevin arrived on the scene, all he could see was one of the woman's white shoes sticking out from under the bus. He quickly discovered the woman was alive and had suffered severe injuries. He crawled up under the bus on the icy ground to take her pulse. After he took her hand, he didn't let go until fire crews were able to lift the bus up and pull her out.

"She was very scared. She asked me not to leave. So I said I would just stay under there with her until we got her out. And she started telling me about her family and where she was headed," Kevin said. "I told her that I would stay there."

"She was afraid she was going to die, and I'm just praying and hoping that the bus doesn't move. We're right next to the tire underneath the bus, and I'm just trying to reassure her, and keep her calm," he said.

Once a rescue crew arrived, the bus was lifted off and a backboard was placed under the woman. She was transported to the hospital and stabilized. Kevin visited the woman in the hospital a few days after the accident.

Compassion and sympathy for suffering seems to be dying qualities today. Be sure you keep them alive and well in your own heart and stay ready to show anyone who may need them.

MY COMFORTER, *there is a place we uniquely connect with You when we suffer and when we hurt with those who do. Thank You that You endured pain here, so that we can know You understand. Help me to watch for the hand to hold today.*

# JUST SPEAK THE WORD

*For we do not have a high priest who is unable to sympathize with our weaknesses, but we have one who in every respect has been tested as we are, yet without sin. Let us therefore approach the throne of grace with boldness, so that we may receive mercy and find grace to help in time of need.* —Hebrews 4:15-16

Leadership and public service offer a unique perspective to life and even to God.

We see in Matthew chapter 8, when Jesus was entering Capernaum, a centurion, a Roman officer in command of 60 to 80 soldiers, walked up to him and said, "Lord, my servant is at my home paralyzed and suffering." Jesus tells him that he will go to his house and heal the man. Next comes an amazing response—both from the centurion and from Jesus.

The centurion responds, "Lord, I'm not worthy for you to come into my house. Just speak the word right here and my servant will be healed. For I am a man of authority, with soldiers under me. If I say 'go,' or 'come,' or 'do this,' it is done."

Jesus was amazed. This guy got it! Jesus said, "In no one in Israel have I found such faith. Go, let it be done for you according to your faith." And the man's servant was healed, with the centurion standing right there in the street with Jesus.

The centurion's experience told him what Jesus could do, if He chose. But a truly amazing aspect of this story is that a Roman centurion believed Jesus was who He said He was. This caused him to feel unworthy to be in Jesus' presence, but his care for his servant gave him the boldness to ask anyway.

Today, know that there is a difference in being arrogant and confident. God knows your heart and wants you to come to Him in confidence and faith. Like the centurion, you already understand authority and chain of command. Now, show Him your faith!

LORD JESUS, *it is amazing to me that I am speaking to the same Healer who healed the centurion's servant. This story encourages me to be confident before You and show You my faith that You are who You say You are.*

# IT'S A PRIVILEGE TO BE INVITED

*Return, O my soul, to your rest, for the Lord has dealt bountifully with you. For you have delivered my soul from death, my eyes from tears, my feet from stumbling. I walk before the Lord in the land of the living.* —Psalm 116:7-9

Wendy is a volunteer on a community nurse team that makes over 2,800 visits annually to people who are living with a terminal illness. They allow patients to stay in their own homes, on their own terms. It's a service provided free to their community.

Wendy tells about her work, "There is no typical day for me. I visit with families and help them cope with what's happening. I see couples that have been together for 40, 50, or 60 years that are facing a future without their soul mate. It's not just about treating the disease, but about focusing on all aspects of their needs. It's a privilege to be invited into these people's lives."

Wendy tells about one of her patients, "Carol has a rare form of incurable cancer. But like many of our patients, Carol wants to be able to live every moment in her own home, in her own way. I spend time with Carol making sure her medication is right for her increasing pain, talking through any concerns she has, and helping her husband understand Carol's condition and needs. This means she actually has time to live, instead of just grappling with her illness. It also means families like hers have the reassurance of knowing they are not alone during this time. I—or another member of my team—is here whenever they need us, day or night."

Carol talks about Wendy, "I couldn't have gotten through the last few months without Wendy. I would be in constant pain with absolutely no quality of life."

It takes a special calling to bring life from impending death. Let this story encourage you to live this day to the fullest. We are all terminal. Some just know sooner than the rest of us.

ALPHA & OMEGA, *You truly are at our beginning and our end. Thank You that we can trust You with both, as well as all the life in between. Help me make today count as I serve.*

# ON MY 23RD MISSION

*You prepare a table before me in the presence of my enemies; you anoint my head with oil; my cup overflows.* —Psalm 23:5

Past presidential candidate John McCain was shot down over North Vietnam in his Skyhawk bomber in October of 1967. Navy pilot McCain was taken prisoner with two broken arms and a broken leg.

In a U.S. News special report, he said, "I was on my 23rd mission, flying right over the heart of Hanoi in a dive at about 4,500 feet, when a Russian missile came up and blew the right wing off my bomber. It went into a straight-down spin. I pulled the ejection handle and was knocked unconscious by the force. I landed by parachute in a lake right in the corner of Hanoi. I was in a dazed condition, wearing an inflatable life preserver."

"Some North Vietnamese swam out and pulled me to the side of the lake and immediately started stripping me. A huge crowd of people gathered; all screaming, cursing, spitting, and kicking at me. When they had most of my clothes off, I felt a twinge in my right knee. My right foot was resting next to my left knee, in a 90-degree position. I said, 'My God! My leg!' One of them slammed a rifle butt down on my shoulder. Another stuck a bayonet in my foot."

During captivity McCain's weight dropped to 100 pounds He spent two years in solitary confinement, and endured torture after torture. He was released at the end of the war and still walks with a limp from his injuries. McCain entered the life of politics, still desiring to serve his nation.

All our POWs and MIAs made the ultimate sacrifice for our freedom. That is what makes our opportunity to serve mean so much. Thank God today for your freedom and the men and women who have, and continue to, make it possible.

RIGHTEOUS ONE, *You understand torture and pain at the hands of captors. You endured much of the same—being nailed to the cross. Yet Your mission was far more than political; it was to save the entire world. Thank You for what You endured in my place. Help me to serve You today.*

# ALIVE—AGAIN

*Are not five sparrows sold for two pennies? Yet not one of them is forgotten in God's sight. But even the hairs of your head are all counted. Do not be afraid; you are of more value than many sparrows.* —Luke 12:6-7

Here are three stories of EMTs bringing people from death back to life by using their quick thinking and trained responses.

Montville, New Jersey police officers Frank Cooney and Carlo Marucci were dispatched to a medical call for a woman unconscious and not breathing. When they arrived, she had no pulse. They quickly administered three shocks and began CPR. The woman's pulse came back and she was transported to the hospital where she made a full recovery. Later, they found out that the woman they had saved was the mother of a fellow officer.

EMT Sean Ward of the Point Borough First Aid Squad was called to the home of a woman whose 3-year-old grandson had fallen into the swimming pool. When he was pulled from the pool, he had been underwater for nearly ten minutes. The boy had no pulse and was not breathing. EMT Ward arrived and began life-saving measures. Because of the fast response and training, the boy is alive with no disabilities.

On a cold January day, Monmouth Beach police officers Aaron Rock and Matthew Clark responded to a call. Upon arriving, they found a 15-year-old boy who had collapsed in his driveway while shoveling snow. The boy was in complete cardiac arrest, not breathing, and no pulse. The officers used an automated defibrillator to shock his heart back into rhythm. The 15-year-old was airlifted to a local hospital where he made a full recovery.

EMTs, like so many public servants, see death far too often, but also have the amazing opportunity to bring people back using their God-given skills. What better job could one have than saving a life?

THE WAY, THE TRUTH, LIFE, *some get to have a second chance at life through CPR and other skills. Today I thank You for every breath. Help me to make mine count for good.*

# YOU INSPIRE US

*Beloved, you do faithfully whatever you do for the friends, even though they are strangers to you.* —3 John 1:5

Country music super-group Lady Antebellum decided to put on a contest where she would give a free prom appearance to a winning high school.

The small town of Henryville, Ind., had been devastated by a 175 mph twister that leveled the local high school. When some of the students found out about the band's contest, they launched a campaign to win. This got Lady Antebellum's attention and they decided to put on a benefit concert to help raise money for the town.

Although the platinum selling band couldn't make it to Henryville's actual prom, the school's 188 juniors and seniors and their dates attended a private "mini-prom" the night before the concert, where the band performed as well.

Hilary Scott of Lady Antebellum told the crowd, "Each and every one of you inspired us." The band even brought a few students on stage to dance. For one night, the teens were able to forget about the tragedy and celebrate their achievement.

The following night—ten weeks after the tragedy struck—the band played a special show in nearby Louisville, Ky., and raised $235,000 for the citizens of Henryville.

Artists and celebrities like this band have a major stage from which to raise both money and awareness, but we must remember that we all have some sort of platform and circle of influence.

It can tempting to think of all we would do if we had money and fame, but the truth is, our character determines what we do with a little or a lot, not our pocketbook or platform.

PROVIDER, *thank You that we don't have to question if You will be faithful. No matter what we do, You are constant. Help me to use the platform You give me for good and to grow in my reach toward people—friends or strangers.*

# EYES ON THE FIELD

*May the Lord reward you for your deeds, and may you have a full reward from the Lord, the God of Israel, under whose wings you have come for refuge!* —Ruth 2:12

Gleaning is an Old Testament concept that refers to the sharing of wealth. In those days, people were permitted to reap the leftover grain around the sides of the field after the harvest, then they would give it to the widows in the community.

In Ruth chapter 2, we meet Boaz. He comes back to his property where the harvest is going on and sees Ruth in the field, asking his foreman about her. Beginning with verse 8—Then Boaz said to Ruth, "Now listen, my daughter, do not go to glean in another field or leave this one, but keep close to my young women. Keep your eyes on the field that is being reaped, and follow behind them. I have ordered the young men not to bother you. If you get thirsty, go to the vessels and drink from what the young men have drawn."

Boaz had heard about Ruth and her commitment to her mother-in-law. He had respect for her and wanted to help. He expressed compassion, protection, and provision for her, as well as the others who were gleaning from his harvest.

Do you make it a practice to share your money? Time? Energy? Care? Do your neighbors, co-workers, extended family know you as someone of strong reputation?

Boaz and Ruth had exceptional reputations because of their character. Think about the concept of gleaning. There are people in your life who need to gain and learn from you. Don't just share what you have, but who you are.

GREAT PROVIDER, *show me who, where, and how You want me to share of all my resources that You graciously give to me.*

# TO GIVE HIS LIFE

*For where your treasure is, there your heart will be also.* —Matthew 6:21

Ever stopped to think why it feels so good to serve others? To do good for our communities and be a positive influence in society? Why is there a natural sense of wanting to help and feel the satisfaction of knowing we have contributed for someone else's gain?

A mother came to Jesus one day and asked if her two sons could sit on His right and left in Heaven. Now that's a proud mama! . . . Too proud.

Jesus told her she didn't know what she was asking and He also told her that those positions weren't His to grant. He continued and used this as a teaching moment. Listen to Matthew 20:26-28.

*"Whoever wishes to be great among you must be your servant,*
*and whoever wishes to be first among you must be your slave;*
*just as the Son of Man came not to be served but to serve,*
*and to give his life a ransom for many."*

We have the desire to serve, because the God who formed us and gave us life came not to be served, but to serve—to give up His life. When we give, serve, and contribute, we are joining God in His activity. We are actively showing and expressing love, which is of His nature. Service connects us to His identity.

EVERLASTING GOD, *You could have revealed Yourself to us in so many ways, but You chose a Servant. May I serve to identify with You and join You in where You are working.*

# SOLES & SOULS

*In all this I have given you an example that by such work we must support the weak, remembering the words of the Lord Jesus, for he himself said, "It is more blessed to give than to receive." —Acts 20:35*

Several years ago, young entrepreneur Blake Mycoskie founded his own company called TOMS Shoes. While competing on the second season of the TV show The Amazing Race with his sister in Argentina, he noticed a style of shoe there called "alpargata." He started wearing these shoes while there. At the same time, as he went through some of the area villages, he noticed how many children had no shoes.

When he began his for-profit shoe company, he also formed a non-profit called "Friends of TOMS." He decided for every pair of TOMS shoes purchased, Friends of TOMS would give a pair away to a child with no shoes. To date, over one million pairs of shoes have been given away to children in over 20 countries worldwide, including to impoverished areas of the U.S.

Every April 5th, TOMS promotes "One Day Without Shoes," encouraging people to go all day without shoes to raise awareness of this issue. Over 250,000 people have committed to take part.

Particularly in metropolitan areas, TOMS shoes have become the shoes of choice for the hip and trendy, many customers not even knowing that somewhere on the other side of the world, a child will be receiving their first pair of shoes.

Businessmen like Blake Mycoskie, and companies like TOMS, prove that money can be made, but lives can also be changed for the better. Wouldn't the world be a better place, if some profit from every company, were converted to a practical plan to help those who can't help themselves? Be sure anything that you have a say in, or are a part of, gives back.

MERCIFUL GOD, *it's ironic that when we give, we feel like we have received—and, often, something far more valuable than a physical gift. Guide me to grow in giving.*

# WHAT WILL YOU DO?

*If you have faith the size of a mustard seed, you will say to this mountain, "Move from here to there," and it will move; and nothing will be impossible for you.*
—Matthew 17:20b

"What are you going to do about the orphans?"

That question, asked by a friend of evangelist Everett Swanson after returning from Korea, forever changed not only his life, but the lives of many thousands of children for over six decades.

Everett traveled to preach the Gospel to troops of the Army of the Republic of Korea.

He saw many children there orphaned by the war and living on the streets, searching for food and shelter. Many lived in garbage dumps, digging for food scraps. As with so many of us when we encounter such a mammoth problem, the potential answer seems so overwhelming that we feel paralyzed and do nothing.

In sharing with a missionary friend about his burden, the question was asked.

The answer birthed Compassion International—a child sponsorship program that impacts the life of a child. The ripple effect, however, can positively touch as many as 30 people around that child. A person can sponsor a child for approximately $35-$40 a month.

Compassion works to not only meet the child's physical needs, but social, economic, emotional, and spiritual as well. The organization works through a local church in each area to partner for a holistic approach to help children. Today, 1.2 million children in 26 countries are impacted daily.

Everett Swanson proved that even though a problem can seem to be insurmountable, answers can be found—one child at a time, one sponsor at a time. And it all started with one simple question: what are you going to do about it?

THE WAY, *I am certainly guilty of looking at many of the world's problems and giving in to discouragement and then giving up. Help me to look at every challenge as an opportunity and every person I meet as an encounter with You.*

# INVISIBLE POWER

*My grace is sufficient for you, for power is made perfect in weakness.' So, I will boast all the more gladly of my weaknesses, so that the power of Christ may dwell in me.* —2 Corinthians 12:9

After a tornado had swept through a small town in Texas, residents were amazed to find a piece of straw had been driven through a telephone pole! How could that be? Something that was so flexible and brittle piercing through something so dense and strong! The secret was that piece of straw took on the strength of the tornado. The straw was able to accomplish what would normally be impossible.

That's the kind of strength you can have, if you'll just allow Christ to live through you. His power can enable you to accomplish the unbelievable.

When you become a Christian, you take on the power of Jesus Christ. With Christ, you have much more strength than you could ever hope to have on your own.

The place that you tap into that power source is your private time in prayer. As you are reading this book each day, try spending more time talking to God about your concerns and burdens. You can also start to read more Scripture than the verse given here each day.

You can stay connected to God all day long, talking to Him whenever you want, but a dedicated, focused time of talking, listening, and surrendering to Him is crucial to keeping and strengthening your connection with Him.

HEAVENLY CREATOR, *teach me to pray. Teach me how to quiet my mind and heart and listen to You. Teach me to value Your Word.*

# THE TIPPING POINT

*You have given me the shield of your salvation, and your right hand has supported me; your help has made me great.* —Psalm 18:35

Tipping Point CEO Eric Zimmer saw the amazing skills that returning military personnel had as they came back into the private sector, so he developed a program called "Solar for Soldiers."

"In a lot of cases, employers who hire vets want to squeeze the military out of them, but we want the opposite: to utilize the discipline and qualities the military has imbued in them. It is our small way of saying, 'Thank you for your service'," stated Zimmer.

That's where five year Marine vet Mark Haake comes in. He had spent time in Iraq and Afghanistan as an aviation electronic maintenance specialist on Huey and Cobra helicopters. After pounding the pavement for jobs and realizing he was going to have to go to college to get the degree to be able to do the type of job that he was already trained to do, he found Tipping Point. His first job was to install 2,800 solar panels on a fleet maintenance building for the city of Columbus, Ohio.

Mark said, "I'm in an expanding field where I can grow new skills based on the ones I learned in the Marines."

Connecting skills and passion to the optimum career setting is one of the greatest challenges in life. And it can also be one of our greatest blessings.

If you are searching today for the right fit for you, pray specifically, asking God to lead you to your spot in the world. If you're already there, then thank Him right now for bringing you there.

LORD OF ALL, *I want to know that I am serving You and mankind in the optimum place I can. Keep me mindful of what You're doing and where You want me to be.*

# THAT'S WHAT'S DRIVING ME

*You visit the earth and water it, you greatly enrich it; the river of God is full of water; you provide the people with grain, for so you have prepared it. You water its furrows abundantly, settling its ridges, softening it with showers, and blessing its growth.* —Psalm 65:9-10

"What's your plan for retirement?" a co-pilot once asked Bill Gross, an international UPS pilot. "I'm going to get a big John Deere four-wheel-drive tractor and a planter," he answered. "I'll drive across North Dakota (where he grew up), pulling into places where it looks like a farmer is having a tough time and say, 'Hey, I'll plant a couple hundred acres for you today, free of charge.'"

But Bill started early, even before retirement. Farm Rescue, a group helping farm families affected by injury, illness, and natural disaster, was born.

Farm Rescue provided assistance to ten farm families in its first year. One example is Merlin Backman who postponed arm surgery for planting season. "I told the doctor, 'I don't know what I'm going to do about the farmwork.' And today Farm Rescue is putting my crop in for me."

Farm Rescue has now helped over 150 farm families in North and South Dakota, Minnesota, and Montana. Their teams of volunteers work shifts of 8 to 12 hours at a time, around the clock, in spring and fall.

Bill added, "Small family farms are dying off. The further they go into debt, the less likely their children will carry on the tradition. That's what's driving me. We're making it possible for farm families to continue on for future generations."

It is vitally important that whatever we invest our lives in is also impacting future generations—not just the here and now. Leaving a legacy casts a piece of who we are into the future.

ALMIGHTY GOD, *I recognize today that You are the creator and the sustainer of all life. As I live today, help me to leave a part of me for future generations.*

# RIGHTEOUS BEFORE ME

*By faith Noah, warned by God about events as yet unseen, respected the warning and built an ark to save his household; by this he condemned the world and became an heir to the righteousness that is in accordance with faith.* — Hebrews 11:7

Even the occasional church-goer knows the story of Noah—the man that God told to build a huge boat, when it wasn't even raining; the man that God told to go and get two of every animal to go on his boat; the man that endured both the criticism of people while he was building the boat, yet had to hear their cries as they drowned in their unbelief. Take a look at these four verses about Noah.

Genesis 6:9—Noah was a righteous man, blameless in his generation; Noah walked with God.

Genesis 6:22—Noah did this; he did all that God commanded him.

Genesis 7:1—Then the Lord said to Noah, "Go into the ark, you and all your household, for I have seen that you alone are righteous before me in this generation."

Genesis 7:5—And Noah did all that the Lord had commanded him.

We tend to remember the ark, the flood, and, of course, the animals, but we cannot miss the reason why God chose Noah to experience all this and literally re-start the human race.

The good news today is that, through Jesus Christ who made a bridge between God and us, you can be called righteous, walk with God, and do all that God commands you, just as Noah did. You have both the opportunity and the power made available to you through Christ. At the end of the day, Noah was just a flesh-and-blood man, but the difference was—he loved God.

SAVIOR GOD, *help me to know today that, I too, can love You as Noah did and obey You as he did as well. Help me to walk with You.*

# GIVE UP ON NOBODY

*So let us not grow weary in doing what is right, for we will reap at harvest time, if we do not give up.* —Galatians 6:9

Warren Buffett, whose net worth is estimated at over $40 billion in 2012, pledged that his money will go to charity when he dies. But he's also funneling millions to charity now—simply by selling a lunch meeting. In 2000, Buffett began the annual auction on eBay with the proceeds going to the Glide Foundation, an organization that serves meals to the needy and runs a church in a poor area of San Francisco.

The first year's winner got the lunch meeting with Buffett for $25,000. Over ten years later, the two-hour meeting has gone for over $2.6 million. The winner can bring up to seven people to dine with Buffett at the Smith & Wollensky Steakhouse in New York.

Since its inception, the event has brought in more than $11 million for Glide. The billionaire investor was introduced to the Reverend Cecil Williams, Glide's founder, by his now deceased wife, Susan, who had volunteered for the charity.

"I was suspicious when I heard my wife raving about this place in San Francisco. What I witnessed was an institution and an individual that really gave up on anybody. They took the people that the rest of the world had forgotten, people who gave up on themselves, and they felt that every human being had a potential."

There are two types of investment in this world—finances and faith. Faith takes nothing physical to begin—just some time and energy with someone to reach out to. So, how does your "portfolio" look in that area? A wealth of love awaits you.

LOVING GOD, *give me eyes to see and ears to hear those who I must pour my life into. May I trust You with the outcome as I give out my time, energy, and gifts.*

# CATALYST FOR COOPERATION

*Nations shall come to your light, and kings to the brightness of your dawn.*
—Isaiah 60:3

No one even loosely connected to American politics would argue that former Presidents Bill Clinton and George W. Bush would be on opposite sides of the fence on the majority of government issues and policies. However, when the earthquake devastated the country of Haiti in 2010, the need for unity became greater than their divisions.

The two came together to form the Clinton-Bush Haiti Fund. By 2012, they raised over $54 million.

The purpose of their collaboration is:

1. Supporting micro-finance institutions
2. Providing small business with financing
3. Providing training and development of the workforce
4. Responding to miscellaneous capital needs that arise

The goal of the Clinton-Bush Foundation is long-term investment and economic recovery—attempting to help the people learn to help themselves. Their goal is to promote the creation of jobs and economic growth, serve as a catalyst for building Haitian capacity, watch as Haitians sustain it, and then remove themselves from the picture.

"The fund is dedicated to supporting the Haitian people's efforts to rebuild their own country. The successes we celebrate are not ours, but theirs," Clinton-Bush Haiti Fund CEO Gary Edson said. "While progress in Haiti can be difficult to measure, the Haitian businesses and workers we are supporting today are hopeful examples of how Haiti can thrive."

We aren't going to get along great with everyone or always agree on issues, but when it comes to service and the greater good, we must lay aside differences to get the job done and take action for those in need, as these two presidents did.

PRINCE OF PEACE, *as we look at the Holy Trinity, we see the great benefit of unity and cohesion. Guide me, no matter my differences with others, to always focus on community and cooperation for the sake of those in need.*

# I KNOW THIS IS GOOD

*But take care and watch yourselves closely, so as neither to forget the things that your eyes have seen nor to let them slip from your mind all the days of your life; make them known to your children and your children's children.* —Deuteronomy 4:9

Thomas is 23 years old and has just graduated from college. For the past two years, he has given some of his time and energy to Julio, a fourth grader, who lives with his mom and younger siblings. As the oldest child in the family, he needed a solid, positive role model. Big Brothers Big Sisters of America (BBBS) is a 100-year-old organization that has the nation's largest donor and volunteer network for mentoring young people. BBBS put Thomas and Julio together.

Whether it is helping with homework, going to the museum, or just hanging out and talking, the two get along great. "I wanted a little brother, because I had an older brother, and now I have a little brother that gives me someone to teach and talk to," Thomas said. "We talk about anything that's on his mind, anything that's bothering him. Just being a big brother feels really right, very natural and good. What I'm doing in volunteering, I know this is good."

Beginning in 1904, BBBS now has programs in all 50 states and 12 countries around the world for children ages 6 to 18.

With global issues like the deterioration of the family, coupled with local crises such as inner city gangs, volunteers like Thomas are changing the world and the legacy of families, one child at a time. Julio's life will never be the same, because of just a few hours spent with a role model who provides care, guidance, and support.

Regardless of your place or position in life, be sure you're investing in the lives of children. There is great return and reward that comes from loving a child.

DEAR SAVIOR, *thank You that You recognized and loved children when You were here to show us their importance to You. Thank You, too, for being my Father and allowing me to be Your child.*

# A FIGHTING CHANCE

*So then, let us not fall asleep as others do, but let us keep awake and be sober.*
—*1 Thessalonians 5:6*

Officer Dale Gordon was patrolling the beach in Pascagoula, Miss., when he got a call for help. A three-year-old girl was swimming at Pascagoula Point when she nearly drowned and was pulled from the water.

"As I approached, I could see a child unresponsive, lying in the sand," Dale said. "The tips of the fingers had turned blue, the toes had turned blue, and the child's lips had turned blue." Officer Gordon immediately began CPR. "I lifted the back of the neck and began giving mouth to mouth resuscitation. After a few minutes of CPR, I felt her chest and it started getting a big, strong heart beat."

Once he felt a pulse, Officer Gordon said all he could do was thank God "because, I knew the child had a fighting chance at that point."

Officer Gordon continued, "It was a high pressure situation and I'm just happy the little girl is alive and well. From what I have been told by family, she is responsive, sitting up, smiling, and it appears she is going to make a full recovery. I look at myself as blessed by God to be able to do something to bring this child back to life."

Every single day, there are tragedies all around us—situations where there isn't an Officer Gordon or he can't get there in time. But, every single day, there are also Officer Gordons who will get up, go to work, and by the end of the day, will save someone's life. Training, alertness, and timing all come together for a happy ending.

Today, that just might be you. Live ready to serve and to save.

ALMIGHTY GOD, *strengthen me today to stay alert, serve, and if called upon, to save.*

# END OF WATCH

*Remember me, O my God, concerning this, and do not wipe out my good deeds*
*that I have done for the house of my God and for his service.* —*Nehemiah 13:14*

ODMP.org is a web site dedicated to fallen officers, titled the "Officer Down Memorial Page" with the byline of "Remembering All of Law Enforcement's Heroes." ODMP is also a non-profit organization dedicated to honoring America's officers.

Approximately 20,000 law enforcement officers have been killed in the line of duty in our nation's history.

In 1996, Chris Cosgriff, a university freshman, read a Washington Post article about the release of a murderer, convicted of slaying two Maryland police officers. Upon learning that this violent criminal served only 16 years for this heinous act, Chris was compelled to find a way to honor fallen officers.

Chris, the ODMP founder said, "When a police officer is killed, it's not an agency that loses an officer, it's an entire nation."

Family, friends, and co-workers can go and write reflections to the fallen officers. For each officer listed, there is also a biography and incident report of the officer's "end of watch."

You can search by state or by year. It is sobering to browse the site to see how many policemen, policewomen, correctional officers, state troopers, sheriffs, sheriff's deputies, and reserve officers have been killed serving and protecting the public.

ODMP supports an initiative called "No Parole for Cop Killers." The program's intent is to ensure that all criminals guilty of ending the life of an officer serve their full sentence without parole.

It is difficult to find a community that has not suffered from this tragedy and loss. Go to ODMP.org and look at your city or area for the officers who have given their lives in service for your community.

LORD JESUS, *You gave us an ordinance to remember Your sacrifice and death through Holy Communion. Thank You for the ways we can remember those who have died in service to our community and nation. Bless those families today.*

# A RIPPLE EFFECT

*In your righteousness deliver me and rescue me; incline your ear to me and save me.* —Psalm 71:2

Growing up in war-torn Democratic Republic of the Congo (DRC), Richard Kitumba often went to bed wondering if he would survive the night. And just as they feared, Richard said, "Soldiers broke into my family's house and we were forced at gunpoint to load all our possessions onto their trucks." He and his family survived the experience and he eventually relocated to the United States as a translator, while countless children were orphaned during the five-year war there.

On trips back to his country, Richard was overwhelmed by the crippling poverty and he knew he must help. In 2007, he founded City of Refuge International, a nonprofit organization that, mainly through individual sponsorships, places DRC orphans in foster homes. In his hometown of Kamina, orphans are placed into foster care, taking care of their clothing, medical, and education expenses.

"I felt compelled to help the children of the DRC, because they are so vulnerable," explained Richard, who now lives in Springfield, Ore., with his family. "The difference we make in the lives of these children is already having a ripple effect on the entire city. You never know—one of these children may end up being a scientist, a physician or a governor someday."

So many people would have fled and never looked back, just being grateful to have escaped, but Richard turned his experience into a motivation to rescue children.

Our best places of service are often those situations that we have walked through ourselves.

SAVIOR, *thank You that You came to relate and translate Your love to us. Thank You for Your rescue and care of our hearts and lives.*

# THEY DON'T FORGET

*I will give, in my house and within my walls, a monument and a name better than sons and daughters; I will give them an everlasting name that shall not be cut off.* —Isaiah 56:5

Billie and Peggy Harris were married just six weeks when he was shipped off to fly a fighter plane during the invasion of Normandy.

He was shot down during a mission over Nazi-occupied northern France.

Billie was first reported missing, but later his body was found and buried.

A government letter later reported Billie's body was to be relocated in an unspecified cemetery.

Months turned into years of trying to get answers as to exactly where her husband was laid to rest. Finally in 2005, the House Armed Services Committee responded that he was MIA, according to the National Archives.

This is where Billie's cousin, Alton Harvey, began to do his own detective work.

Through his search, they found Billie's body had been buried at the Normandy American Cemetery and Memorial. After six decades, Peggy's mystery was finally solved. But the story doesn't end there.

In the Normandy town of Les Ventes, the main road is named "Place Billie D. Harris." Three times a year the townspeople, led by the mayor, walk the road and commemorate Billie's sacrifice. Ninety-one-year-old Guy Surleau tells the story of when Billie's plane was hit, he fought to crash his plane in the woods to avoid the villager's homes. Even diving to his death, he saved the lives of townspeople. Their gratitude for the American intervention and Billie's sacrifice remains to this day.

Peggy now travels to Les Ventes annually to join them in their memorial of her husband. "They don't forget," Peggy somberly stated.

Our men and women who give their lives in service leave behind survivors, who give up part of their hearts for the rest of their days.

DELIVERER, I *pray You bless each of those husbands, wives, and children whose loved ones gave their lives in service to our nation and for our freedom. May Your care and comfort touch them today.*

# BAND OF BROTHERS

*He trains my hands for war, so that my arms can bend a bow of bronze. You have given me the shield of your salvation, and your right hand has supported me; your help has made me great.* —Psalm 18:34-35

When 26-year-old Major Dick Winters was among 13,000 other paratroopers, about to enter his first battle in what would be the largest amphibious attack in history—the invasion of Normandy, he had no idea he was also going to be in command.

Easy Company's commander was killed in the jump.

Just eight hours after landing, Major Winters led a dozen men in an attack on Brecourt Manor in France where 50 German soldiers were entrenched, guarding an artillery battery and its four heavy guns shelling Omaha Beach. The major led an attack on the fixed position that is still taught at West Point today. They destroyed all four guns, then Major Winters personally seized the military maps, revealing the German army's positions all along the Nor-mandy coast. It is important to note that none of Easy Company had ever been in battle before.

The popular TV series, "Band of Brothers," was inspired by these events. Major Winters was awarded the Distinguished Service Cross, the Army's second highest medal for valor. He retired to his hometown of Lancaster, Pa., and died at age 92. In Saint-Marie du Mont France, a statue of Major Winters was erected to honor him and all the junior officers who led American men on D-Day.

It seems that most often when service culminates in heroics, it is in a spontaneous circumstance where training and courage merge into perfection. This is exactly why so many lauded as heroes insist they are not. Know today that you, serving in your role, are making a difference and making history—for someone.

FAITHFUL & TRUE, *whether calculated or spontaneous, guide me to make a difference in any situation You place me in. May I be found faithful when my moment comes.*

# GOT GPS?

*All our steps are ordered by the Lord; how then can we understand our own ways?*
*— Proverbs 20:24*

The invention of the GPS—or Global Positioning System—is revolutionizing lives everywhere. Our smart phones now tell us where we are and how to get where we're going. People with little or no sense of direction don't have to be lost anymore. Just program in the start address and the end address and you can know exactly where to go, turn, and stop. All you have to do is follow the instructions and you can arrive at your destination safely.

What if someone gets a GPS installed in their vehicle or has it on their phone, but then either never turns it on or never figures out how it works? What if they never take the time to punch in where they want to go?

When you become a Christian, you receive the Holy Spirit who will direct your decisions and direction. Call it "God's Positioning System."

You can choose to ignore God's voice and do what you want, but why would you want to do that?

God wants to lead you through life, every twist and turn, start and stop. Prayer is the "app" for that faith GPS.

THE WAY, *lead my steps today. Show me Your way. Let me walk with You, not falling behind or running ahead.*

# LIKE A FREIGHT TRAIN

*For the Lord searches every mind, and understands every plan and thought. If you seek him, he will be found by you. —1 Chronicles 28:9b*

When Firefighter Jeff Novack arrived at a burning West Baltimore apartment building, he quickly realized there were people trapped inside.

Before other firemen could get their hoses set up to begin to battle the blaze, Jeff rushed in. He found and carried out an unconscious 86-year-old woman and handed her to paramedics. He had heard screams coming from the third floor and rushed back in.

Just then, flames shot up the steps "like a freight train," Jeff recalled. He jumped into an open apartment and through the thick smoke, felt his way along the wall for a way out.

He crawled out a window, dangling by his fingertips, then he felt a wave of intense heat roll over his arms. Fire was shooting out above him and Jeff knew he must let go. He fell three stories onto a cement sidewalk, suffering from second-degree burns on his arms, while also breaking his shoulder and hip.

The cause for the fire? Arson—set by a jealous woman after a lover's quarrel. The veteran fireman said he hopes his story will stop anyone from committing arson, adding, "She wanted to hurt one person, but she ended up hurting many more."

Whether natural, accidental, or intentional, when a fire threatens lives, firefighters must go into action. The reason for the flames makes no difference until every life is saved.

Do others' motives sometimes affect your desire to serve? It's understandable for it to be a factor. But there is usually a greater good that matters even more.

Be faithful to serve—regardless of the circumstances.

SAVIOR, *motive drives so much for us all. Help my own motives to be pure and focused on the big picture—that there are needs to be met and lives to be changed.*

# HOUSE OF HEROES

*The angel of the Lord encamps around those who fear him, and delivers them.*
—Psalm 34:7

Air Force veteran Leonard Sarbin and his wife Sharon have always been do-it-yourselfers when it came to house and yard projects. "I put the roof up myself," Leonard said as he nudges his wife of 48 years. "We remodeled a bathroom. We put a wall up and took the wall back down," Sharon remembered.

But as Leonard's back problems worsened, it became nearly impossible for him to take care of his home.

The Sarbins no longer have to worry about the work that has piled up. Over 50 volunteers were hard at work in the Saturday morning heat, helping complete projects the couple had been unable to do. Many of the volunteers were happy to serve a man who had served his country many years ago.

"It's a wonderful opportunity to be able to work and provide service to help our brother any way we can," said volunteer Michael Chastain.

The Sarbin's North Augusta home was chosen by House of Heroes, a non-profit that helps fix up and repair homes of elderly or disabled veterans.

"There are little things, even changing light bulbs, that are such a problem for some of our veterans," said House of Heroes Volunteer Coordinator Sam Shehane. "By giving back this way, it's just a small way to say thank you." And tasks that have needed attention for years are suddenly taken care of in a matter of hours at the hands of volunteers.

Leonard and Sharon say they can't thank the volunteers enough. "God has sent us a legion of angels," Leonard said.

If an angel is a messenger of God, then certainly these folks are sending a message of hope and love to those who have sacrificed and served for our country.

CORNERSTONE, help *me to see each day as a mission I am sent out to accomplish, so that I might do the work of angels.*

# HUMILITY PLAYS INTO IT

*The fear of the Lord is instruction in wisdom, and humility goes before honour.*
*—Proverbs 15:33*

At the annual recognition awards for the Western Massachusetts emergency services community, there was a lot to consider. In the past year, they had faced a hurricane, tornado, snowstorm, and even an earthquake. This was, of course, amidst hundreds of other crises where people needed medical attention in an emergency.

Robert Hassett, Springfield's emergency preparedness director, stated, "Everything they did, it was so professional and done with such care and competency. I'm overwhelmed. The EMTs and paramedics are often overlooked. This is a group of people that do their jobs, do it competently and professionally, and then move on to the next one. They don't often give you a chance to say thanks."

City Council President Daniel J. Corliss added, "Humility plays into it. These are individuals who are not looking for recognition. In the best possible sense of what being a public servant is about, emergency care providers as a group are interested mostly in treating people who need help."

Laura Machado, who was named Paramedic of the Year, said she did not know what she did that allowed her to be singled out among her peers. Laura originally wanted to be an athletic trainer, but after her first emergency medical training class she knew what she wanted to be.

One 20-year-veteran on the team stated, "Even today the job, though hard and often unpleasant, is still fulfilling. I love it. When you work with a great group of people, it makes the job enjoyable."

A crucial factor in effective service is a strong team. Be pro-active in encouraging and motivating all those you work with.

HOLY ONE, *teach me to not be concerned with getting credit, but with gaining connection with my team. Help me to choose humility over honor.*

# THAT WAS THE WAY HE WAS

*Suffering produces endurance, and endurance produces character, and character produces hope, and hope does not disappoint us, because God's love has been poured into our hearts through the Holy Spirit that has been given to us.* —Romans 5:3b-5

Sergeant Dennis Weichel, 29, of the Rhode Island National Guard, was riding in a convoy in eastern Afghanistan when some children were spotted in the road ahead, picking up shell casings, which are recycled for money. The soldiers in the convoy got out of their vehicles to get the children out of the way of the heavy trucks coming later. The huge, armored MRAPs, or Mine Resistant Ambush Protected Vehicle, can weigh as much as 16 tons.

An Afghan girl darted back onto the road to pick up some more casings. Weichel spotted the girl and managed to get her out of the way, but he was run over by the heavily armored truck. He later died of his injuries.

Lt. Colonel Denis Riel, a spokesman for the Rhode Island National Guard, said, "I have heard nothing but incredible stuff about this kid. He was the living embodiment of the Army: courageous, selfless, and loyal. This one is a significant loss."

Staff Sgt. Ronald Corbett said, "He would have done it for anybody. That was the way he was." The father of three was posthumously promoted to sergeant and received the Bronze Star for heroism.

What motivated Dennis to risk his life? Was it being a father? A soldier? Or maybe it was just built deep into his character? Likely, it was all of these things.

Today, whatever God is working to build into your character, cooperate fully. God knows what is best for us and, as with Sergeant Weichel, knows how to produce some amazing traits.

MIGHTY GOD, *in life and in death, I want to be known as a person of great character. And I know it is produced slowly over time, one decision at a time. Help me today to make wise choices in all that I do.*

# LOOSEN CHAINS

*Learn to do good; seek justice, rescue the oppressed, defend the orphan, plead for the widow.* —Isaiah 1:17

In the seventh grade, Zach Hunter was studying Black History Month and the abolitionists of years past.

He told his mother, "If I had lived back then, I would have fought for equality and against slavery."

Then his mother told him that slavery was still going on in the world and that 27 million people are still subjected to slavery in some form. In fact, there are more slaves today than in the 1700s and 1800s.

Zach learned that most slavery today has to do with money and debt. A family may allow a child to go with a family friend who promises a good job to help meet their needs. The child soon discovers this "friend" has sold him/her into slavery. Often the parents are misled to believe their child will have better living conditions or an opportunity for an education. Instead, the child becomes a slave.

Sometimes slavery results from family debts, which causes them to have to work in a brickyard all their lives. Sometimes little girls are made to work in brothels and boys are forced to roll cigarettes all day long.

Zach Hunter decided to take action. Through his church and school, he launched Loose Change to Loosen Chains, a fund-raising for social justice efforts around the world. The movement has enabled the release of many trapped in slavery.

Be grateful for your freedom today, as you have found out that millions are deprived of theirs. And use your freedom for good.

MERCIFUL GOD, *the suffering in the world can be overwhelming and subjects like human trafficking can seem a world away. For every rescue being planned and carried out, may You provide and protect to bring freedom.*

# WHY DID YOU PICK US?

*Then the righteous will answer him, "Lord, when was it that we saw you hungry and gave you food, or thirsty and gave you something to drink? And when was it that we saw you a stranger and welcomed you, or naked and gave you clothing? And when was it that we saw you sick or in prison and visited you?"*
—Matthew 25:37-39

A pastor in St. Louis, Mo., was going through his daily mail when he found a hand-written letter addressed to the church.

He did not recognize the return address or the name. As he opened the letter, a dollar bill fell out. He picked up the bill and read the words written by a woman, "My marriage has ended. My children don't love me anymore. I don't think I can go on much longer. Would someone please call me? I have given up hope."

The lady's name and phone number were written at the end.

The pastor showed the letter to his wife, then they called the woman and set a time to meet with her together. After several weeks of consistent counseling and help, the woman gave her life to Jesus and became a Christian.

Finally, the pastor asked her the question he'd been waiting to ask for weeks, "Of all the churches in this entire city, why did you pick our church?"

The lady smiled and answered, "I didn't just send a letter to your church. I sent that same letter with a dollar bill in each to 25 churches. You were the only one that called me."

There is an old saying that goes, "The world is changed by those who show up." How true that is. We don't always have to have a plan, program, or a committee to help people, just a willing, caring heart.

SAVIOR, *give me eyes to see You and the courage to show up.*

# ARE YOU OK?

*I have good advice and sound wisdom; I have insight, I have strength.*
—*Proverbs 8:14*

Post-traumatic stress disorder (PTSD), has typically been associated with the battlefield. But it is now being diagnosed in civilian first responders, such as search-and-rescue personnel, paramedics, police, and firefighters.

For example, Michael Ferrara developed PTSD from three decades as a search-and-rescuer, ski patrol officer, paramedic, and firefighter in Aspen, Colo.

Images from those rescues started playing over and over in his mind. "Little by little, it just started to build, and then one day, the slideshow of all these events started running in my head and I couldn't control it," Michael said. He handled it by isolating himself. "I didn't leave the house and I began using prescription drugs intended for physical ailments for my emotional trauma."

Hampton Sides, of Outside magazine, writes, "It's only recently become apparent that PTSD is rampant among the community of first responders. They see these horrible things—often people that they know. Now it's OK for first responders to come forward and try to deal with it before it becomes acute, like it did in Michael's case. We have to recognize that having this stuff mess with your head is not abnormal."

Michael adds, "You're not supposed to see stuff like this. And what we need to do is break through the culture by someone like myself stepping up and saying, 'Hey, it happened to me,' and I'm going to ask you: 'Are you OK?'"

If any of this sounds familiar to you, or reminds you of a friend that you serve with, reach out and get help. It's OK to not be "fine." You can search PTSD on the web for counselors who specialize in this area.

COUNSELOR, *help me to realize when I am not doing well emotionally, mentally, or spiritually, that there is no shame in getting help. Lead me to get help when I need it, so I may continue my service to others.*

# OVERCOMING OBSTACLES

*We have gifts that differ according to the grace given to us: prophecy, in proportion to faith; ministry, in ministering; the teacher, in teaching; the exhorter, in exhortation; the giver, in generosity; the leader, in diligence; the compassionate, in cheerfulness.* —Romans 12:6-8

When a soldier is hurt in war, recovery stateside means many months in a hospital bed. Rehabilitation therapy, boredom and restlessness become huge negative factors.

Tim Donley is a young Marine who lost both legs and severely injured his right arm after an IED attack. He was sent to Walter Reed Army Medical Center in Maryland for months of treatment.

Keeping up with his family and friends—even from a distance—was crucial to Tim's recovery and an important ingredient in regaining a healthy mental state.

The Wish Upon a Hero Foundation and other support charities provide iPads to the hospital. The apps, games, email, and Internet on one small device provide positive stimulation, as well as a way to connect with loved ones.

Winnie Pritchett, the mother of a young man serving in Afghanistan, saw the tablets as a great resource for the soldiers overseas, since they have no TV or cell phones. She started an organization called iPads for Soldiers. She, with the help of many other benefactors, has sent over 500 units to Afghanistan.

Whether a company buys a single tablet or 40 people give ten dollars each, meeting the needs of soldiers with such a simple solution makes a huge difference. It just takes an organization like WUAH or a lady like Winnie Pritchett to put some creativity and energy behind connecting a need with the right resources.

Today, pay attention to the needs around you and look for ways to connect with answers.

PROVIDER, *it is encouraging to see others creatively meet needs for people so worthy to receive, yet are too often forgotten. Guide me to watch for anywhere I can connect resources with needs.*

# NOT FORGOTTEN

*"You shall love the Lord your God with all your heart, and with all your soul, and with all your mind, and with all your strength." The second is this, "You shall love your neighbour as yourself." There is no other commandment greater than these.*
—Mark 12:30-31

There is a tradition among the members of all four branches of the military. When ambulances or airplanes carrying wounded military personnel stop to load or unload their precious cargo, everyone in the area lines up to honor, reach out, and encourage the fallen.

Military personnel will say there is no greater honor than to meet the wounded warriors. Their mission in that moment is to show gratitude for the soldiers' service and sacrifice.

They line up on the tarmac at airbases all over the world, even when they're off-duty. They touch the stretchers carrying wounded troops, shake hands, salute, or give a respectful glance, but every person is communicating: "I know what you're going through and you are not forgotten."

God designed us to need human contact and compassion, especially in times of tragedy or distress. He also gave us the desire to express that care to others as well.

Even though our culture increasingly encourages isolation and an every-man-for-himself attitude, recognitions, like the military have chosen to do, are needed and necessary by all of us.

Today, make eye contact with people, no matter how busy you are. Show respect and care for those you encounter. Communicate to people, both verbally and nonverbally, that they matter to you and that they are not forgotten.

LORD JESUS, *when You walked among us, You touched people daily in so many ways. It is so easy to get caught up in my life and my problems. Help me to see those around me as You would and treat them as You would.*

# HERO'S HIGHWAY

*Go through, go through the gates, prepare the way for the people; build up, build up the highway, clear it of stones, lift up an ensign over the peoples.* —Isaiah 62:10

"In Iraq during an operation called Phantom Fury near the city of Fallujah, injured U.S., Iraqi, and coalition soldiers were arriving faster than they could be processed in the emergency room," said Colonel John Mitchell.

"We had patients waiting outside in the elements and it began to rain on the second day. After several attempts to cover the patients, medical teams erected a tent cover on a frame."

A couple of years later, with the tent still in place, a 20x30 American flag was placed underneath the ceiling, so the soldiers lying on stretchers could see the reason they were fighting and sacrificing. The tent also received a name—Hero's Highway.

In just four years, 30,000 patients passed through Hero's Highway and underneath the American flag.

The old saying, "Necessity is the mother of invention" has long been true. Necessity brought about the tent, but people also need inspiration and motivation to keep going under difficult circumstances.

The flag and the name, Hero's Highway, was born out of that place of deep purpose and calling. America has long been a beacon of freedom throughout the world and stories such as this are historical snapshots of that shining light.

Look for ways to inspire and motivate your brothers and sisters that you serve with. We are so much better together than we ever are alone!

HOLY TRINITY, *help me to meet the needs of those around me, but help me also to inspire the hearts of those I touch. Please pour into me, as I pour out to others.*

# ICU AT 35,000 FEET

*But for you who revere my name the sun of righteousness shall rise, with healing in its wings.* —Malachi 4:2

Captain Aaron Lapointe of the Mississippi Air National Guard is piloting the C-17 globe master plane for the long flight from Ramstein Air Base in Germany to Andrews AFB in Washington. This plane, however, is unique because it is a flying ICU—intensive care unit—for wounded soldiers.

Pumps, tubes, and bags hang from metal racks turned into hospital beds. The most severely wounded will likely not remember the flight, but most have spent several days being stabilized before the long flight home.

The state and care of these troops is contingent upon the skill of the surgeon, flight nurse, and respiratory technician aboard the flight.

"At a hospital, if you need a cardiologist, or any other medical specialist, all you have to do is call him. When you are flying 35,000 feet over the Atlantic Ocean, you can call a specialist for advice, but they are not coming to the bedside to help you," said Air Force Lt. Colonel Raymond Fang, the trauma director at Landstuhl Regional Medical Center in Germany.

He and other medical professionals say the Critical Care Air Transport teams are some of the best in the world and planning ahead for the trip makes the difference.

Working in an ICU is a major challenge for any doctor or nurse, but running a unit at 35,000 feet over the ocean sounds like a job only for our military.

It seems that no matter how challenging or difficult our job may be, someone else has a tougher one. Today, be grateful for where you serve and for those with whom you serve.

GREAT PHYSICIAN, *it is amazing to know all the specialty jobs of service and those who add an element of risk and challenge to an already stressful job. Bless those today who take these on. Thank You for where I serve and those I serve with.*

# WHAT A WONDERFUL FEELING

*The trees of the field shall yield their fruit, and the earth shall yield its increase.*
*They shall be secure on their soil; and they shall know that I am the Lord.*
—*Ezekiel 34:27a*

Austen Pearce learned to garden on a small patch of ground in his backyard in Maricopa, Ariz. At age 10, he started volunteering at a local food bank and noticed the produce being sold was often not fresh. He began to wonder why fruits and vegetables couldn't be grown locally, so they would be fresh when given to the families.

Austen lobbied his city for a community garden, and within months, a farmer had donated an acre of land, as well as much-needed irrigation. A master gardener helped Austen plan his plots. From March to July, Austen and his band of volunteers raise tomatoes, cucumbers, okra, and similar crops. 7,000 pounds of donated produce were harvested during the first year alone. "I would love to see such gardens in more cities," said the teenage Austen. "Why stop in Arizona?"

"I was inspired to take that concept and extend it to something that could physically help people in need," he explained. "I wanted people to know that they were cared about and could be helped by members of their own town. To see the appreciation of all of the families as they received the produce was overwhelming. What a wonderful feeling it is to help other people."

By the age of 12, Austen was recognized as one of America's top ten youth volunteers. At 14 years old, he was supplying 200 needy families with fresh produce.

Taking good ideas and making them better is a natural and necessary part of serving people. Inspiration is like dropping a pebble into a lake; the effect can be far-reaching, whether being the volunteer or the recipient, giver or receiver.

OUR VINE, *we are indeed the branches that can do nothing without You. Keep me inspired; keep me inspiring others.*

# I STILL DON'T KNOW HIS NAME

*Yet surely my cause is with the Lord, and my reward with my God.*
—Isaiah 49:4b

"I remember it quite vividly," said Marine First Sergeant Michael Barrett. "It was at Al Anbar province, Iraq, just south of Ramadi. Our vehicle was struck by an IED. It was too dangerous to get a helicopter in there." He miraculously escaped the fireball that followed the blast.

Michael ended up being placed on the hood of a vehicle for the trip out of the danger zone. "My lieutenant and an Army medic showed up out of nowhere," Michael said.

"I still don't know who that soldier is to this day. So there are three of us on the hood of a truck and convoyed back to the base. The trip took 15 minutes, but it was the longest trip of my life. I lost about four pints of blood, shattered my femur, had burns on my right wrist, face, and blew my right ear drum," said the First Sergeant.

"We all roll the dice every day. Any one of us could be killed at any second of the day. We all know that, and we would gladly do so in defense of our country," he said.

Michael now works with other Marines who have been injured and flown back to the U.S. at the National Naval Medical Center in Bethesda, Md.

Sergeant Barrett was treated by a medic whose name he never even knew. Every day, people serve and save others, while those who are saved never even know the names of their benefactors.

Anonymity is often a part of the job description of service, with no recognition or reward. The knowledge that the work impacted a life is often the true and only motive.

DELIVERER, *there are so many people who have directly and indirectly touched my life. Strengthen me to focus on my service and work; never the credit or my name.*

# WE'VE GOT TO DO SOMETHING

*O Lord, you will hear the desire of the meek; you will strengthen their heart, you will incline your ear to do justice for the orphan and the oppressed, so that those from earth may strike terror no more. —Psalm 10:17-18*

In 1999, just after their daughter had started her freshman year in college, Tom and Stacey Branchini received a call that their daughter Alexa, 18, had been raped at her dorm on the campus of Boston University. While her attacker was arrested later that night, his trial didn't take place until 18 months later.

During the months prior to the trial, the family faced a traumatic legal process. Tom and Stacey flew to Boston for each part of the trial.

"We were appalled to learn how poorly Alexa was being treated by the system," said Stacey.

Alexa, who had to testify at the month-long trial, said, "I wouldn't have testified if my family hadn't been with me."

Travel expenses and lost income mounted. "What would people do if they couldn't afford this?" asked Tom. "We've got to do something."

Two years later, the Branchinis started the "It Happened to Alexa Foundation" to help families who must endure the same hardship.

The foundation raised over $100,000 and helped over 200 victims and their family members.

Alexa is now pursuing a Ph.D. in criminal justice and is dedicated to assuring rape survivors that they are not alone.

One of the amazing facets of the human spirit is not accepting defeat and being determined to not be a victim, even while being victimized.

Brave individuals, like Alexa, turn tragedy into triumph and pain into perseverance. They motivate us to do the same.

MIGHTY GOD, *it is difficult to imagine such a nightmare. Thank You for the supernatural strength and grace You give people like Alexa and her family to endure hardship. As hard times come, help me to respond as they did.*

# FEELING A PART OF LIFE

*I want their hearts to be encouraged and united in love, so that they may have all the riches of assured understanding and have the knowledge of God's mystery, that is, Christ himself, in whom are hidden all the treasures of wisdom and knowledge.*
—Colossians 2:2-3

Sylvia Jones shared a story about her experience as a community volunteer:

"I was employed full time at a busy job and also newly married, but I gave of my time at a mental institution in our town. The joy I found and the satisfaction I felt was overwhelming.

"To my surprise, I found out that a friend of my parents from many years back was a resident of this facility, and that when I was a baby, this lady had wanted to babysit me as she was unable to have children.

"I brought her up to date with pictures. Together, after much time, we had closed up the years. I was told that she would have been able to be released from the facility, but because she had no family to go to, she couldn't leave.

"I was able to bring her to my home on two occasions for afternoon refreshments, and I saw the joy of this lady feeling a part of life.

"I have never forgotten this volunteering experience. This lady later passed away, but in my sadness I did find fulfillment for these small acts of kindness. These little things made a difference to her.

"I felt so humbled by this, and I give all thanks and praise to my Lord for directing me and for my mother telling me the story of why this lady was where she was."

So many who volunteer find there is a much higher purpose for their contribution than they ever thought possible. It may be found out quickly or may take some time, but giving sacrificially always has hidden blessings.

EMMANUEL, *I know You have blessings planned for me in my work. Help me to live expectantly of what You have planned and look for those that I will bless.*

# IN HIS NAME

*You did not choose me but I chose you. And I appointed you to go and bear fruit,*
*fruit that will last —John 15:16a*

Raymond Mitchell, a 73-year-old clerk at a supermarket, was shocked when a young man walked up and handed him an envelope with $50, saying, "This comes from Mr. Hal Reichle, who has appreciated your service for a long time."

The grocery bagger was targeted by SSSSH—Secret Society of Serendipitous Service to Hal.

The group honors Hal Reichie, an Army helicopter pilot who died at age 27 during Operation Desert Storm. He painted homes while families were on vacation, sneaked groceries onto front porches, and once persuaded a banker to give a car loan to a needy pal. Known for his contagious generosity, the soldier inspired these random acts of kindness—in Hal's name, not their own. They have been known to pick up dinner checks, pay bills, and paint a garage.

"We plant seeds of happiness," said Roger Cram, Hal's close friend and now the informal head of the group. "We hope to have the whole world pulling Reichles."

To be a part of SSSSH, one must perform an anonymous good deed and describe it in a letter to Cram.

"No signature or return address on the letters or else we throw them away," he insisted.

"One person used a disability check to buy refreshments for work-release prisoners who were cutting grass and another bought cable TV for a paraplegic."

The young man who surprised Raymond said, "It's all very exciting. I've never had more fun than I had turning over that envelope."

As followers of Jesus Christ, we are to be a people loving in tangible ways in His name. We live and serve today, our deeds by and through Him.

LORD JESUS, *this story is inspiring, but I must do these same things in Your name, by Your Spirit. This is a part of the abundant life that You promised.*

# WATCHING FOR SIGNS

*No testing has overtaken you that is not common to everyone. God is faithful, and he will not let you be tested beyond your strength, but with the testing he will also provide the way out so that you may be able to endure it.* —1 Corinthians 10:13

A man knew the only way his new diet was going to work was if he took a different route to his office and didn't make his daily stop at the donut shop anymore.

One day, he was deep in thought and accidently took his old route. He was about to turn around, but thought, "Maybe this is a sign from God that He wants to reward me." So the man said a short prayer, asking God, "If this is what You want, then let there be a parking spot right in front."

Sure enough, on the fifth time he drove around the block, a parking space opened up!

There are many scenarios where we try to justify our choices.

"If that shirt is on sale, I'll know I'm supposed to buy it."

"If I'm so tired that I don't wake up in time, I'll know it was okay for me to miss church."

"If that person isn't home, I'll know it's OK to not talk to them and get things right."

Fooling yourself to rationalize and compromise in little things will always lead to failing in the big decisions. We laugh at the man who sees a parking spot open for the fifth pass around the block as a sign from God, but the parking spots eventually turn into blind spots!

Where are you teaching yourself to compromise or even to blame God with "signs" and "tests?" Stopping now might save your life—or even someone else's. Be careful of your motives when you pray. Keep your prayers focused on God.

DEAR LORD, *heal my blind spots. Help me see the places where I rationalize and compromise and give those areas to You.*

# THE IMPORTANCE OF WHAT WE DO

*A gift opens doors; it gives access to the great.* —Proverbs 18:16

Operation Gratitude annually sends 100,000 care packages filled with snacks, hygiene products, entertainment items, and personal letters of appreciation, all addressed to individually named U.S. Soldiers, Sailors, Airmen, and Marines deployed in harm's way.

The mission is to lift morale, bring a smile to a service member's face, and express to our Armed Forces the appreciation and support of the American people.

Each package contains donated products valued at $125 and costs the organization $15 to assemble and ship. Assembling of packages occurs at the Army National Guard armory in Van Nuys, Calif.

Since its inception, Operation Gratitude volunteers have shipped more than 800,000 packages. The long-term goal is called March to a Million—an effort to ship 1 million packages to our service men and women.

Through collection drives, letter-writing campaigns and donations of funds, Operation Gratitude provides civilians a tangible way to express their respect and appreciation to those in the U.S. Military.

One soldier wrote, "It truly means a lot to know we have so many supporters back home who take the time to send us really neat stuff. It literally brought tears to my eyes when I opened my last care package and it was from a second grade class. The kids poured their feelings out in drawings and letters and really made me think of the importance of what we do day to day over here."

If you are interested in sending a package, or if you are in the military or have a family member in the military and wish to request a package, go to the Operation Gratitude web site.

PROVIDER, *there are so many small, yet tangible ways to encourage and help those in service. Help me to consistently put love into action through my own life.*

# STANDING TOGETHER

*…from whom the whole body, joined and knitted together by every ligament with which it is equipped, as each part is working properly, promotes the body's growth in building itself up in love.* —Ephesians 4:16

For several years, U.S. law enforcement agencies have been battling the growing drug cartel in Mexico. These efforts also reach into Central America, Colombia, and Brazil. The span of the drug trade is rivaled only by the violence and brutality.

In just one day in the Houston, Texas, area, the FBI and U.S. Marshals seized $750,000 in U.S. currency, 322 pounds of marijuana, 13 kilograms of cocaine, 37 weapons, 10 vehicles, and they arrested of 33 individuals.

Thomas Hinojosa, acting special agent in charge of the Houston Division, DEA stated, "The DEA, and all of our law enforcement partners, will continue to aggressively disrupt and dismantle the ruthless drug trafficking organizations and their partners in crime who are operating on both sides of the Texas/Mexico border."

Robert Rutt, special agent in charge of ICE-Homeland Security Investigations in Houston said, "The priority here is fighting transnational gang violence and drug trafficking in the U.S. by Mexican led cartels who profit through violence and fear."

"This operation is a glowing example of the success that can be achieved when all agencies stand together to combat those who deal in drugs, weapons, and violence," stated U.S. Marshal Elizabeth Saenz.

Whether law enforcement, volunteers, or military, the power of working together and pooling resources has proven to be one of the most effective tools that human beings have. Who can you reach out to today— both to help and to receive help?

GOOD SHEPHERD, *teach me to look for ways to more effectively reach across any dividing lines around me to join together with those whom I could help and those from whom I need help.*

# I WILL BLESS YOU

*After these things the word of the Lord came to Abram in a vision, "Do not be afraid, Abram, I am your shield; your reward shall be very great." —Genesis 15:1*

In Genesis 12:1, we see God's call to Abram: "Now the Lord said to Abram, 'Go from your country and your kindred and your father's house to the land that I will show you.'"

God basically told Abram to pack up his family and hit the road. Now, most of us would have a million questions of God, wouldn't we? Which direction? How long will we be gone? How are we going to live? Where will my kids be going to school? What address do I give the post office for forwarding?

What God said next to Abram in verses 2 and 3 likely ended any questions he had. "I will make of you a great nation, and I will bless you, and make your name great, so that you will be a blessing. I will bless those who bless you, and the one who curses you I will curse; and in you all the families of the earth shall be blessed."

So, what was Abram's response? Verse 4 states, "So Abram went, as the Lord had told him." And, when you go on reading, Abram became Abraham and God did just as He had promised.

It is easy to make these Bible characters into supernatural heroes that either didn't have a choice or were somehow far above who we are. That is simply not true. They were humans with a choice—just like us.

Is God calling you to anything new? It may be across the street or across the world, but always be open to God's leading. As with Abraham, there is great blessing in the sacrifice.

GREAT I AM, *in a very real way, You are the road of life, leading me, yet being my Path as well. Please surround me with Your love and life, as I walk with You.*

# SHE HELD HER OWN

*You who live in the shelter of the Most High, who abide in the shadow of the Almighty, will say to the Lord, "My refuge and my fortress; my God, in whom I trust." —Psalm 91:1-2*

It was supposed to be a routine health and welfare check at the Arizona State Prison in Tucson where 550 inmates are incarcerated.

Correctional Officer Laurel Kennedy was making rounds in the Santa Rita unit when an inmate grabbed her and pulled her into his cell, threatening to slash her neck if his demands were not met. The inmate had taken a disposable razor and managed to get the plastic guard off to expose the blades.

Warden Fizer and a team of negotiators stood at the open door of the cell, trying to keep him calm. The warden and other officers said Laurel's ability to keep cool in such a volatile situation helped save her life.

"I'll tell you, she's a hero," said Sergeant Tracy Hubbartt. "She held her own. I don't know if I could. Hopefully I don't have to find out."

Warden Fizer added, "She performed incredibly. She was very courageous. "It's the worst case scenario an officer can face and that any staff members in the department can face, tough for everyone to deal with. She's a mother with four kids and that would have been really tough to have something happen to her."

The inmate was talked down by the staff and by Officer Kennedy; no lives were lost.

A job of service that puts your life at risk daily will always be about more than a paycheck. It has to be a calling. There is assurance in good training, and there is assurance in whose hands you are held, that fortress of God.

STRONG TOWER, *protect and bless those today who serve in harm's way. Give them strength to make a difference, even at the risk of harm.*

# THE SITUATION IS DIRE

*A bad messenger brings trouble, but a faithful envoy, healing.* —Proverbs 13:17

Doctors Without Borders is an international medical humanitarian organization created in 1971. Today, they provide independent, impartial assistance in more than 60 countries to people whose survival is threatened by violence, neglect, or catastrophe.

A team in southern Sudan gave this report from an area where over 30,000 refugees are trying to survive: "Every day we go to the small tented clinic. We have to ensure we are seeing the most severe cases. Yesterday, just before we were going to leave the first site, there was a small child who was brought in gasping and in a state of medical shock. We managed to save that child, a timely reminder for me of why we are here and what we are able to do, even in the toughest circumstances.

"In just one week we conducted a total of 537 consultations at both refugee locations. Over half were for diarrhea. Of the 342 children who were screened for malnutrition, 130 of them were malnourished. We are also seeing the first cases of malaria. People are living close together and, with the rain, the temperature is dropping—so we are bound to see pneumonia, especially in young children.

"The situation is dire. These people need to be moved right now to a suitable place where they have food, water, and shelter; where their health can be assured. Time is not on their side."

So many in our world are without the basic resources needed to support human life. Getting resources from where they are abundant to areas where they save lives is crucial.

As you serve right where you are, consider also getting involved in an organization that helps those on the other side of the world.

HEALER, *help me to expand my worldview, not be overwhelmed, but to focus on places where I can help. Show me where and to whom I should place my resources.*

# IT REALLY IS THAT SIMPLE

*For I was hungry and you gave me food, I was thirsty and you gave me something to drink, I was a stranger and you welcomed me.* —Matthew 25:35

Greg Arnold is an entrepreneur in Ocean Springs, Miss., who had a calling to minister to men in today's American culture. One of the projects he launched was Livebold, an on-line digital magazine with articles designed for discipling men of faith on a vast array of topics. As his readership grew, Greg wanted to connect this new tribe of mobilized men to a greater purpose.

Reading Jesus' words in Matthew 25, Greg decided that feeding the hungry would be the focus of this new effort. So foodFIGHT was born.

Greg shares the vision, "Millions of people are fighting for food around the world, while millions waste enough food to end world hunger. So, we asked, what would happen if we turned a simple trans-action into hunger relief? We then developed a brand and product that was strictly focused on feeding people. When an organization starts a foodFIGHT, they challenge their peers to make a single transaction. Buy a shirt, save a life. It really is that simple. Whether you buy one shirt or a case, all of the profit goes directly to feeding people."

Any time or any place that we are given a platform, we can use it for good and a broader purpose. Many people are just waiting for some direction to help people in need, especially when it is made so simple. What is your platform? How many are in your circle of influence? Determine today how you can use it to create something that makes a difference.

DEAR GOD, *lead me to be creative and think "outside the box" for ways I can make a difference in my circles of influence. Teach me to lead out in making a difference.*

# THE WORLD HAD CHANGED

*Happy is the nation whose God is the Lord, the people whom he has chosen as his heritage. The Lord looks down from heaven; he sees all humankind. From where he sits enthroned, he watches all the inhabitants of the earth.* —Psalm 33:12-14

President George W. Bush was thrown into the first great crisis of the 21st century on 9-11. No president since Abraham Lincoln had seen such loss of life on American soil. No president since James Madison had seen the nation's capital city successfully attacked.

Scott Pelley interviewed President Bush about the details of that morning.

Sept. 11, 2001, started with the usual routine. In Sarasota, Fla., for an appearance at an elementary school, the president was up before dawn on his four-mile run. Later at the school, he was told about the first plane just before sitting down with a class of second graders to watch a reading drill. "I thought it was an accident," said the president. "I thought it was a pilot error."

The president's chief-of-staff Andy Card stepped in and told the president, "A second plane hit the second tower; America is under attack."

President Bush recalls, "We're at war and somebody has dared attack us and we're going to do something about it. I realized I was in a unique setting to receive a message that somebody attacked us and I was looking at these little children and all of the sudden we were at war. I can remember noticing the press pool and the press corps beginning to get the calls and seeing the look on their face. And it became evident that the world had changed."

There are freedoms in our society that 9-11 changed forever, but one thing will never change: the spirit of Americans who commit that "we will do something about it." In the midst of military action plans, President Bush also spoke to the nation about his faith in God and encouraged the country to be in prayer. He welcomed the prayers of the world.

Every day, all over the world, Americans are taking action for freedom—at home and abroad.

AUTHOR OF LIFE, *thank You for our freedom and for the constant sacrifice so many make in their lives, and in death, to keep it. May I prayerfully do my part, to serve where I should, with gratitude and grace.*

# SECRET WEAPON

*I will go before you and level the mountains, I will break in pieces the doors of bronze and cut through the bars of iron, I will give you the treasures of darkness and riches hidden in secret places, so that you may know that it is I, the Lord, the God of Israel, who call you by your name.* —Isaiah 45:2-3

Polish Colonel Ryszard Kuklinski risked his life and the safety of his family to protect Poland from the Soviets during the Cold War by spying for the United States. From 1972-1981, Kuklinski provided more than 40,000 pages of Polish and Warsaw Pact documents to the CIA.

In 1972, Kuklinski decided to take action to help Poland. He wrote a letter to the United States Embassy in Bonn, Germany, offering to provide information. The letter eventually made its way to CIA headquarters. And soon, Kuklinski's double life as a spy began.

Over the course of nine years, the Polish colonel passed vital information regarding Soviet plans, Polish military plans, and the Communist party to the CIA through many covert drops. He was given the codename "Gull" for his love of the sea and provided with materials for secret messages, as well as a special camera to photograph documents.

During his many years of spying, he lived in constant fear of being discovered and the consequences from that. The colonel eventually contacted the CIA and asked them to extract him and his family from Poland. They were safely relocated to the United States in 1981, shortly before martial law was imposed on Poland.

The CIA viewed him as one of the most successful spies in history to win the fight to end communism.

Many people have lived double lives in sacrifice for the greater good of their nation and, ultimately, the cause of freedom. These stories of great bravery give us inspiration in our own service to devote our one life to the good of humankind. Do you know that God goes before you in your work? With that knowledge, show bravery for His Kingdom.

OUR INTERCESSOR, *You came to earth being fully God, yet fully man. You felt the pain of humanity through Divine power. Thank You that You relate to us now and have won the war to gain our freedom.*

# IT TAKES A COMMUNITY

*May God Almighty bless you and make you fruitful and numerous, that you may become a company of peoples. —Genesis 28:3*

Belva Davis bought her first home at age 50. She purchased a Cape Cod-style house in a Detroit suburb, moving away from the inner-city.

Just two years in, she lost her job, and soon fell behind on her mortgage payments. After a period of unemployment, she found new work and began to try to catch up, but her lenders refused to cut her any slack. They threatened foreclosure, even though she was once again making regular payments. The company wanted the balance of her missed payments right away.

People suddenly moving away because they had lost their homes wasn't a unique sight in Belva's neighborhood.

So at the homeowner's association meeting, she told of her plight. She told her neighbors she loved her community and didn't want to leave. Everyone agreed with her. So, she and her neighbors began to organize protests and hand out flyers. They posted interviews and updates on YouTube. They even went to the city council. As a final resort, all the neighbors bombarded the bank president with emails and phone calls. Finally, after nine months of hard work, the bank agreed to restructure Belva's loan.

Belva said, "If more people would band together, people could stay in their homes. But one person can't do that by herself. It takes a community. And it's certainly a way to get to know your neighbors!" In their stance, the sin of greed was exposed to the light of truth.

Community is a powerful asset. How engaged are you in your community? There are people in needs all around us. As we serve, may we each be responsible to keep the unity in our community. May we be His light of truth and a community of faith.

OUR ADVOCATE, *help me to be a contributor in the community around me. Guide me to give and receive inside the circle where You have placed me.*

# IN THE MIDST OF CHAOS

*He called a child, whom he put among them, and said, 'Truly I tell you, unless you change and become like children, you will never enter the kingdom of heaven. Whoever becomes humble like this child is the greatest in the kingdom of heaven.*
*—Matthew 18:2-4*

Noah Jones' parents, Nathan and Sara, had become foster parents. Noah found out that in his area of Kentucky approximately 600 foster kids had to change families every year. When one of these kids had to move, the temporary "suitcase" was a trash bag. Most of these children showed up at their new homes with all they owned in a garbage sack. This bothered Noah.

"Packing kids' belongings into garbage bags is like telling them that their stuff has no more worth than trash," Noah shared. So, with the help of his parents and two younger sisters, he began to collect suitcases and duffel bags.

He wrote letters to local churches, placed ads in local newspapers, and on radio stations. Within a few months, the family was averaging 500 suitcases and duffels a week, getting them into the hands of foster care caseworkers as soon as possible.

Noah soon began also to offer backpacks filled with personal items such as shampoo and soap, and a toy for the younger ones.

Noah said, "My hope is that by giving the children things that are just theirs, they will feel a little control in the midst of chaos." He has also convinced local caseworkers to always use bags and never trash bags again. His mom adds, "If a 10-year-old can see a problem and create a solution, how much more can we do as adults?"

There are many "small" problems in the world that we miss. Commit to seeing a simple solution to an invisible problem sometime this next month. It just might change someone's world—including your own.

HEAVENLY SPIRIT, *give me your eyes to see the things that others may miss. Help me to find simple solutions, like Noah did, to help those in need around me.*

# IT'S ONE MORE

*I will satisfy the weary, and all who are faint I will replenish. —Jeremiah 31:25*

Nevada has one of the lowest high school graduation rates in the nation—only about half actually receive diplomas.

Neddy Alvarez, a high school principal, decided to do something about it. He invited school officials and community volunteers out on Saturdays to talk to students and their parents. The target was dropouts and those with poor attendance, at risk of dropping out.

"We're trying to reclaim our students, and that's the whole purpose of this initiative," said Neddy. "If it's just one student, it's one more that we can put on a program to graduate. We speak to the parents. 'Why isn't your child coming to school? They need to come to school. We want them to graduate.'

"It was a very positive thing for me to go out and visit with the parents and their children. It's great to see the smile on their faces. 'You really want us to come back?' 'Yes, we want you to come back. You know, we need you at school. It's for your future. There's a reason why you need to graduate.'

"It's changing a whole mindset in a school like ours that's at risk."

The more "every-man-for-himself" our culture gets, the less people care about others. But, that also causes people like Neddy Alvarez to "stick out." Taking the initiative and making extra effort to reach out can change lives forever. Such action can affect generations by breaking a cycle of poverty or illiteracy. Caring more for others, going the second mile, serving above self has been a counter-culture model since the time of Jesus.

COUNSELOR, *help me to "stick out" in this world, loving the unlovely, giving hope for the hopeless, and reaching out to the untouched.*

# HEALING FROM THE CEILING

*Immediately he stood up before them, took what he had been lying on, and went to his home, glorifying God. Amazement seized all of them, and they glorified God and were filled with awe, saying, 'We have seen strange things today.' —Luke 5:25-26*

In Mark 2 and Luke 5, there is an amazing and humorous story of commitment among friends.

Jesus was in someone's home and so many people were inside and gathered outside, trying to get to Him, that there was no hope of getting in. There were four friends who had brought their paralyzed buddy on a makeshift stretcher for Jesus to heal him. They surveyed the situation and decided the only possible entry was through the roof. So, they all got on the roof and started digging. Can you imagine being in that house when pieces started falling into the inside and the sun began to peak through?

They managed to get a hole carved out large enough to lower their friend down to Jesus in the house. When He saw their efforts and obvious faith, Jesus simply said, "Son, your sins are forgiven." The man was healed. Now, imagine being one of those four friends, holding that rope, looking down at your buddy. Then imagine hearing Jesus' words and seeing your friend get up off that mat and walk out!

Some Pharisees or Sadducees were there and saw the entire scene. All they could do was question Jesus' claim of forgiving sin and accuse Him of blasphemy.

Contrast the men who dug a hole in the roof for their friend and the men who ignored the miracle and criticized the motive.

The world will always have winners and whiners and gripers. Take a quick look around your life and be sure you're always digging a hole for a friend and not the one critiquing the method.

HEALER, *I want to be that kind of friend, committed on that level. Protect me from a critical and negative spirit. Help me to be a "hole digger" for my friends.*

# MORE TIME TO BOND

*Whoever has two coats must share with anyone who has none; and whoever has food must do likewise. —Luke 3:11b*

A few days after Hurricane Katrina, Lisa Klein read that a Louisiana church was asking for baby clothes for displaced families.

"I instantly knew I'd found a way to help," she said. She pulled together boxes of outfits that her daughter had outgrown and spread the word to friends. Within days, 200 pounds of baby items were ready to be shipped to New Orleans. Lisa thought, "If that's what I can do in four days with a few friends, what if I really put my mind to it?"

Lisa soon started the non-profit group, Loved Twice, to collect gently used baby clothes for distribution to hospitals, prenatal-care clinics, and shelters. "These women have to worry about having the finances to feed the baby, buy diapers, and pay rent. We try to alleviate some of that stress, hoping it will give the mothers more time to bond with their babies."

The group's six collection bins gather roughly 1,000 pounds of clothing every month. Volunteers sort the garments into boxes—so far over 28,000 pounds of clothing to newborns in need. Her dream is to rent a warehouse as a headquarters, allowing her to handle more clothing and more volunteers. "I'm so happy to be able to spread awareness," she said. "These babies deserve to be warm and clean."

It has been said many times that America could feed and clothe the world with its left-overs and hand-me-downs. While that may be somewhat of an exaggeration, if any nation could try, we could.

People like Lisa Klein decided to give it a shot. What do you have that needs to be Loved Twice?

MY SOURCE, *guide me to be a good steward of all You have blessed me with and may I bless others with what I have.*

# THE WAR AT HOME

*The Lord your God, who goes before you, is the one who will fight for you, just as he did for you in Egypt before your very eyes.* —Deuteronomy 1:30

Eric Smith, 27, was in the Navy for six years, working his way up to Petty Officer Third Class. He enlisted at 17 years old, and by 19, was leading a four-man team at a 20-bed ICU battle zone. After serving two tours of duty, performing emergency medical procedures on wounded soldiers in Iraq, he came home to find that his unique life-saving skills could not be recognized by U.S. medical facilities.

Smith mops floors at the MedStar Union Memorial Hospital in Baltimore. He said, "All the things I was trained to do are going to waste. It cost the Navy, the American people, really, a million dollars and nearly six years to train me. And it's lost."

Smith now has decided to earn his EMT certification which, coupled with his military training, will allow him to use his skills and finally be able to make a reasonable living, after being unemployed or underemployed since returning home.

He adds, "The war at home is tougher than the war overseas."

Our returning vets have a wealth of knowledge and skill, coupled with qualities like discipline and loyalty. God can take any experience and teach us skills and life lessons.

The private sector must make efforts to utilize these great Americans who can continue to make her great. The next time your business or anyone you know is hiring, consider our veterans as an amazing resource. We can honor those who serve us; as they have served with honor and righteousness.

MIGHTY GOD, *one thing that has always been true in this sinful world is that life is not fair. Stories like this one today, just prove it. Guide me, Lord, to make all that I touch as fair and right as I am able.*

# ACTIVE AGENT OF GOOD

*But the meek shall inherit the land, and delight in abundant prosperity.*
—*Psalm 37:11*

Dr. Jan Karski led an amazing life with his final assignment being a university professor at Georgetown University. He kept his classes spellbound as he shared from his unique life experiences. Here are just a few examples: —Survived being captured by the Russian army, but escaped prior to the Katyn Forest Massacre where 8,000 Polish officers were executed. —Escaped by jumping from a Nazi train speeding through Poland. —Joined the Polish Underground, carrying coded messages across Europe into France. —Survived being captured and tortured by Nazi agents. —Jumped from a German hospital window to escape certain death by the Nazis. —Witnessed the genocide led by Hitler at an extermination camp. —Traveled across Nazi-occupied Europe to reach London where he briefed the British War Cabinet on his experiences. —Finally, came to America and spoke with President Franklin Delano Roosevelt.

Wanda Urbanska, director of the Jan Karski U.S. Centennial Campaign reported, "He went on to a distinguished career as an educator—one who was not bitter, but who reached out to the better angels in us all—for being active agents of good in the world, for building bridges between communities at odds with each other."

Men like Dr. Karski, through their commitment, sacrifice, and bravery, helped defeat the atrocities of Hitler during World War II. Thank God that there are men like this raised up in every generation. May we be inspired today by Dr. Karski and those who serve as he did.

LIBERATOR, *may my life make this kind of difference in this generation.*

# CAN'T IMAGINE NOT DOING IT

*The blessing of the wretched came upon me, and I caused the widow's heart to sing for joy. I put on righteousness, and it clothed me; my justice was like a robe and a turban. I was eyes to the blind, and feet to the lame. I was a father to the needy, and I championed the cause of the stranger.* —Job 29:13-16

Caitlin Crommett began volunteering at Hospice Care of the West in Foothill Ranch, Calif., spending her time filing, but also singing at memorial services. Inspired by the movie Patch Adams, Caitlin envisioned a group that could grant wishes to terminally ill patients.

Soon, Dream Catchers was born.

Her parents had saved up money for her to go to Catholic High School, but Caitlin requested that she go to a local public school, so she could have the money to start her organization.

The first beneficiary was Ann Klein, whose husband, Bernard, was a hospice patient. Ann said, "We had sailed every weekend for years. I said, 'If I get Bernard on a sailboat one more time, he'll really love it.'"

Soon after, Caitlin met with a family in a nearby harbor. When the crew of the $600 chartered 82-foot double-mast schooner lifted Bernard aboard, "he started laughing," Ann said. "It was the first time we had laughed together in a long time."

Caitlin plans to continue Dream Catchers when she attends Notre Dame University. "I can't imagine not doing it," she said.

Helen, a Dream Catcher recipient with lung cancer, said of Caitlin, "It's marvelous. You hear about all the bad things kids are doing and never the good things [like this]."

For decades, our culture has begun devaluing the elderly and dying. Reversing a societal trend such as this takes courage, but also creates a great blessing for all those involved. Showing love, faith and respect to those who are dying right up until their moment of passing is a celebration of life and love at its finest. How are you serving the least, the lost and the last?

THE LIFE, *our dying makes life have value. An end makes the journey have purpose. Today, may I live and not just survive. May my moments have meaning as I serve others in your name.*

# LAND OF THE FREE

*Keep these words that I am commanding you today in your heart. Recite them to your children and talk about them when you are at home and when you are away, when you lie down and when you rise. Bind them as a sign on your hand, fix them as an emblem on your forehead, and write them on the doorposts of your house and on your gates.* —Deuteronomy 6:6-9

---

*"The only man who makes no mistake is the man who does nothing."*
—President Theodore Roosevelt

*"If you want to make enemies, try to change something."*
—President Woodrow Wilson

*"A pessimist is one who makes difficulties of his opportunities and an optimist is one who makes opportunities of his difficulties."*
—President Harry Truman

*"There is nothing wrong with America that the faith, love of freedom, intelligence and energy of her citizens cannot cure."*
—President Dwight Eisenhower

*"For whoever wants to save his life will lose it, but whoever loses his life for me will save it."*
-Jesus Christ

---

It is tempting and easy to become paralyzed in the face of all the problems in our world today. Yet, each generation in our nation has faced its own unique challenges and, through perseverance and sheer grit, managed to press forward to make this nation great. We should, as they did. We can, as they did. We will, as they did.

MIGHTY GOD, *guide me to accomplish no less than what You desire for me to be about today.*

# THE HUMAN CONNECTION

*For everything there is a season, and a time for every matter under heaven.*
—Ecclesiastes 3:1

Christine French, a senior at the time at George Washington University, was the coordinator of Intervention and Cultural Services at the University's Office of Community Service. To back up her title, she volunteers at Martha's Table, an organization that helps at-risk families, My Sister's Place, which helps domestic violence victims, and RAINN (Rape, Abuse, and Incest National Network), where she serves as a hotline operator.

Back home in Omaha, Neb., she helps out at an interfaith agency that helps high school students develop tools to fight injustice, discrimination, and hate.

Growing up in a Catholic family, service and volunteering were always a part of life.

"I remember my mom driving me to the retirement home when I was in eighth grade to play UNO and Bingo every week," she recalled. "It was so much fun. My life has been deeply enhanced by service."

So, what makes Christine such a great volunteer?

"I think it's that I listen to people. Often, all people really need is someone to listen to them and validate their feelings," said Christine. "We just want human connection and to know that we are loved and valuable. That is what I can do for others and it's more important than the fact that I am a hard worker or a critical thinker." In asking if she has any advice to give to someone interested in volunteering, she answers, "You bet. Do it! It is so valuable." We are indeed called to love our neighbor, whoever that might be.

Time is such a precious commodity and, thusly, one of the greatest gifts we can give. Whether it's 4 hours a month or 20 hours a week, the gift of service is never wasted, but maximized.

MIGHTY COUNSELOR, *help me to remember that I can do nothing about yesterday or tomorrow, that all I have is today. May I use the gift of today wisely.*

# WHATEVER IT TAKES

*The Lord is good, a stronghold on a day of trouble; he protects those who take refuge in him.* —Nahum 1:7

Robert Edwards of the Maquoketa Fire Department and Rescue Squad started hacking away at the rock wall with a chisel. Two people were trapped in a cave at Maquoketa Caves State Park and this first responder had to walk and crawl about 300 feet just to get to the pair.

"There was a 90-degree turn that you had to take to go down a small corridor, about 10 to 12 feet away, before you could actually get to them," Edwards said. "We had to remove some rock before we could actually get around that turn." Edwards became concerned that his exhaustion and the poor air quality might lead to his getting stuck in the cave as well. "It was a very confined space. All the dirt and dust just lingered in the air. I would stop for a little bit, let every-thing settle, talk to them to see how they were doing, and then I would continue again," Edwards reported.

About three hours into the ordeal, the woman was pulled free from the cave. But it was 20 hours before the male explorer was rescued.

When lives are on the line and time is precious, the reasons someone got into trouble or what it takes or how long it takes to get them out are of little consequence. A life must be saved. As you go through your days, remember that many you will encounter are in trouble emotionally, mentally, and spiritually. They may not appear to be in need of rescue, but they are. Your care and kindness can offer a unique gesture for those today.

SAVIOR, *may I be Your light today to all those I encounter. By smile, hand, or kind word, may I offer help to a hurting world.*

# UNUSUAL BACK-UP

*And though one might prevail against another, two will withstand one.*
—*Ecclesiastes 4:12a*

Joe Archer, a resident of Bloomington, Ind., was out mowing his lawn one afternoon when he noticed a Monroe County Sheriff's deputy who appeared to be in trouble. Inside the car, Deputy Beverly McKnight was struggling with a suspect that she was transporting to the Monroe County Jail.

Detectives said the man somehow got his handcuffs in front of his body while in a seat belt in the back of Beverly's SUV. He was able to get his arms around her neck as she was driving, then went for her gun. The gun went off, narrowly missing Deputy McKnight's leg. Archer said he heard Beverly scream and rushed to help.

"I opened the door and jumped on the suspect's back. I put him in a headlock and pried him off the deputy," Joe Archer said. He also told detectives that he heard the man tell the deputy that she "wouldn't get out of the car alive."

Deputy McKnight, her husband, and their three children personally thanked Joe for his brave actions. Monroe County Sheriff's Department officials also commended him and said "he'll be formally recognized by the sheriff."

What if Joe Archer had decided to "look the other way" or to "not get involved?" It is possible that the sheriff's office might have one less deputy and three children might not have a mom. It is also possible that other innocent people may have been hurt had the suspect escaped. What an unplanned gift from a good Samaritan.

In a world that seems to just get crazier, we must be watching for where we are needed every day, just like Joe Archer, who was just planning on mowing his lawn.

STRONG TOWER, *help me to watch for You, to see where You need me and who I should help today.*

# EVERYTHING HAS CHANGED

*I will exult and rejoice in your steadfast love, because you have seen my affliction; you have taken heed of my adversities.* —Psalm 31:7

Maria was born in Brazil into a family of five children. She was also born with a cleft palate. Her parents separated when she was just a baby, her father choosing two of her siblings to live with him. Her mother chose two others. Neither wanted Maria, now abandoned by her family.

The city services called her grandmother, who agreed to raise her granddaughter.

As Maria grew older, her classmates teased her, saying, "You're crippled. Stay away from me." Maria wouldn't even play with children in her neighborhood, because of her embarrassment, keeping her mouth covered with her hands in public.

Maria's grandmother was determined to find help for her granddaughter. She first approached the mayor of her city, who was also a doctor. Eventually, a government official directed her to Operation Smile, a non-profit organization that exists on donations and volunteer teams of medical personnel.

When she arrived at the medical mission in Fortaleza, 5-year-old Maria immediately captured the hearts of all the volunteers. After her surgery, she laughed and smiled.

"I'm so very happy," said her grandmother. "She plays, runs, talks. She is completely different. Everything has changed for the best. She is not ashamed anymore. She always said that she is beautiful, that she is gorgeous. It was everything we have ever wanted."

A medical team of volunteers can literally change the lives of many children in a single trip. Just $240 can fund an operation for a child. Over 200,000 to date have been performed—just another way that skilled expertise can join donated time and energy to make a life-changing difference in someone's world.

GREAT PHYSICIAN, *it is so difficult to understand the injustice in the world—especially to children. Help me to stay focused on being an answer and helping people—one life, one heart at a time.*

# ARE YOU LISTENING?

*Be still, and know that I am God! —Psalm 46:10a*

In 1 Samuel 3, we see that Samuel was a boy who helped Eli with his duties in the Temple. One night Eli and Samuel were asleep in the Temple, where the ark of the Covenant of God was stationed.

Suddenly, Samuel heard someone call his name. The boy got up and ran to Eli and said, "Here I am. You called me." Eli, surprised, said, "I did not call you. Go back and lie down." So Samuel, a little confused, obeyed.

Again the boy heard, "Samuel!" So he got up and went to Eli again, saying, "Here I am. You called me." Yet again, Eli said, "My son, I did not call. Now go back and lie down."

A third time, Samuel heard his name. Puzzled, but trying to be obedient to his master, the boy got up, went to Eli, saying, "Here I am. You called me." It was at that moment that Eli realized that God was calling Samuel. Eli told the boy, "Go and lie down and if God calls you again, say, "Speak, Lord, for your servant is listening."

God not only called Samuel, but appeared before him, calling his name, "Samuel! Samuel!" So Samuel, doing as Eli had told him, answered, "Speak, Lord, for your servant is listening."

This story has a bit of intrigue, mystery, and even comedy as Samuel kept hearing his name. After all, who else would be in the temple in the middle of the night?

A great way to begin your personal prayer time is with the words, "Speak, Lord, for your servant is listening." And then, sit quietly and listen.

ALMIGHTY GOD, *I want to hear Your voice and learn to know when it is You speaking to me. Help me to hear You above the noise of the world and obey.*

# THE WINDOWS OF HEAVEN

*For where your treasure is, there your heart will be also.* —*Matthew 6:21*

Were you aware there is one Scripture in the Bible where God tells us to test Him? You might be surprised the area He said this about.

Malachi 3:10—Bring the full tithe into the storehouse, so that there may be food in my house, and thus put me to the test, said the Lord of hosts; see if I will not open the windows of heaven for you and pour down for you an overflowing blessing.

Historically, it is understood that a tithe is 10% of our resources. God asks that we give Him back 10% of our income for use in "my house." The most positive way to view this is to not focus on having to give God 10%, but yet being grateful that He lets us keep 90%!

What if we all tested Him as He commanded here? What if we all gave 10% of our incomes? There would be no need for government programs for the poor, because the church and other ministries could singlehandedly take care of poverty and many other social ills of our day.

Regardless of your personal spiritual beliefs, no one would question that giving back of our financial resources is a good and positive activity to help those who are in need. May God push the "windows of Heaven" open for you and may God "pour down for you an overflowing blessing."

MY PROVIDER, *thank You that You allow me to keep 90% of what I make. Teach me to give. Teach me to be a good steward of all You allow me to manage.*

# OTHER THAN LUCK

*The angel of the Lord encamps around those who fear him, and delivers them.*
—Psalm 34:7

Paramedics arrive at so many scenes where tragedy has occurred, but sometimes they get to experience a miracle.

In Albany, N.Y., 4-year-old Hasim Townsend, was left home alone in his apartment building by his mother. He stood on his bed and leaned too hard against a window screen, which then gave way.

He fell 11 stories and bounced off a metal awning about 12 feet from the ground, then into a courtyard. When he landed, witnesses said he immediately tried to stand up.

When paramedics arrived, they had to hold the boy still. He suffered a broken skull, a broken leg, and a few minor injuries. "I'm amazed the kid's alive," Police Chief James Tuffey said.

After being taken to a hospital, the boy was able to talk with doctors. "It's an incredibly good sign that he was talking and I can't attribute it to anything other than good luck," said the attending doctor in the emergency department. Ironically, the boy ended up in the same pediatric intensive-care unit at Albany Medical Center where his mother worked as a receptionist. She was charged with endangering the welfare of a child.

A 4-year-old falling out of an 11-story window and surviving has to be more than "good luck." Those angels had to work extra hard to soften that landing. There are situations that occur every day that makes absolutely no sense outside of a God who watches over us all.

GREAT SHEPHERD, *I don't understand how You see all of us and take care of all that You do, but I am grateful You are ever on the watch and that miracles still happen every day.*

# COMMITTING TO COMMUNITY

*I desire that you insist on these things, so that those who have come to believe in God may be careful to devote themselves to good works; these things are excellent and profitable to everyone. —Titus 3:8*

A federally funded study revealed that middle America has the cities with the country's highest volunteer rates—the percentage of people who freely devote their time to help their communities. In Minneapolis-St. Paul, Milwaukee, Omaha, Tulsa, Columbus, and Cincinnati, at least one-third of the population volunteers each year.

According to the three-year study, four major factors tend to encourage high volunteer rates: attachment of a community (such as high levels of home ownership), low commute times to and from work, high education levels among the population, and the presence of nonprofit organizations.

"These factors tend to build social capital and to directly or indirectly encourage volunteering," the report stated.

Minneapolis was number one where more than 40% of the population volunteers. In Milwaukee, which has the eighth-highest volunteer rate (about 35%), there are more than 600 nonprofit groups for every 100,000 residents.

The study also found that areas with high poverty rates, a high percentage of multi-unit housing, and high population density tend to have low volunteer rates. No city in California or the Northeast made it into the top 10. In the South, only Charlotte made the list.

Of course, studies reflect generalities, patterns, and reasons, but the truth remains that a volunteer in a top city or one from the bottom of the list gets the same satisfaction from engaging in their community.

Whether you join a team of 100 or begin a brand new effort with two, working to make a difference counts. Regardless of where you live, make your life count by making every day count!

MIGHTY KING, *time is such a valuable and precious gift. Help me to make the best use of my time and continually give value to my days.*

# EAGLES AND CLOWNS?

*How very good and pleasant it is when kindred live together in unity!*
*—Psalm 133:1*

In 1974, members of the Philadelphia Eagles football organization joined with the owners of a Philadelphia McDonald's restaurant to create the first Ronald McDonald House. Ten years later, Ronald McDonald House Charities was established in memory of Ray Kroc, McDonald's founder. Today, there are over 300 Ronald McDonald Houses around the world and over 40 Mobile Care Units.

Ronald McDonald House program provides a "home away from home" for families, so they can stay close by their hospitalized child at little or no cost. The organization believes nothing else should matter when a family is focused on healing their child—not where they can afford to stay, where they will get their next meal, or where they will be able to stay. When a child is hospitalized, the love and support of family is as powerful as the strongest medicine prescribed.

Families are stronger when they are together, which helps in the healing process. By staying at a Ronald McDonald House, parents can also better communicate with their child's medical team and keep up with complicated treatment plans. They can also focus on the health of their child, rather than grocery shopping, cleaning, or cooking meals.

When businesses and corporations, that have little in common, can come together to impact and improve lives, linking up with thousands of volunteers, it is an amazing and unlikely partnership. The overriding truth about service and volunteerism is we are so much stronger together than we could ever be alone. "A cord of three is not easily broken" —Eccl. 4:12.

Are there any partnerships or connections you might make that could strengthen an existing work or possibly create something brand new to meet an unmet need?

MERCIFUL GOD, *You are always about addition and multiplication of resources. When we join with You, while cooperating with each other, we can all win.*

# IT'S A PROCESS, NOT A PLACE

*As God's chosen ones, holy and beloved, clothe yourselves with compassion, kindness, humility, meekness, and patience.* —Colossians 3:12

Psychologists at the University of California tested over 500 people by asking them to commit to practicing kindness for ten weeks.

They were asked to do things like hold doors open for strangers, give their place in line to others, do the dishes without being asked, and other acts to place others first. The idea was to promote good interactions with other people to see if it would improve the person's self-image.

The results were people that performed a variety of kind acts showed an increase in personal happiness and the ones who continued on reported increased benefit.

One psychologist that led the study said, "Happiness is the process, not the place. So many of us think that when we get everything just right, obtain certain goals and circumstances, everything will be in place and we will finally be happy, but once everything is in place, we still need new goals and activities."

The foundation and heart of service is kindness. If service is done for personal empowerment or gratification, it will eventually fizzle out. But the by-product of service is personal satisfaction. Why? Because it's the right thing to do!

The best and most inspiring factor in service is to honor and follow Christ and His lifestyle. Walking daily with Him keeps us focused on the right goals and activities.

As you serve, be kind. As you're being kind, serve. The two are intertwined.

HOLY GOD, *when I'm focused on me, I get miserable fast. But when I stay focused on You and others, my world seems right.*

# EVERY MOMENT

*He said to them, "When you pray, say: Father, hallowed be your name. Your kingdom come. Give us each day our daily bread. And forgive us our sins, for we ourselves forgive everyone indebted to us. And do not bring us to the time of trial.'*
—Luke 11:2-4

A man was overheard praying, "Dear Lord, so far today, I've done really well. In fact, I'm doing great! I haven't gotten frustrated, talked bad about anyone, lost my temper. I haven't been greedy, grumpy, nasty, selfish, over-indulgent, or told anyone off yet. I'm so proud!

"But in just a few minutes, God, I'm going to get out of bed, and from then on, I'm going to need a lot more help. Thank you. In Jesus' name. Amen."

Isn't it amazing how we can be doing so well and then, in a heartbeat, everything changes and it's downhill fast?

Following God is a choice you make every single day, situation by situation, moment by moment.

Just like the man in today's story who knew he needed God's help as soon as he got out of bed, commit today to Him, and then remember tomorrow to do the very same thing. And the next day, and the next, and the next.

MY REDEEMER, *when I rise, when I lie down at night, and all in between, guide me, lead me, help me to be all You have created me to be.*

# AS YOU PASS, PRAY

*The Lord answer you in the day of trouble! The name of the God of Jacob protect you! —Psalm 20:1b*

A statewide bulletin had made law enforcement in St. Joseph, Mo., aware that a man wanted for a brutal homicide was on Interstate 70 near Concordia.

Sergeant Mark DeGraffenreid and Corporal Ryan Smith responded in separate vehicles. As the man's car was spotted, Ryan deployed a tire deflation device in the event the suspect fled from the initial traffic stop. Seeing this, Sergeant DeGraffenreid activated his emergency lights to initiate the stop. The suspect drove into the median crossover, stopped, and then began firing multiple rounds at Sergeant DeGraffenreid, striking his patrol vehicle several times. The Sergeant stopped and returned fire, as the suspect fled at high speed in the northbound lanes. Trooper Douglas Fessenden then joined the pursuit.

When his vehicle's right rear tire became flat, the suspect pulled to the shoulder. He then released a barrage of gunfire at the officers, striking their vehicles. Sergeant DeGraffenreid's windshield exploded. Just as Trooper Fessenden exited his car, a bullet entered the windshield and splintered the steering wheel. As Corporal Smith exited his car, a round shattered the driver's door window.

Sergeant DeGraffenreid and Trooper Fessenden returned cover fire, re-entered their vehicles, and put distance between themselves and the threat. After a period of time with no shots fired by the suspect, the officers determined he had taken his own life.

For state highway troopers, no stop can be routine. In our increasingly violent culture, their lives are on the line far too often. Try this: anytime you pass an officer, pray for him/her. Their families would appreciate it.

PROTECTOR, *please cover our law enforcement officers who place their lives on the line in service daily. As I pass each one, may I pray.*

# WHY I DO WHAT I DO

*The words of the mouth are deep waters; the fountain of wisdom is a gushing stream.* —Psalm 18:4

On a Saturday evening in Racine, Wis., Julie and her four kids decided to take a quick swim with neighbors in their backyard pool. The adults, having just counted heads, looked away from the children for seconds to apply insect repellent.

And then it happened. Baker's 7-year-old son started screaming. His 3-year-old brother, Danny, had slipped under the water. He wasn't breathing. "I turned around and he was lifting him up to his sister," Julie recalled. "He was blue with no pulse. It was terrible."

Racine County Dispatcher Emily Johnson answered their 911 call. Emily, like all of the county's dispatch technicians, had recently received additional emergency medical dispatch training. After immediately sending rescuers from the Union Grove-Yorkville Fire Department to the home, Emily walked the adults through the steps of child CPR. "I need you to put one hand on the forehead and put the fingers of your other hand under the bony part of the chin and gently tilt the head back. Do you see him breathing at all? I want you to roll the baby onto his side and hold the baby's feet," Emily said.

They followed Emily's instructions to the letter and a few seconds later, little Danny was breathing. "Julie, he's breathing," an adult can be heard saying to his mom during the call. "He's breathing, honey. He's going to make it."

"It's the best feeling in the world," Emily said. "It's why I do what I do."

Emergency dispatchers have saved many lives through a phone line. Staying calm and instructing in detail is an amazing gift and service to all those in crisis. Help in this crisis was at the end of the phone line; help for you and me today is at the end of a prayer line.

OUR ADVOCATE, *in my own communication, help me to stay calm and level-headed, responding correctly and gently to all those I encounter today.*

# TOGETHER, WE CAN SAVE A LIFE

*Religion that is pure and undefiled before God, the Father, is this: to care for orphans and widows in their distress.* —James 1:27a

Single mom Regina was sound asleep in her apartment building in Salt Lake City with two-month-old Laila. She was awakened around 2 a.m. to cracking sounds coming from the structure. The building was shifting, having already dropped six inches, and all the residents had to be evacuated. So, where does a young mother and a baby go in an emergency like this?

A Disaster Action Team of Red Cross volunteers showed up and took them to a local shelter. Regina told the Red Cross, "I was so glad to have a place to sleep! I was tired and the baby slept great through this whole thing." The Red Cross provided shelter to 11 people who were displaced by the failing apartment.

The residents expressed gratitude to the Red Cross for setting up a shelter and showing them that someone cared. One neighbor, who was 8 months pregnant at the time, was especially grateful for a big breakfast the next morning.

Every year, thousands of people receive Red Cross help after they are affected by a disaster, such as fires, earthquakes, and floods.

Most people are very familiar with the American Red Cross logo and are accustomed to seeing it on the news when disaster strikes. It can easily be a sight we take for granted, until our family or community needs the help. To folks like Regina and Laila, it becomes very personal when suddenly there's no one to help and nowhere else to go. Is there a cross in your life that you seek when there is nowhere else to go?

ALMIGHTY GOD, *help me to watch for the widows and orphans (and single moms) inside my circle of influence. Help me to help them.*

# AN INTENSE 20 SECONDS

*The Lord will keep you from all evil; he will keep your life. The Lord will keep your going out and your coming in from this time on and for evermore.* —Psalm 121:7-8

Ever think a courtroom deputy's job is boring? Anytime, anywhere that dangerous inmates are exposed to the public can turn a quiet day in court into chaos.

In Louisville, Ky., County Circuit Court Judge Judith McDonald-Burkman was wrapping up loose ends on a case, when courtroom video shows Kristopher Bacanskas, dressed in an orange prison jumpsuit, bursting through a side door beside the jury box, with his hands wrapped around the neck of Sheriff's Deputy Mark Bryant.

Assistant Commonwealth Attorney Josh Schneider and another deputy in the courtroom rushed to help. "It was an intense 20 seconds," Josh said. It took three men to hold down the 6'4" 260-pound inmate. "I was just trying to hold his hands," Josh said, so Bacanskas couldn't grab hold of Deputy Bryant's weapon.

Yates said when Bacanskas saw Deputy Bryant crack the door to his holding cell to bring another inmate to the courtroom, the inmate rushed him, pushed him through the cell door, then slammed him through a second door that leads to the courtroom, which typically remains unlocked.

The judge pushed an emergency panic button hidden behind the bench, which calls other law enforcement to the courtroom to help. Several officers in the building responded in seconds. The inmate was eventually subdued, shackled, and taken back to jail. Thanks to the officers' quick response, no one was seriously hurt in the incident.

Any law enforcement officer stands between the public and danger anytime. The uniform and the badge change the person inside into a representation of an authority to be respected, a literal shield to protect the public. Who is at the end of your 'panic button'? Who comes to you at a time of need? Are you on the end of someone's 'panic button'? Where is God in this?

MIGHTY ONE, *may I protect those in my care. Bless and protect those who act as humans shields daily between the innocent and evil.*

# IN HER OWN BACKYARD

*Take delight in the Lord, and he will give you the desires of your heart.*
—Psalm 37:4

Most people have heard of Special Olympics, possibly attended an event, or know an athlete who participates, but many do not the origin of this unique organization.

It was the early 60s and Eunice Kennedy Shriver had noticed how people with intellectual disabilities were treated unfairly and unjustly. She also took note that most playgrounds were not designed for them to be able to play.

She decided to put on a summer day camp for children with intellectual disabilities in her own backyard. The goal and vision was to figure out what they were able to do in sports, not focusing on what they could not.

The vision and the movement grew and in the summer of 1968, the first International Special Olympics Games were held at Soldier Field in Chicago. Approximately 1,000 athletes took part in track, field, and swimming events.

In 1971, the U.S. Olympic Committee gave the organization official permission to use the Olympic name. Today, at the World Summer games, over 7,000 athletes compete from over 170 countries. Of course, local Special Olympic events occur regularly all over the nation and the world.

Most of us associate the name Kennedy and Shriver solely with politics and money. What an amazing legacy Eunice left for both famous family names by being the catalyst for Special Olympics.

Every entity such as Special Olympics begins with a burden. Then the burden ignites with passion to give feet to the dream. What if God wanted to give birth to an international movement through you?

To whom do you have a passion to reach? You never know what God can do with a desire and a dream.

COMFORTER, *it's so easy to think the big accomplishments will come from someone else. Thank You for the reminder that You can and will bless my dreams and desires to serve.*

# HE SPOKE SOFTLY

*Be strong and bold; have no fear or dread of them, because it is the Lord your God who goes with you; he will not fail you or forsake you.* —Deuteronomy 31:6

Pro surfer Bethany Hamilton shares about her now-famous shark attack, "It came, literally, out of the blue. I had no warning at all; not even the slightest hint of danger. The waves were small and inconsistent, and I was just kind of rolling along with them, relaxing on my board with my left arm dangling in the cool water. I remember thinking, 'I hope the surf picks up soon.' That's all it took—a split second. I felt a lot of pressure and a couple of lightning fast tugs. Then I watched in shock as the water around me turned bright red. Somehow, I stayed calm. My left arm was gone almost to the armpit, along with a huge crescent-shaped chunk of my red, white, and blue surfboard.

"I remember most clearly what the Kauai paramedic said to me in the ambulance: He spoke softly and held my hand as we were pulling out of the beach parking lot. He whispered in my ear . . . "

The verse the paramedic spoke to Bethany is today's Bible verse.

When Bethany was attacked, she had friends with her and her family soon joined her at the hospital, but the words that she recalls most are the words spoken by the paramedic.

Regardless of your role in service or where you serve, your attitude, words, and actions can make such a difference to the people around you. Whether you are with someone for seconds or days, you can have a huge impact!

HEALER, *help me to always be mindful that my words and attitude make such a difference with the people I serve and deal with. Help me to, like Bethany's paramedic, reflect Your heart for people.*

# I'LL GIVE YOU THE RECRUITS

*Like good stewards of the manifold grace of God, serve one another with whatever gift each of you has received.* —1 Peter 4:10

In St. Louis, police officers have come together to help promote literacy among local children by forming the Books-and-Badges program. In fact, being a tutor for a child is mandatory for becoming a city police officer. For nearly a decade, police recruits have been partnered with children.

Founder Karen Kalish got the idea while riding with a police officer years ago on the 7 p.m. to midnight Saturday shift. "It was so boring," she said. "There was really nothing going on." But the experience led her to learn that many criminals cannot read.

She approached the chief of police at that time with the idea of pairing officers with children who struggled with reading. "He told me you can't have the police, because they need to be on the streets. But I'll give you the recruits," Karen said.

The director of the police academy welcomed the idea. "Our mission is to prevent crime and serve the public and we're not always using traditional strategies to do that," he explained. "Clearly this has an impact that's difficult to measure, but it makes a difference," he said.

"Our hope is that it gives the recruits sensitivity to their job as more than just arresting individuals, but making relationships with the community. We want them to work with these kids now, so they don't see them later." Teaching a child to read forever changes their horizon.

By the St. Louis police making community service a mandatory part of job training, they are setting an example of involvement and prevention. What are some creative connections that you and your teammates could make? What are some new avenues to make a difference right where you are? Where do you feel God is leading you?

COUNSELOR, teach *me to watch for new places to connect and to serve. Guide me with Your creativity to see my work with new eyes.*

# YOU'RE READY TO GO

*Each will be like a hiding-place from the wind, a covert from the tempest, like streams of water in a dry place, like the shade of a great rock in a weary land.*
*—Isaiah 32:2*

In Pike County, Ala., volunteer fireman Glenn Adkins has been fighting flames for more than 25 years. "When the pager goes off, you're ready to go," said Adkins.

On this particular day, a 165,000 square-foot assembly plant has caught fire around 3:30 a.m. "This was the very first fire I was in charge of," he said.

Glenn is in command of an army of 12 volunteer fire departments with some 60 volunteer firefighters.

After intense fighting, about seven hours after the initial call came in, the fire was brought under control. In the end, the blaze got the best of the $16 million metal building.

"We did save some of the equipment they could work with. We saved the welding department and the paint shop. It's disappointing, but it's hard to get in on a fire that big," said Glenn.

So what does Glenn Adkins do to make a living when he's not fighting fires for free? He's a chicken farmer.

Even though the fireman job has no pay, no benefits, and no retirement, he adds that just the thought of trying to save lives and property is good enough. Alabama has some 10,000 volunteer firefighters.

This nation is held together by a giant army of volunteers, whether it be for local support or international relief. Be encouraged today that many stand alongside you to serve in so many places and roles. Most volunteers do so in response to a calling; share your calling today with friend, family member, or co-worker.

LIVING WATER, *it's amazing how regardless of biography and geography, all of us who serve humankind are everywhere! Bless today all those who give, love, fight, and protect.*

# LOVE OF A LITTLE GIRL

*I am about to do a new thing; now it springs forth, do you not perceive it? I will make a way in the wilderness and rivers in the desert.* —Isaiah 43:19

Allison Winn, 10, a resident of Denver, spent 14 months recuperating from treatment of a brain tumor. Their family dog, Coco, became a huge comfort and security for Allison. So much so that it gave her an idea.

"Coco helped me feel better. She would cuddle with me when I didn't want to play."

Allison told her parents that she wanted to help other sick kids find the same kind of comfort. She started raising money by selling lemonade and homemade dog biscuits in front of her house. By the end of that summer, she had raised nearly $1,000—enough to adopt, train, and spay or neuter two dogs and give them to children with cancer.

Two years later, corporate groups and civic organizations gathered to make dog treats at a Denver kitchen for Allison's cause. She named her brainchild, the Stink Bug Project, after a picture she drew commemorating the end of her chemotherapy.

Stink Bug now helps families adopt pets from the Colorado Correctional Industries Prison Trained K9 Companion Program, where inmates teach commands to rescued dogs. To date, the program has raised enough for the adoption of ten dogs.

"I wanted to do a million adoptions, but my mom made me lower it," she said. "Allison has figured out how to help—in a way that no one else has," Allison's mom said proudly. "It took the love of a little girl to wrap all that together into one amazing package."

Let Allison's story encourage you today to keep on making a difference. Turn opportunity into action!

CREATOR GOD, *help me to stay faithful to what You have already called me to. Keep me fresh and focused. But also keep me mindful of new places You want to take me too.*

# JUST BEING A MOM

*Deliver me, O Lord, from evildoers; protect me from those who are violent, who plan evil things in their minds and stir up wars continually.* —Psalm 140:1-2

Louise Zoller arrived 45 minutes early to pick up 2-year-old Hannah at the day-care center in Cape Coral, Fla. As she walked in, Louise overheard a cell phone conversation: "Yes, there's a man outside. I believe he has a gun."

Throughout the day-care center, teachers gathered children into restrooms. Just then, a man with a gun walked past Louise. "Where is [she]?" the man demanded. Suddenly the intruder turned toward the bathroom and Louise realized he was hunting Hannah's teacher, Christine Dunn.

She saw the man step into the bathroom and a shot rang out, followed by the sound of screaming children. Louise rushed in and grabbed the man's arm. He shoved her to the floor. She again saw the man raise his arm. Again the gun went off. Louise grabbed the man's arm with both hands and pulled him into the hallway. She knocked the gun from his hand, then tossed it toward the front lobby.

Louise raced to the lobby, scooped up the pistol, and ran outside. "I have it, I have it," she shouted to the police, and she threw the weapon to the ground.

Officers rushed into the building, where they found Dunn dead in the bathroom. Her 2-year-old daughter, Allyson, as well as the other children, were all physically unharmed.

The man was angry about his divorce and his inability to see his daughter without supervision.

Cape Coral mayor Eric Feichthaler formally recognized Louise Zoller saying, "That kind of heroism is very rare."

Louise simply explains, "I was just being a mom." This is clearly a demonstration of "no greater love."

There are few forces on earth stronger than a mother's love and her desire to protect her children.

MY DELIVERER, *it is awesome to think of the many situations daily where ordinary people do extraordinary things to overcome and stop evil. Thank You that You have overcome, and that one day, evil will be no more.*

# BUT THEY COME BACK ANYWAY

*So God created the great sea monsters and every living creature that moves, of every kind, with which the waters swarm, and every winged bird of every kind. And God saw that it was good. —Genesis 1:21*

Alongside Tampa Bay's Sunshine Skyway Bridge, Mark Maksimowicz and his sister, Janice Whitmore, "fish" for what earlier visitors have tossed: fast-food wrappers, dirty diapers and other debris. They, along with their cousins Jeff and Vince Albanese, are the founding members of the Green Armada. Their personal mission is to clean up the coastlines around Tampa, St. Petersburg, and Clearwater, Fla.

On a typical day, they haul up to 700 pounds of trash to the dump. For Mark, the Green Armada is the fulfillment of a dream he's had for more than 10 years. So far, the cousins have spent about $100,000 of their own savings to launch their endeavor. Jeff quit his job to devote himself to the effort full-time, as did Janice. And they've attracted 700 volunteers.

Mark said, "What kills you is, we clean it to where you wouldn't mind sitting there and a week later, it's like we never cleaned this area up."

But they come back anyway, hoping someday they'll reach their long-term goal: that so many others will be inspired to clean up the waterways—and more important, stop and think, before littering—there will be no need for a Green Armada.

Some people look at Mark, Janice, Jeff, and Vince and question why someone would spend so much time, energy, and money in what, too often, seems like a losing battle. But that's the beauty of finding a passion. And evidently, 700 people agree with them. They personally sacrifice to care for the gift of the Creation.

LIVING WATER, *no matter what any of us choose to do to change the world, it is so easy to get overwhelmed and think it doesn't matter. Keep me focused on what I can change, what the goal is, and those who stand with me to make a difference.*

# FLAG DAY

*Declare among the nations and proclaim, set up a banner and proclaim, do not conceal it . . . —Jeremiah 50:12*

On June 14, 1777, the Continental Congress replaced the British symbols of the Grand Union flag with a new design featuring thirteen white stars in a circle on a field of blue with thirteen red and white stripes—one for each state. This flag was the one that was alleged to have been made by the Philadelphia seamstress Betsy Ross, who was an official flag maker for the Pennsylvania Navy. The number of stars increased as the new states entered the Union, but the number of stripes stopped at fifteen and was later returned to thirteen.

In June 1886, Bernard Cigrand made his first public proposal for the annual observance of the birth of the flag when he wrote an article entitled "The Fourteenth of June" in the Chicago Argus newspaper. Bernard's effort to ensure national observance of Flag Day finally came when President Woodrow Wilson issued a proclamation calling for a nationwide observance of the event on June 14, 1916. However, Flag Day did not become official until August 1949, when President Harry Truman signed the legislation and proclaimed June 14 as Flag Day. In 1966, Congress also requested that the president issue an annual proclamation designating the week in which June 14 occurs as National Flag Week.

Flags and banners have long been a rallying point for people—a symbol to represent an identity and history. The U.S. flag represents many lives and many events in a rich history of freedom, sacrifice, and courage. Today, thank God for what our flag represents and your opportunity to be a part of its present and future.

CORNERSTONE, *thank You for our flag and all she represents—the sacrifice and service of so many. Thank You for the rich legacy that I can be a part of and add to.*

# MY PEOPLE, MY GOD

*May the God of steadfastness and encouragement grant you to live in harmony with one another, in accordance with Christ Jesus.* —Romans 15:5

Ruth 1:11-19—Naomi said, "Turn back, my daughters, why will you go with me? Do I still have sons in my womb that they may become your husbands? Turn back, my daughters, go your way, for I am too old to have a husband. Even if I thought there was hope for me, even if I should have a husband tonight and bear sons, would you then wait until they were grown? Would you then refrain from marrying? No, my daughters, it has been far more bitter for me than for you, because the hand of the Lord has turned against me."

Then they wept aloud again. Orpah kissed her mother-in-law, but Ruth clung to her. So she said, "See, your sister-in-law has gone back to her people and to her gods; return after your sister-in-law."

But Ruth said, "Do not press me to leave you or to turn back from following you! Where you go, I will go; where you lodge, I will lodge; your people shall be my people, and your God my God. Where you die, I will die—there will I be buried. May the Lord do thus and so to me, and more as well, if even death parts me from you!"

When Naomi saw that she was determined to go with her, she said no more to her. So the two of them went on until they came to Bethlehem.

Ruth showed a deep respect and love for Naomi, for which God blessed her.

As our culture becomes busier and we become more isolated from each other, human qualities such as loyalty and commitment may become scarce. Work toward unity in all that you do. Be a bridge builder on every team you serve. Let loyalty be a trait for which you are known.

FAITHFUL ONE, *thank You for building a bridge to our hearts. Help me to gain a reputation for loyalty and unity in all that I do.*

# SAFELY HOME

*May he defend the cause of the poor of the people, give deliverance to the needy, and crush the oppressor.* —Psalm 72:4

In 1984, police could enter information about stolen cars, stolen guns, and even stolen horses into the FBI's national crime computer, but not stolen children. Because of The National Center for Missing & Exploited Children, that is no longer true. More missing children come home safely today, and more is being done today to protect children, than any time in the nation's history.

In 1984, the U.S. Congress passed the Missing Children's Assistance Act that established a National Resource Center and Clearinghouse on Missing and Exploited Children. On June 13, 1984, President Ronald Reagan officially opened the center during a White House ceremony.

The center has become the leading nonprofit organization in the U.S. working with law enforcement to address the problems of missing and sexually exploited children. As many organizations that operate on a massive scale, volunteers play a crucial role. Some work directly with the center while others distribute the information. There are multiple opportunities to get involved.

What better activity could anyone be a part of than being than helping rescue missing children? Clearly the Creator wants our families to be healthy and intact.

The next time you see a flyer or ad of any kind with missing children's pictures, look a little closer. An army is looking for them and could use your help.

GREAT SHEPHERD, *thank You for the people who work tirelessly to find these children. Bless and strengthen them. Thank You that You came to rescue us as Your children.*

# STAND TOGETHER

*May you be made strong with all the strength that comes from his glorious power, and may you be prepared to endure everything with patience, while joyfully giving thanks to the Father, who has enabled you to share in the inheritance of the saints in the light. He has rescued us from the power of darkness and transferred us into the kingdom of his beloved Son, in whom we have redemption, the forgiveness of sins.*
—Colossians 1:11-14

Ever see the animated movie Finding Nemo? There's a scene where the fish "swim down" together to get out of a fisherman's net.

Well, that really happened.

A school of herring caught in a trawler's net refused to give up without a fight—and sank a 10-meter boat.

The trawler, called Steinholm, was fishing off Norway's northern coast when the six-member crew made a huge catch of fish. When they tried to haul in the net, the entire school of herring swam for the bottom of the sea, capsizing the ship.

"I have been fishing since I was 14 and I have never seen anything like it," said Skipper Geir Nikolaisen. The crew members tried cutting the net loose, but were forced to abandon the ship, which sank in ten minutes.

One or two herrings could never have sunk that boat.

You, too, can achieve what seems impossible when you meet regularly with other Christians to pray, talk about what God is doing in your life, and be accountable to each other as you confront your weaknesses. We stand together, not alone!

ALPHA & OMEGA, *You made us to need each other. Lead me to join with others, help others, and stand strong in Your name.*

# I HEREBY COMMISSION YOU

*Then Gideon built an altar there to the Lord, and called it, The Lord is peace.*
—Judges 6:24a

The story of Gideon is a great encouragement for us.

We meet him in Judges 6—"Now the angel of the Lord came and sat under the oak at Ophrah, which belonged to Joash the Abiezrite, as his son Gideon was beating out wheat in the wine press, to hide it from the Midianites. The angel of the Lord appeared to him and said to him, 'The Lord is with you, you mighty warrior.'

"Gideon answered him, 'But sir, if the Lord is with us, why then has all this happened to us? And where are all his wonderful deeds that our ancestors recounted to us, saying, "Did not the Lord bring us up from Egypt?" But now the Lord has cast us off, and given us into the hand of Midian.'

"Then the Lord turned to him and said, 'Go in this might of yours and deliver Israel from the hand of Midian; I hereby commission you.'

"He responded, 'But sir, how can I deliver Israel? My clan is the weakest in Manasseh, and I am the least in my family.'

The Lord said to him, 'But I will be with you, and you shall strike down the Midianites, every one of them.'"

When this angel, sent by God, calls Gideon a "mighty warrior," he doesn't take the compliment, but questions what is happening to his country? When God commissions him, his response is "Me? How can I do this?" Then God promises He will be with Him.

Be encouraged today that God is in the business of taking ordinary, fearful, doubting men and women and doing extraordinary things with their lives. Do you relate to Gideon? Good! Let Him work in and through You today.

ALMIGHTY GOD, *I want to be called a mighty warrior for You. Help my doubt and fear. Turn it to faith and courage.*

# WRITE A NEW EPITAPH

*So if anyone is in Christ, there is a new creation: everything old has passed away;*
*see, everything has become new!* —2 Corinthians 5:17

Toward the end of the nineteenth century, Swedish chemist Alfred Nobel was reading the local newspaper one morning and was shocked to see his own obituary mistakenly printed there! It called Nobel the "merchant of death."

As a pacifist, he had invented dynamite in the hopes that it might actually end wars sooner, but of course, it just made for one of the first weapons of mass destruction.

Alfred's older brother was actually the one who had died, but the event had a profound effect on him.

Alfred decided he wanted to be known for something other than inventing another way to kill people, so he initiated the Nobel Peace Prize, an award for scientists and writers who foster peace. He said, "Every man ought to have the chance to correct his epitaph in midstream and write a new one."

If you were to die today, what would your family and friends say about you?

Are there some "old things" in your life that need to "pass away?"

Is there an attitude, such as rebellion, or a sin that you need to give up? Write out a prayer to God, telling Him how you feel and what you need. Tell him about that which affects your witness for Him, and ask Him to help you with it. Then start praying.

Journaling is a great practice and discipline for your prayer time. Write down your prayer requests and God's answers. Documenting your spiritual journey can help you to grow spiritually and it can be a rich blessing.

REDEEMER, *each day brings a new start with You. Help me to let go of yesterday to fully embrace today, letting go of the old and receiving the new.*

# UNCONDITIONAL LOVE

*Therefore be imitators of God, as beloved children, and live in love, as Christ loved us and gave himself up for us .. —Ephesians 5:1-2a*

In North America, tens of thousands of children cannot stay with their birth families. These children—often labeled unadoptable or hard to place—are mostly school-aged. Some are brothers and sisters who need to be placed in homes together. Some have been exposed to drugs or other harmful situations. Others have medical issues that require care and attention. Most have physical, mental, or emotional difficulties. Yet all of these children need loving families.

The North American Council on Adoptable Children is committed to meeting the needs of waiting children and the families who adopt them. The council was started nearly 40 years ago by adoptive parents. They believed that all children have the right to a permanent, nurturing, and culturally sensitive family. A desire for unconditional love by an adult committed to them for life is a part of their mission.

The council relies heavily on a volunteer network to maintain a presence in every state and throughout Canada. Proximity to someone involved with the organization is vital to supporting families and providing homes for children.

Support groups provide the opportunity for parents to share information, experience, and emotions with one another. The need for support after the adoption is critical and parents regularly turn to support groups to find this help. Parent groups are an inexpensive and effective means of providing and expanding post-adoption services to families.

In a very real way, all of us start out this life as spiritual orphans, needing adoption by a Heavenly Father who can lead us through life.

Regardless of your background or family, maybe you have more in common with these children than you might think?

FATHER, *thank You that when we were spiritually orphaned by our choosing, You came to adopt and bring us into Your family. As I live and grow, may I look more and more like You.*

# HAD THEY NOT BEEN THERE

*How you have helped one who has no power! How you have assisted the arm that has no strength! —Job 26:2*

San Jose, Calif., EMTs Brian Newton and Shawn Ellis were on duty when they noticed something unusual. They turned their ambulance around quickly and called in a possible fire.

Payal Hazari, 17, was sleeping upstairs inside her home. "[The EMT] just came into my room like, 'Ma'am, your house is on fire,' and that's when I got scared and I was like, 'is this real? Am I dreaming?'" she said.

"I see that the flames were flickering out of the doorway and that thick black smoke began to just completely fill the hallway," Shawn said. "All of this happened before fire crews were able to arrive at the home.

"As they found out, the fire was spreading very quickly and had they not been there to take action, the outcome would have been very different," San Jose Fire Department Chief William McDonald said.

Pallavi Hazari, Payal's mother, said, "They really saved two lives. I can't imagine life without her, so it's a life for both of us."

Payal's family gave handwritten cards to both men. "I wanted to thank them, but I don't know how to, because it's just so big," Payal said. "You can't thank them enough. There is no way you can pay them back for what they've done."

Whether it be an EMT, policeman, fireman, trooper, soldier, or a citizen Good Samaritan, when a life is saved, family members and friends are also saved from grief and devastation from the tragic loss of a loved one.

Pallavi is right. Saving one life is saving many others as well.

SAVIOR GOD, *thank You for the reminder that when we touch any life, we are also helping all those whose life that person is connected to.*

# A PLACE IN HISTORY

*The Lord bless you and keep you; the Lord make his face to shine upon you, and be gracious to you; the Lord lift up his countenance upon you, and give you peace.*
—Numbers 6:24-26

One hundred Connecticut National Guard soldiers deploying to Afghanistan to perform aircraft maintenance stood at attention with their flags inside the hangar at the Groton-New London Airport, while national, state, and local officials told them how much they are appreciated. Soldiers posed in front of a Black Hawk helicopter as their family members snapped pictures with their cell phones.

"After more than 10 years of war, responding to our nation's call is not new to members of the Connecticut National Guard," said Major Gen. Thaddeus J. Martin, commander of the state National Guard. The deployment could last up to 400 days.

Major Raymond Chicoski of Colchester, a Black Hawk pilot who will be testing helicopters, said the group has outstanding technical capabilities and is equipped like few others.

Leaving home is tough, he said, but the National Guard does an excellent job of preparing families.

A wife of Chief Warrant Officer James Muthig said that her husband, a 56-year-old pilot on his third deployment, would not be happy if he wasn't doing his duty. She added, "You do what you have to do."

"Never in the history of this nation have so few men and women borne the burden of battle for so long," Blumenthal said. "You deserve a place in our history."

Every day, our soldiers are moving to and from assignments all over the world. You can't set foot today in an airport without seeing our fighting men in uniform. For every service man or woman you see, there is a family somewhere missing, praying, and hoping for a swift and safe return. They deserve our gratitude, our prayers and thanks as well.

PRINCE OF PEACE, *please bless and protect all of our fighting men and women all over the world today. And bring a special blessing and comfort to all of their families.*

# A SIMPLE BOUQUET

*To provide for those who mourn in Zion—to give them a garland instead of ashes, the oil of gladness instead of mourning, the mantle of praise instead of a faint spirit. They will be called oaks of righteousness, the planting of the Lord, to display his glory. —Isaiah 61:3*

Hotels, weddings, and many corporate events spend big money on beautiful flower arrangements, but often within just a few hours are finished with them.

Nancy Lawlor was sitting in the lobby of the Waldorf Astoria Hotel, marveling at the towering floral displays. She aske, "Where do they go at the end of the day?". The answer was "into the dumpster."

Nancy volunteered to take them away. Once the hotel agreed, Lawlor delivered $2,000 worth of large pink bouquets to a New York City hospital. "It all started with one person saying 'yes'," she said.

Nancy started her nonprofit organization, FlowerPower, which has distributed more than $2.5 million worth of flowers to hospitals, rape crisis centers, nursing homes, and rehabilitation clinics.

The bouquets last several days, often broken down into many from one large arrangement, giving patients a healthy dose of good cheer.

"I've seen thousands of people transformed all over a simple bouquet of flowers that originally would've been thrown away," said Nancy.

"FlowerPower is passionate about altering our society's culture by transforming the way we relate to our sick and dying elders," said Nancy. "We provide opportunities for volunteers to make bouquets and give them to our elders."

Nancy's efforts bring a whole new meaning to recycling. And, in reality, those flowers are far more noticed and appreciated by her recipients. Her actions expand on the story found in Matthew 25, "I was sick and you visited me".....with flowers!

Just paying attention in our world and asking the right question can connect resources to those who can truly use them.

CREATOR GOD, *every day You take the discarded and abused and turn them into beautiful, useful gifts. Whether a flower, a kind word, or an act of service, help me to cooperate with You to bring beauty into the world.*

# SAFEGUARDING AMERICA

*Where there is no guidance, a nation falls, but in an abundance of counselors there is safety.* —Proverbs 11:14

The Department of Homeland Security has many people to protect our nation at the highest level of security. One such person is U.S. Coast Guard Petty Officer Bonnie Wysocki.

On a ten-month deployment to Iraq and Kuwait, she served as an inspector with the Coast Guard's Redeployment Assistance and Inspection Detachment (RAID), helping to ensure the safety of military containers being shipped back to the United States.

The only woman on her team, Petty Officer Wysocki was mobilized as an inspector for hazardous materials. She traveled around the region to inspect and seal containers and check cargo for compliance with international shipping standards—ensuring that hazardous materials such as acetylene, oxygen, fire extinguishers, batteries, radioactive instruments, and fuel were properly loaded and labeled.

In this capacity, Petty Officer Wysocki and her team played a critical role in making sure that troops and their equipment could return home from Iraq, or redeploy to Afghanistan, safely. This team has at the core of its mission, safety and the good stewardship of resources.

For more than 220 years, the Coast Guard has safeguarded America's maritime interests and natural resources on our rivers and ports, on the high seas and around the world.

The last decade has brought many changes to our nation. New challenges have come from a new war. The Department of Homeland Security once again displays America's ability to quickly respond and enact a defense toward any enemy.

As an American, you are a part of one of the most blessed and strongest legacies in history. Is your team being good stewards of what has been provided for them?

*I AM, You have blessed this nation in countless ways. Thank You for all those who work daily on so many fronts to keep us safe and also fight evil around the world.*

# SERVING THE HEART

*"Because the poor are despoiled, because the needy groan, I will now rise up," said the Lord; "I will place them in the safety for which they long." —Psalm 12:5*

Former police detective Rob Michaels saw the national statistics for suicides and divorces among law enforcement officers and firefighters, and he knew he must do something.

A veteran of the Virginia National Guard serving on the military police battalion and then as a patrol officer for the Norfolk, Va., Police Department, Michaels knew well the emotional and psychological aftermath caused by consistently witnessing crimes and accidents. He references an FBI report that states every 17 hours a law enforcement officer takes his/her life, and 75 percent of police officers and 87 percent of firefighters are divorced.

In response to these issues, Michaels started Serve & Protect, a non-profit organization whose motto is "serving the heart of those who protect." The group operates the 24/7 Coast2Coast Serve & Protect Crisis Line. Counselors can provide immediate help to first responders who call in.

"It's my firm contention that the best chaplains come from first responders," said Rob. "They understand the job and the emotions. They get it."

Rob has also begun a Bible study program called "Guns and Hoses," which can be implemented anywhere by a facilitator, as well as a program for the spouses of first responders.

When God calls people to serve and protect, it just makes sense that He calls others to help the ones that are called. If you are a first responder and know you need some help, it's OK to ask.

When you reach out for help, God will provide it for you.

HEALER, *if I broke my leg, I wouldn't hesitate to go to the doctor. Help me when my heart or my spirit gets broken to reach out and get help then too.*

# DECLARATION OF DEPENDENCE

*Have regard to your servant's prayer and his plea, O Lord my God, heeding the cry and the prayer that your servant prays to you today.* —1 Kings 8:28

George Washington kept a prayer journal. Below is one his entries. Note that these are just two sentences.

O eternal and everlasting God, I presume to present myself this morning before thy Divine majesty, beseeching thee to accept of my humble and hearty thanks, that it hath pleased thy great goodness to keep and preserve me the night past from all the dangers poor mortals are subject to, and has given me sweet and pleasant sleep, whereby I find my body refreshed and comforted for performing the duties of this day, in which I beseech thee to defend me from all perils of body and soul.

Increase my faith in the sweet promises of the gospel; give me repentance from dead works; pardon my wanderings, and direct my thoughts unto thyself, the God of my salvation; teach me how to live in thy fear, labor in thy service, and ever to run in the ways of thy commandments; make me always watchful over my heart, that neither the terrors of conscience, the loathing of holy duties, the love of sin, nor an unwillingness to depart this life, may cast me into a spiritual slumber, but daily frame me more and more into the likeness of thy son Jesus Christ, that living in thy fear, and dying in thy favor, I may in thy appointed time attain the resurrection of the just unto eternal life bless my family, friends, and kindred.

Humility, gratitude, repentance, dependency, and submission are all unmistakably qualities displayed here. Take a moment to meditate on Washington's words again and frame your own prayer from his.

O eternal *and everlasting God–*_____

# BEFORE THE THRONE

*Let us approach with a true heart in full assurance of faith.* —Hebrews 10:22a

*A Police Officer's Prayer*
*Author Unknown*

*Lord, I ask for courage*
*Courage to face and conquer my own fears*
*Courage to take me where others will not go*
*I ask for strength*
*Strength of body to protect others*
*Strength of spirit to lead others*
*I ask for dedication*
*Dedication to my job to do it well*
*Dedication to my community to keep it safe*
*Give me, Lord, concern for all those who trust me*
*And compassion for those who need me*
*And, please, Lord, through it all, be at my side*

Today, no matter your place of service, be encouraged and pray for courage. Be strong, while you pray for strength. Dedicate yourself, while you ask for more dedication. Stay close to those you love, while you stay close to God.

GREAT I AM, *You are my source of all that is good and all that I need. Give me courage. Strength. Dedication. May I love others as You love me.*

# THE WAY OF WORSHIP

*Surely the righteous shall give thanks to your name; the upright shall live in your presence.* —Psalm 140:13

God created us to worship Him—to find our significance and value in Him alone. Sin and disobedience toward God turns us from Him and towards another person, activity, or thing.

That is also worship, but the Bible calls it idolatry when we replace God.

Worship is a deep and intimate act, and it is in Scripture that worship takes on physical form in the life of David.

As you read these verses from Psalms, view them as simple expressions of love toward your Heavenly Father.

Worship is inward and outward, regardless of what we worship. Express your love toward God today. He is expressing His love to you.

*But I, through the abundance of your steadfast love, will enter your house, I will bow down towards your holy temple in awe of you.* —Psalm 5:7

*I will give to the Lord the thanks due to his righteousness, and sing praise to the name of the Lord, the Most High.* —Psalm 7:17

*I will give thanks to the Lord with my whole heart; I will tell of all your wonderful deeds.* —Psalm 9:1

*So I will bless you as long as I live; I will lift up my hands and call on your name.* —Psalm 63:4

MIGHTY KING, *one day when I stand in Your presence, I know I will have a reaction to Your holiness. Help me today to express that to You right here, right now.*

# LIFE'S CHALLENGES, GOD'S VICTORIES

*For nothing will be impossible with God.* —Luke 1:37

As a newborn, Jon Sheptock's mother never even held him. She gave him up to the authorities.

After being adopted by Christian parents, Jon struggled as a teen with thoughts of suicide and he wrestled with hopelessness and fear.

Jon is unique.

He was born with no arms and his right leg shorter than his left. Yes, absolutely no arms—his body ends at his shoulders.

Through the love of his parents, Jon gave his life to Christ and soon discovered that nothing is impossible with God. Jon began to sing and share his story at churches and schools. Today, Jon travels and ministers all over the world. He is married and has three daughters. His ministry's motto is: Making life's challenges, God's victories.

Today's verse is the last sentence that the angel spoke to Mary after he told her she would have a child. Mary had asked how a virgin would bear a child. This verse explains how anything miraculous happens—like a man with no arms having a beautiful family and traveling the world sharing and singing.

We're all "handicapped." We're all "challenged" in some way. Living in a world full of evil and chaos as sinners causes this in us all. It comes down to what we focus on and what we believe about ourselves.

What are your handicaps? Your challenges? Maybe it is something as serious as Jon Sheptock's life.

Regardless, let today's story and verse inspire you to press on and live the life God intends for you. Make life's challenges into God's victories, because nothing is impossible with God.

HEAVENLY FATHER, *thank You for every blessing that You have given me. Help me to stay focused and use all You give for Your glory.*

# TO HIM WHO CAN

*If my people who are called by my name humble themselves, pray, seek my face, and turn from their wicked ways, then I will hear from heaven, and will forgive their sin and heal their land.* —2 Chronicles 7:14

As a drought gripped the state of Georgia, Governor Sonny Perdue was doing all he knew to do to provide much-needed water to the residents of his state, as well as mandate conservation. He had ordered statewide water restrictions and launched a legal battle for the release of water from federal reservoirs, even appealing directly to the president.

Having done all he knew to do in the physical realm, Governor Perdue, along with Lieutenant Governor Casey Cagle, held a prayer meeting outside the Capitol building in Atlanta.

Several hundred people, including a few local pastors and priests, gathered together. "We've come together here simply for one reason and one reason only: to very reverently and respectfully pray up a storm," Perdue charged. "It's time to appeal to Him Who can and will make a difference."

As one might suspect, a small band of protesters gathered to protest a religious observance on government property.

There is an old saying: "There are no atheists in foxholes." This, of course, alludes to war when, just before engaging the enemy, prayer seems natural and necessary. The governor could have held a private assembly with no political risk, but appealing to God at a time of crisis overshadowed any threat.

There is certainly a time for private prayer, but there is also a time to band together for public prayer. The next time you are in a situation where you know everything physical has been done and help must come from elsewhere, be bold and lift up a prayer to the One Who holds the answers.

MIGHTY KING, *how it must make You feel when You can and are willing to help and we won't ask You. Help me to be bold and come before You anytime, anywhere.*

# GRANTED AND ACCEPTED

*Seek the Lord while he may be found, call upon him while he is near; let the wicked forsake their way, and the unrighteous their thoughts; let them return to the Lord, that he may have mercy on them, and to our God, for he will abundantly pardon.*
—ISAIAH 55:6-7

During the presidential term of Andrew Jackson, a postal clerk named George Wilson robbed a federal payroll from a train and killed a guard.

The court convicted him and sentenced him to hang. But public sentiment against capital punishment during that time was running high. This was also his first conviction, so a movement began to convince President Jackson to pardon him. Eventually, Jackson agreed.

To everyone's shock, George Wilson refused the pardon. Since this had never happened before, the Supreme Court was asked to rule as to whether someone could refuse a presidential pardon.

Chief Justice John Marshall handed down the court's decision that stated, "A pardon is a parchment whose only value must be determined by the receiver of the pardon. It has no value apart from that which the receiver gives to it. George Wilson has refused to accept the pardon. We cannot conceive why he would do so, but he has. Therefore, George Wilson must die."

George Wilson was hanged. Pardon, declared the Supreme Court, must not only be granted, it must be accepted.

God is humankind's judge, but He is merciful.

Isaiah understood that God offers to sinners, condemned to an eternity in hell, a pardon for all sin. Notice what has to happen before the pardon comes—Isaiah said, "Let him turn to the Lord . . ."

HOLY JUDGE, *thank You for making a way for me to come to You—both now and in eternity. I believe on You for forgiveness of sin. I believe in You for salvation.*

# MORE PRECIOUS TO ME

*Whoever pursues righteousness and kindness will find life and honor.*
—*PROVERBS 21:21*

Danny DeLaRosa, a street cleaner for the city of Alvin, Texas, found a bank bag on the side of the road. He opened the bag to find over $7,000 in cash.

No one was nearby. So, did he act like he had won the lottery? Pay off some bills? Go on a shopping spree? Vacation? No.

He turned the bag into his boss back at Town Hall, who was able to determine that the bag belonged to a local donut shop owner.

The owner had put the bag on top of his car, then forgot it was there, and drove off. DeLaRosa said he was "stunned" to see thousands of dollars in the bag. But he said he wasn't tempted to keep the money. The owner of the donut shop was shocked that someone was "still honest."

So why was Danny not tempted? He answered, "My honor was more precious to me than the money."

Danny made the choice to pursue righteousness—the right way—and he found honor. His boss, his wife, and all those who heard about his actions spoke of integrity about his life and choice.

Is that worth more than $7,000? You can't put a price tag on qualities such as love, honor, and truth.

An old saying goes: "Integrity is doing the right thing, even when no one is watching." Isn't it ironic how some of the strongest temptations can come when no one is watching? Whether alone or with others, pursue God's ways over your own preferences.

In the long run, it will always be worth it.

RIGHTEOUS ONE, *give me strength when I am alone to hold fast to my integrity, to say "no" when I should and say "yes" when I should. Teach me to pursue Your ways.*

# QUARTER CENTURY OF LIFE

*Who among all these does not know that the hand of the Lord has done this? In his hand is the life of every living thing and the breath of every human being.*
*—Job 12:9-10*

Gunner's Mate 2nd Class Danny Dietz entered the United States Navy in 1999. After graduating from Recruit Training Command and Gunner's Mate school at NATTC Pensacola, Fla., he transferred to Basic Underwater Demolition/SEAL Training and graduated. He then attended Basic Airborne Course at Fort Benning, Georgia, SEAL Qualification Training and SEAL Delivery Vehicle Training. From there he reported for duty at SEAL Delivery Vehicle Team TWO in late 2001.

Danny was assigned to Task Unit BRAVO as pilot of the secondary SEAL Delivery Vehicle. During a rigorous pre-deployment work-up, he honed his skills to become one of the best pilots at the command.

He was assigned to Task Unit CHARLIE as a primary Special Reconnaissance Team member and the Communications Department Head. In April 2005, Danny deployed to Afghanistan to support Naval Special Warfare Squadron TEN and the Naval Special Warfare community's prosecution of the Global War on Terror.

During his service Danny was awarded the Silver Star, Purple Heart, Navy and Marine Corps Achievement, Combat Action Ribbon, Good Conduct Award, National Defense Service, Global War on Terrorism Expeditionary, Global War on Terrorism Service, Sea Service Deployment, Expert Pistol, and Expert Rifle.

Danny died in an ambush during Operation Red Wings in Afghanistan. He is survived by his wife.

At just 25 years old, Danny had accomplished much—more than many people do in three times that amount of time.

If you are alive today, you can still change anything with which you are not pleased. Your Creator has a great plan for your life. Talk to Him about it today.

CREATOR, *yesterday is gone, tomorrow never comes, so help me to make today count. Help me to follow You.*

# INDEPENDENCE DAY

*For you were called to freedom, brothers and sisters; only do not use your freedom*
*as an opportunity for self-indulgence, but through love become slaves to one another.*
*—Galatians 5:13*

The legal separation of the 13 colonies from England occurred on July 2, 1776. The Second Continental Congress revised the wording and approved the Declaration of Independence on July 4.

John Adams wrote these words to his wife, Abigail, "The second day of July, 1776, will be the most memorable epoch in the history of America. I am apt to believe that it will be celebrated by succeeding generations as the great anniversary festival. It ought to be commemorated as the day of deliverance, by solemn acts of devotion to God Almighty. It ought to be solemnized with pomp and parade, with shows, games, sports, guns, bells, bonfires, and illuminations, from one end of this continent to the other, from this time forward forever more."

As we know, July 4, the day of approval of the declaration, became the actual holiday, but what a prophecy Adams made of what this day would look like, year after year, in America.

Whether you are enjoying the holiday with family and friends or you're in service and on duty far away, reflect today on the many great blessings we share in being United States citizens.

Thank God for the privilege of being a part of one of the greatest nations in history. Express gratitude today, too, for the opportunity to serve your country in your area of responsibility.

MIGHTY LIBERATOR, *thank You for freedom—physical and spiritual. Thank You that You provide both. I am grateful for my nation and I renew my desire to serve her.*

# WE SHALL PREVAIL

*The Lord has heard my supplication; the Lord accepts my prayer.* —Psalm 6:9

The following is a prayer that Franklin Roosevelt prayed on D Day, June 6, 1944:

*Almighty God: Our sons, pride of our nation, this day have set upon a mighty endeavor, a struggle to preserve our Republic, our religion and our civilization, and to set free a suffering humanity.*

*Lead them straight and true; give strength to their arms, stoutness to their hearts, steadfastness in their faith. They will need Thy blessings. Their road will be long and hard. For the enemy is strong. He may hurl back our forces. Success may not come with rushing speed, but we shall return again and again; and we know by Thy grace, and by the righteousness of our cause, our sons will triumph.*

*Embrace these, Father, and receive them, Thy heroic servants, into Thy kingdom. And for us at home, fathers, mothers, children, wives, sisters, and brothers of brave men overseas, whose thoughts and prayers are ever with them, help us, Almighty God, to rededicate ourselves in renewed faith in Thee in this hour of great sacrifice. Give us strength, too, strength in our daily tasks, to redouble the contributions we make in the physical and the material support of our armed forces.*

*With Thy blessing, we shall prevail over the unholy forces of our enemy. Help us to conquer the apostles of greed and racial arrogances. Lead us to the saving of our country, and with our sister nations into a world unity that will spell a sure peace—a peace invulnerable to the schemings of unworthy men. And a peace that will let all men live in freedom, reaping the just rewards of their honest toil.*

GRACIOUS FATHER, *I recognize that prayer changes things. Help me to affect my future by giving today to You.*

# THEY KNOW NOT

*But love your enemies, do good, and lend, expecting nothing in return. Your reward will be great, and you will be children of the Most High; for he is kind to the ungrateful and the wicked. Be merciful, just as your Father is merciful.*
—Luke 6:35-36

The April 1942 air attack, launched from the aircraft carrier Hornet and led by Lieutenant Colonel James H. Doolittle, was the most daring operations undertaken by the United States in World War II.

Of the eight men the Japanese captured, three were executed and five were imprisoned. These men were regularly beaten, tortured, and starved by their captors. One of the men, Jacob Deshazer, said, "My hatred for the enemy nearly drove me crazy. My thoughts turned toward what I had heard about Christianity changing hatred between human beings into real brotherly love. I begged my captors to get me a Bible and when the emperor of Japan told them to treat us better, I finally got one."

The sentence that changed Jacob's heart was Jesus saying, "Father, forgive them, for they know not what they do."

After the war was over and he was released, Jacob attended seminary, then he and his wife served as missionaries in Japan for over 30 years. He eventually met the Japanese pilot that led the attack on Pearl Harbor. The two became friends and Jacob led him to Christ.

Through every generation, Christianity has countless stories of people who have every human right to hate, yet because of Christ, they love. Jacob Deshazer made a decision to love His God more than he could hate his enemies. He replaced hate with love. Bitterness with Grace. Revenge with peace.

You will have opportunities to hate throughout your life. Christ offers you a higher road, a better path. Choose His way—the way that leads to His love.

AUTHOR OF LOVE, *it is so easy to hate when people hurt us. Thank You for offering a different path, a better way. Teach me to love as You do, for on my own, I cannot.*

# ALL ABOUT YOUR MINDSET

*And the peace of God, which surpasses all understanding, will guard your hearts and your minds in Christ Jesus.* —Philippians 4:7

Brandon Rollins and three members of a drug task force had been conducting surveillance and making arrests when they stopped at a Lancaster, S.C., restaurant.

As they were eating, an armed robber burst in, demanding money from the front register. Brandon reports, "All four of us jumped up, dropped our forks, and got out our guns."

As the suspect began firing, a bullet lodged into Brandon's side. "I knew I'd been shot. I pulled my hand away and saw all the blood covering my hand," said Brandon. I said, 'I've been hit'"

At that moment, he remembered advice from his police training, "If you're thinking about pain and good-byes, it means you're alive."

The other officers told Brandon to lie down on the floor, but he wouldn't. "I started thinking about what I could do to survive. I slowed down my breathing. It's all about your mindset."

The other officers apprehended the shooter.

One of the first things Brandon did after leaving the hospital was make a phone call to the trainer to thank him. "It's hard to tell the impact you have on others and I wanted to make sure he knew that a thought he put in my head was what helped save my life and take me home to my family," Brandon said.

Any time, but particularly in a time of crisis, what we think, and how we think, can make a difference in the outcome. Do you tend to think negatively or critically? Combining positive thinking with realism and faith can not only improve your life, and just might save your life.

SAVIOR, help me to stay positive in a negative world. Help me to focus on construction and not destruction. Guard my mind.

# WE'VE GOT EACH OTHER

*The second is this, "You shall love your neighbour as yourself." There is no other commandment greater than these.* —Mark 12:31

As the worst fire in Colorado history was burning up 26 square miles, 30-year veteran Mike Wittry was running the staging area in the parking lot of a local business.

He and his wife had already been evacuated from their neighborhood.

As he waited for his assignment to go out to fight the fire, the call came over the radio that his subdivision was on fire. Mike took his wife's hand, looked at her, and said, "We've got each other." But Mike, like most of the other firefighters, was focused on saving others' homes and not his own.

Because approximately 350 homes had already been destroyed, the fire marshal made the call to evacuate over 32,000 people.

As the fire raged on, thousands of lives were saved as a result of his decision. The National Guard had also committed more than 150 soldiers to help Colorado Springs police return to their normal rounds.

After Mike heard his neighborhood had caught fire, he reported to the staging area. They could see flames shooting into the night. "Guys were excited and wanted to get on the fire," Mike said. "I had 150 guys milling around. Everybody wants to be on the next engine to go out." Mike later found out that his home was spared from destruction, although a bit charred.

The heart of service is putting others first, even when it can potentially mean devastating personal loss. Community servants focus on the greater good over the private gain.

Be encouraged today that this mindset pervades all those who serve with you.

LORD OF ALL, *thank You for the community of first responders and other service personnel that line the fabric of this nation. Thank You that each focuses on the good of all.*

# THAT'S THE BEST REWARD

*The horse is made ready for the day of battle, but the victory belongs to the Lord.*
—*Proverbs 21:31*

Ed Deitch decided to run in the Blue Ridge Half Marathon in Roanoke, Va., with his daughter. Even though he was in shape and prepared for the race, just before crossing the finish line, he collapsed in full cardiac arrest.

"I'm so thankful that we were where we were when that happened," his daughter said.

Roanoke City Battalion Chief David Bishop was in charge of organizing medical first responders. He had set up two ambulances at the finish line. "The runners hear the footsteps of the competitors behind them and I think, right at the finish line, they push themselves," said EMT Jesse Wilson, Jr.

Jesse and two other first responders were staged close by when Ed fell to the ground. Even though Jesse and the other responders work for different organizations, Jesse said they provided a textbook case on treatment. "Each person got in their role, everybody knew where they needed to be, and it really helped for the outcome for Mr. Deitch."

Once Ed made it to the hospital, they all came to see their patient. "It was a very emotional scene. How do you thank someone who literally brought you back from the dead? It was just an incredible moment in my life and, to this day, I think about those guys all the time," said Ed. "To see that gentleman be able to walk and talk and be with his family— that's the best reward," said one of the EMT's.

The combination of smart planning and willing personnel saves lives every day. And for first responders, a saved life means a good day.

SAVIOR, *thanks for a story of good news and a happy ending. Thank You for the opportunities I have had and will have to provide the same for someone.*

# I WANT TO BE THERE TO HELP

*For the needy shall not always be forgotten, nor the hope of the poor perish forever.*
—Psalm 9:18

The First Response Team of America is a non-profit organization that has crisscrossed the country many times in a specialized fleet of disaster recovery equipment, providing free aid to as many as 40 disaster sites over the last few years.

Founder Tad Agoglia talks about the organization, "The First Response Team's priority are those first days before traditional help arrives. When we arrive on the scene sometimes, it is hard for these community leaders to really believe that we are there for free. When they see the equipment working, the light towers going up, and the roads starting to clear, they realize that we are good people and that we are coming with no strings attached to help them.

"They need tools and resources that they don't have themselves. And they welcome us into the community because they need the help. The roads need to be cleared so emergency workers like firefighters and search-and-rescue teams can come in and find the people and extract them to safety. They need lighting, so they can see.

"There is just something inside of me that feels compelled to help. When I watch the news, and I see those super cells go right over small communities, I know that people are going through some of the most traumatic times they have ever experienced in their lives, and I want to be there to help."

The spirit of America is alive and well today in the hearts of people just like Ted Agoglia—and you.

GOOD SHEPHERD, *keep me inspired and motivated to keep on keeping on. No matter who goes—I will. No matter who won't—I will.*

# THE BIG PICTURE

*We know that all things work together for good for those who love God, who are called according to his purpose.* —Romans 8:28

A sole survivor of a shipwreck washed up on a small, deserted island. He cried out to God to save him. Every day he scanned the horizon hoping to see a ship and see his prayers answered, but he saw nothing. Accepting his fate, he pulled together enough limbs and brush to build a small hut and put the few things he had found from the shipwreck inside.

Then one day, after going inland to hunt for food, he came over the last sand dune to see his little home in flames, the smoke rolling up into the sky. He fell to his knees, crying out in anger to God, "Why? No help, no rescue, and now I lose everything!"

The fire burned late into the night.

Early the next morning, to his amazement, he saw a ship on the horizon and watched as it came closer and closer. He was rescued.

"How did you know I was here?" he asked the captain.

"We saw the smoke from your signal fire," he answered.

Sometimes tough circumstances in life are doorways to new beginnings. The immediate circumstances may seem disastrous to us, but God sees the big picture and knows everything is working together for our ultimate benefit.

We tend to be stretched and grow through tough times.

Are you experiencing trouble right now? Do you feel like the man in the story? Know that God wants the absolute best for you. Trust Him!

SAVIOR, *I need to remember to thank You when things go well, but to trust You when times get tough. Remind me that You are there and love me—no matter what.*

# WITHOUT A SAFETY NET

*A bad messenger brings trouble, but a faithful envoy, healing.* —Proverbs 13:17

Every year, hundreds of people attempt to climb Mount Everest. Due to extreme snow, ice, and fierce winds, the climbing season only lasts a few weeks. About 2,000 people have successfully climbed to the summit. And many have died. Many more have been injured in falls or simply because their bodies can't handle the thin oxygen supply.

Enter Dr. Luanne Freer, an emergency room physician, and a team of volunteer assistants who provide medical care to climbers and Sherpa guides.

"What we're doing benefits both the climbers and the Sherpa's," said Dr. Freer. "They needed expert health care and they did not have it until we set up our clinic."

At an altitude of 18,000 feet, Dr. Freer's Everest Base Camp Medical Clinic consists of a 12x20-foot tent. The base camp is where climbers start, return, and stage their climbs. There are four higher elevation camps, but those aren't equipped for medical emergencies.

"This is medicine without a safety net, and no patient has died inside our clinic," said Dr. Freer. "That is what wilderness medicine comes down to—thinking outside the box. Our aim is to give the best care we can, even though we're practicing emergency medicine in a very unusual setting."

Many think that if someone chooses to risk their life simply for a thrill or for adventure that they must also weigh the risks. But people who are called to serve often merge their own sense of adventure with the needs created by those like them.

GREAT PHYSICIAN, *thank You for gifting people with, not only the skills to heal, but the heart to heal. Bless those today who care for the sick—anywhere they are.*

# WHAT THIS MEANS TO ME

*But when you give alms, do not let your left hand know what your right hand is doing, so that your alms may be done in secret; and your Father who sees in secret will reward you.* —Matthew 6:3-4

Ever heard of Larry Stewart? If you lived in Kansas City between 1979 and 2006, you probably have.

Right around Christmas, 1979, Larry was fired from his job. It was a very cold day, so he went to a drive-in restaurant. There he noticed a carhop.

He recalled, "It was cold and this carhop didn't have on a very big jacket, and I thought, 'I think I got it bad. She's out there in this cold making nickels and dimes.'"

So he gave her $20 and told her to keep the change. "Suddenly I saw her lips begin to tremble and tears begin to flow down her cheeks, as she said, 'Sir, you have no idea what this means to me.'"

That started an annual tradition of Larry secretly giving away money.

Larry eventually made a fortune in the cable television and telephone industry. It is estimated that he gave away $1.3 million in those 27 years, mainly handed out to random individuals in $100 bills.

After being diagnosed with cancer, Larry began training other secret Santas by giving them $65,000 to hand out, aside from the money he handed out himself.

Remember—Larry Stewart's first act of kindness was when he had very little and had lost his job. It is also interesting that, with a heart to help people by giving out free money, he himself became a millionaire.

An old saying goes: "You can never out give God."

Always strive to grow in giving. It is one of the greatest blessings we can take part in—for yourself and others.

GIVER OF *GOOD GIFTS*, I want the heart of a giver and help me to trust You with the outcome.

# HIS OWN DECISION

*And it is by God's will that we have been sanctified through the offering of the body of Jesus Christ once for all.* —Hebrews 10:10

Tomas Lopez, 21, was on duty at his job as a Florida beach lifeguard. A person ran up to Lopez and told him a man was drowning in an unprotected part of the beach. Even though it was outside his jurisdiction, Tomas ran down the beach, swam out, hooked the man with one arm, and successfully pulled him to shore. An off-duty nurse tended to the swimmer until paramedics arrived. The man was taken to a local hospital in critical condition, but alive.

After his incident report came before his superiors, Tomas was informed that violating his area of jurisdiction and saving the man in an unprotected area were grounds for dismissal and he was terminated.

"We have liability issues and can't go out of the protected area," his supervisor told reporters. "What he did was his own decision. He knew the company rules and did what he thought he needed to do."

As the story broke, the company responsible for the lifeguards issued a statement saying that they acted hastily and offered Tomas his job back. But Tomas declined. And as a show of solidarity, nine other lifeguards quit.

"I'm not going to obey such a ridiculous rule," Tomas said.

Someone called to save lives has no boundaries, regardless of the reasons or risks.

Tomas would rather live with violating a rule and a liability clause than to live with a man's death on his conscience forever. As our world and its systems get more complicated, there have to be those who are just willing to do what is right—no matter the cost.

SAVIOR, You *didn't come to save us the way everyone expected You to or thought You would, but on Your own terms. Thank You for taking care of sin and death forever and always—for me.*

# HUMBLE HERITAGE

*The Lord our God be with us, as he was with our ancestors; may he not leave us or abandon us, but incline our hearts to him, to walk in all his ways, and to keep his commandments, his statutes, and his ordinances, which he commanded our ancestors.*
—1 Kings 8:57-58

A prayer by Thomas Jefferson for the United States was recorded by a historian on March 4, 1801 in Washington, D.C.

Almighty God, who has given us this good land for our heritage; We humbly beseech Thee that we may always prove ourselves a people mindful of Thy favor and glad to do Thy will. Bless our land with honorable ministry, sound learning, and pure manners.

Save us from violence, discord, and confusion, from pride and arrogance, and from every evil way. Defend our liberties, and fashion into one united people, the multitude brought hither out of many kindreds and tongues. Endow with Thy spirit of wisdom those whom in Thy name we entrust the authority of govern-

ment, that there may be justice and peace at home, and that through obedience to Thy law, we may show forth Thy praise among the nations of the earth.

In time of prosperity fill our hearts with thankfulness, and in the day of trouble, suffer not our trust in Thee to fail; all of which we ask through Jesus Christ our Lord. Amen.

Respect for God and authority has been degraded in our society, but it was undeniably clear in the writings of our nation's architects. Having just established their independence, they were extremely grateful for their newfound liberties.

Today, thank God for your country and echo Jefferson's prayer to be grateful in times of prosperity and attain strength in difficult times.

SOVEREIGN LORD, *bless and protect our nation. Lead us in times of blessing and hardship. All of which I ask through Jesus Christ, our Lord. Amen.*

# TAKE A MINUTE TO BOW

*Yours, O Lord, are the greatness, the power, the glory, the victory, and the majesty; for all that is in the heavens and on the earth is yours; yours is the kingdom, O Lord, and you are exalted as head above all.* — 1 Chronicles 29:11

Sherry Hedge had been an ER nurse at Rush University Medical Center for over ten years. After 9-11, she made the decision to serve her country by joining the U.S. Army Reserves. She signed her papers, took her oath, and then announced to the ER staff and her mother that she had joined.

She served in Kosovo and two tours in Afghanistan. For her second deployment to Afghanistan, at the rank of captain, she served on a mobile surgical unit for the infantry on the front lines of battle. She eventually left the service due to injuries sustained from repeatedly jumping from helicopters to retrieve wounded soldiers.

After two years on the front lines, Sherry returned to the ER at Rush. Chicago police and fire vehicles led a "welcome back" motorcade to honor Sherry.

As the crowd gathered in the hospital atrium, she said, "If we can just take a minute to bow our heads for the 4,000 plus soldiers that are not here today, for the 1700 soldiers who have lost their lives in Iraq, and the 13 soldiers that lost their lives at Fort Hood. Can we take a minute to bow and say a prayer for them and their families?"

The news and Internet are filled every day with glory seekers and fame attracters. A common trait of a public servant is to deflect glory. As followers of Jesus Christ, we are to go one step further—we not only deflect, but reflect glory. If it comes to us, we send it back to the One deserving of the glory and good from our lives. Today—deflect and reflect!

GLORIOUS ONE, *I confess the blessings and gifts I receive come from Your hand. Thank You. May I deflect glory from me and reflect it back to You.*

# A TEAM EFFORT

*Heal me, O Lord, and I shall be healed; save me, and I shall be saved; for you are my praise.* —Jeremiah 17:14

At a seventh-grade football game in Texas, a boy suddenly collapsed on the field. Coaches, Tim Spoonemore and Brad Averitte rushed onto the field and quickly realized the boy was unresponsive with no pulse. While a parent took over CPR, Tim left to get one of the school's automated external defibrillators (AED).

Rita White, a school nurse, ran onto the field. She also happened to be the person that trains district employees to use the AED. The device was brought onto the field and Rita began to administer aid to the boy.

"I saw his stomach start moving and that was just the greatest thing," Coach Spoonemore said. The player was then rushed by helicopter to a nearby Children's Medical Center.

"It was a team effort. Everyone was here. Everyone had a very important part. No one person is a hero," said Rita.

School Superintendent Ray Lea added, "Everybody there was in tears and just really shocked. This is just unheard of at a junior high school football game. It was surreal. I couldn't be any more proud of my staff to perform the way they did and rescue this young man. I don't think the young man would be here without the AED."

The distribution of AEDs to public places has saved many lives. Think through your own community and inquire about the location of AEDs where you live, work, and play. If you're a first responder and not yet trained in its use, consider adding that to your resume´. Trained personnel are crucial, but strategic equipment can be just as important.

STRONG HEALER, *thank You for those who are trained to save and thank You for the advanced technology to literally bring people back to life. We are the helpers, while You are the Healer.*

# THERE IS NO OTHER

*If you obey the commandments of the Lord your God that I am commanding you today, by loving the Lord your God, walking in his ways, and observing his commandments, decrees, and ordinances, then you shall live and become numerous, and the Lord your God will bless you in the land that you are entering to possess.*
—*Deuteronomy 30:16*

The following is an excerpt from President George H. W. Bush on his inaugural address, January 20, 1989.

"My first act as president is a prayer. I ask you to bow your heads.

"Heavenly Father, we bow our heads and thank You for Your love. Accept our thanks for the peace that yields this day and the shared faith that makes its continuance likely. Make us strong to do Your work, willing to heed and hear Your will, and write on our hearts these words: 'Use power to help people.'

"For we are given power not to advance our own purposes, nor to make a great show in the world, nor a name. There is but one just use of power, and it is to serve people. Help us to remember it, Lord.

"The Lord our God be with us, as He was with our fathers; may He not leave us or forsake us; so that He may incline our hearts to Him, to walk in all His ways that all peoples of the earth may know that the Lord is God; there is no other."

So many of the principles and promises we read in the Old Testament that God gave to Israel can be applied to any nation that will accept and receive them. God desires to bless His people, including entire nations that will follow Him.

Pray that our nation would "walk in all his ways" and "know that the Lord is God."

JEHOVAH GOD, *lead me in Your ways. Help me to know You. Help me to know— and show—that You are God.*

# FIVE DAYS LATE

*Let me abide in your tent forever, find refuge under the shelter of your wings. For you, O God, have heard my vows; you have given me the heritage of those who fear your name. —Psalm 61:4-5*

In 1950, Douglas S. Mackiernan became the first CIA officer killed in the line of duty.

As an Army meteorologist serving in western China, Douglas caught the attention of the Strategic Services Unit of the War Department—the forerunner of the CIA. His expertise in radio equipment, photography, and organic chemistry made him a worthy candidate for the unit.

The unit asked Douglas to provide information on Soviet and Communist Chinese activities.

When the CIA was created in 1947, he became an agency employee.

When the situation in Xinjiang began to deteriorate in 1949, other members of the CIA left, but Douglas stayed behind.

When the Xinjiang government accepted the authority of the Communist government in Beijing, Douglas wired CIA that he was escaping southward.

Douglas' team traveled across deserts and mountains until they entered Tibet.

The CIA asked the State Department to get Tibet's clearance for the safe passage of Douglas and his group, and the agency urged the department to get clearances to Lhasa as soon as possible.

One morning, six armed Tibetans on horseback encountered the group and killed Douglas and two others.

The Tibetans looted the belongings of the dead men and took the others prisoner. As they rode away, they met the government messenger from Lhasa on his way to inform the soldiers to welcome Douglas and his party.

The messenger was five days late.

Our nation's history is full of heroes whose stories are buried deep in our lineage. Whether we know their names or not, we now carry on their legacy. Greatness and gallantry flow through our veins. Live like a hero!

OUR FATHER, *only You know the number of our days and what our lives will accomplish by the end. Guide me to make every day count and make a difference.*

# ALL TOGETHER BOYS

*For I have set you an example, that you also should do as I have done to you.*
—*John 13:15*

During the early years of our nation, a rider on horseback came upon a squad of soldiers who were trying to move a heavy piece of timber.

A corporal stood by, giving loud orders to the men to "heave."

No matter how hard the men struggled and no matter how loudly the corporal yelled the instructions, the timber would not budge. It was just too heavy for the squadron of soldiers.

The rider asked the corporal, "Why don't you help your men?"

"Me? Why, I am a corporal, sir!"

Getting down from his horse, the stranger got in the middle of the men, grabbed the piece of timber along with the soldiers, and said confidently, "Now, all together boys! Heave!"

The timber began to move and slid into place.

The stranger walked quietly back to his horse, mounted, looked sternly at the corporal, and ordered, "The next time you have a piece of timber for your men to handle, Corporal, send for the commander-in-chief." Then he rode away.

The horseman was George Washington, commander-in-chief of the Continental Army.

The world has long misunderstood leadership to mean one who does not labor and only gives the orders to those who do.

Leaders who are respected lead by example and by serving those they lead. Anywhere that you are privileged to lead, be sure that you are the kind of leader that you would want to follow.

ALMIGHTY GOD, *I am grateful that You came and gave us not only a Person to look to for an Example, but principles and precepts to live by. Help me to lead as I follow You.*

# SOMETHING WASN'T RIGHT

*Therefore prepare your minds for action; discipline yourselves; set all your hope on the grace that Jesus Christ will bring you when he is revealed.* —1 Peter 1:13

**❝**I knew something wasn't right when I saw his hat on the ground," said Sergeant 1st Class Michael Kinzie, a 20th Support Command soldier, who was driving on Interstate 95 when he noticed flashing lights on a police car on the side of the road. Kinzie could see State Trooper Mike Hamer struggling to get out of his car.

Hamer had responded to a call regarding a pedestrian on the highway. As they talked in Hamer's patrol car, suddenly, the suspect lunged to grab Hamer's gun.

"While I was fighting back, he got the safety off the gun. That's when the gun discharged into my leg," Hamer said. He was able to reach his backup weapon, shoot the suspect, and get out of his car.

Kinzie placed a 911 call, drove to the next exit, and turned around. Hamer credits Kinzie and two others with saving his life.

"Because of his actions, Emergency Medical Services was able to get to the scene quickly," said Hamer, who fully recovered from his injuries.

James De Ford, the northern Virginia field lieutenant told Kinzie, "Because of you and the two other people, Trooper Hamer is alive." Kinzie responded, "I always try to put myself in the position to help others."

There are times that the world is divided into two groups—those who will and those who won't. Of all the people who passed that day on Interstate 95, three took action. That action likely saved the life of a trooper.

As you live your life and go about your days, be one who will, who takes action for others.

STRONG TOWER, *even when I'm tired or don't feel like getting involved, motivate me to take action. To be one who will!*

# WE CAN'T PROTECT YOU

*Strength and dignity are her clothing, and she laughs at the time to come. She opens her mouth with wisdom, and the teaching of kindness is on her tongue.*
—Proverbs 31:25-26

Paula Lucas, a native Californian, was married to a Lebanese man and living in Abu Dhabi.

She and her sons were recipients of physical and psychological abuse from her husband.

In 1999, believing she had rights as a U.S. citizen, she went to an officer at the American Embassy and detailed the abuses that she and her three children were enduring. But in the United Arab Emirates, beating up your wife and kids is not illegal. The officer told her the embassy could not protect her there.

"I was naive," said Paula.

So, when her husband left town, she forged his name on a permission-to-travel paper and a check in order to escape to the states.

She settled in Oregon where she lived off welfare checks.

Her husband eventually found her, but she fought a custody battle and won.

In 2001, she started Americans Overseas Domestic Violence Crisis Center. Through funding from the Department of Justice, Paula launched a toll-free hotline in 175 countries to support hundreds of American families in other countries with counseling, travel assistance, legal services, and relocation.

At least one family returns safely home to the United States each month with Paula's help.

The combination of personal experience, empathy, and a desire to change a part of the world can turn a personal crisis into support and victory for hundreds, or even thousands.

We all have a calling to meet needs in the world. If you don't know yours, God will show you, if you ask. If you do know, be inspired today to fight on.

DELIVERER, thank *You that when we call on You, You are always available to help. For strength, support, and even rescue. Bless those today who are trapped in horrible circumstances. May there be more Paula's—both to save and support.*

# FOR THE LONG HAUL

*Now as you excel in everything—in faith, in speech, in knowledge, in utmost eagerness, and in our love for you—so we want you to excel also in this generous undertaking.* —2 Corinthians 8:7

Peter Gallagher and Jack Wilson, both teenagers who love playing video games, found out that U.S. troops overseas have rare access to game systems. So the teens decided to put collection boxes in local schools, churches, and fire stations.

"It was amazing how many people had old games lying around," said Jack.

They also ask the kids who donate their games to write a short note to a soldier.

Before long, "Games for Heroes" was born with Peter and Jack collecting new and used handheld video games and gaming systems, sending them to soldiers stationed in Iraq and Afghanistan.

"A lot of the troops are not much older than us. The games help take their minds off things," said Peter. The troops have let them know how much fun the games bring and some soldiers re-gift their systems when their stints are up, leaving them behind for others to play.

In two years, Sony, Electronic Arts, Capcom, and G-Net donated about 1,000 games enabling the charity to distribute more than $100,000 in games and systems to troops.

"We're in this for the long haul," said Peter. "We'll ship games to our heroes until the last soldier comes home."

Finding true purpose in life is a key many never find. Locking in on a reason to wake up and live life each day is an amazing gift. It doesn't have to be a complicated plan, in fact, often those who find purpose, discover how simple it is.

Find, live, or pass on your purpose today. God definitely has it for you.

FATHER GOD, *it is so inspiring to see the creative and unique ways that people, even teenagers, find to give back and to serve. Lead me in creativity as I serve to keep life fresh and on the edge with You.*

# YOU CAN'T BUY THIS

*But Ruth said, "Do not press me to leave you or to turn back from following you! Where you go, I will go; where you lodge, I will lodge; your people shall be my people, and your God my God." —Ruth 1:16*

Woody Davis has been helping people in Corbett, Ore., for over 50 years.

He's operated a snowplow, chopped wood, repaired farm equipment, and been a kind of jack-of-all-trades to everyone in the town.

"He's the epitome of something dear," said members of the community. "You have to chase him down to pay him sometimes." "He's uncommon, he's special, he's a gift that this community has had all these years."

Woody was diagnosed with ALS—Lou Gehrig's disease—and doctors told him he doesn't have long to live.

This small community is now repaying him for his thousands of good deeds. They now cut and stack his firewood for winter and fix up his old pickup. Someone even built him a beautiful wooden box and invited the whole town to sign it.

Woody's son, Clint, said, "Bill Gates could not come to Corbett and buy this. You can't buy the love that people have poured out for Dad."

"What do you think of what everybody's been doing for you?" a reporter asked.

"I feel blessed that I'm dying slowly because people have a chance to express to me how they feel," Woody responded.

God always provides the resources, but has full intention that we take care of each other, living in community. He designed us to need each other and to desire that kinship. Who is taking care of you? Who are you taking care of? Be grateful today for both.

RESURRECTION & THE LIFE, *thank You today for every circle I am privileged to stand in. Guide me to bless and receive blessing in each.*

# BIG DREAMS

*He fulfills the desire of all who fear him; he also hears their cry, and saves them.*
—Psalm 145:19

During her junior year of college, Whitney Johnson chose to volunteer in an orphanage in Khayelitsha, one of South Africa's most destitute areas.

At the orphanage, she learned that most of the children were infected with HIV at birth.

"The clinics are overcrowded and under-resourced," Whitney said. "I saw so many kids dying. When I left South Africa, all I wanted to do was go back and change what I had seen."

After graduation, Whitney founded Ubuntu Africa, a nonprofit organization, to provide services for HIV-positive kids. She secured a building to house the endeavor.

The staff includes a counselor, social worker, nurse, cook, and a handful of volunteers, ensuring that each child has access to the proper medication, a free healthy meal, and emotional support.

"One child, Sipho, a nine-year-old boy with HIV, arrived at our center with a black eye and cuts all over his face. He was the victim of repeated sexual and physical abuse," Whitney said. "He was so malnourished, he looked like he was five years old."

"So many people think that HIV is a death sentence, and it's not. There's so much that can be done. In fact, in the five years since the center opened, not one of the 200 kids in the program has died. It's challenging in this environment, but these children deserve to have big dreams," Whitney said.

If we believe that a loving, involved God calls His followers to His work, then we trust He has someone targeted for every cause and every mission. Our goal is to find our place in His work and serve.

DIVINE HEALER, *I want my life to count, to accomplish my mission and purpose in Your Kingdom.*

# THE EXTRA $93

*Ah Lord God! It is you who made the heavens and the earth by your great power and by your outstretched arm! Nothing is too hard for you.* —Jeremiah 32:17

Carolee Hazard of Menlo Park, Calif., was in line at the grocery store when the woman in front of her said she couldn't find her wallet and was visibly very upset.

Carolee offered to pay her $207 grocery bill, gave the woman her address, and told her just to send her a check.

Afterwards, she posted on her Facebook page, "I'm feeling both good and a little stupid," referring to the likelihood that she would never get her money back.

But a check arrived in the mail for $300 and a note of sincere thanks from Jenni Ware. Ware told Carolee to use the extra $93 to "get a nice massage."

Carolee went back online and asked her friends to recommend a better use for the money. One friend suggested a donation to Second Harvest, an area food bank. She thought that was the best suggestion and matched Ware's original $93 with her own money.

The idea went viral. A child gave 93 cents. A single mother donated $9.30 from her last $25. By the end of its first year, the newly founded "93 Dollar Club" had raised $100,000 for Second Harvest.

"We want to raise $200,000 this year," Carolee declares. Soon after, the "93 Dollar Club" received its largest donation yet—$9,300.

What if Jenni hadn't forgot her wallet? What if Carolee had ignored the situation? What if Carolee had just spent the money? Circumstances happen around us every day that, on the surface, appear to be accidents or random events, but as they play out, we see they were actually incredible blessings waiting to be bestowed. Watch for yours!

SOVEREIGN GOD, *help me, teach me to look past the circumstances for what You may be doing inside a situation. I want to see You at work in my life.*

# THAT'S THEIR LEGACY

*For the righteous will never be moved; they will be remembered for ever.*
—Psalm 112:6

The ground-breaking ceremony for the Vietnam Veterans Memorial was held on March 26, 1982 in Washington, D.C.

Today the long black wall stands etched with the names of more than 58,000 Americans who were killed or missing in action in Vietnam.

Jan C. Scruggs, founder and president of the Vietnam Veterans Memorial Fund, conceived the memorial and helped raise more than $8 million to build it.

She said, "It's a great example of three million people who were willing to do what their country asked them to do. These are people who loved their country—and that's their legacy."

At the 30-year anniversary of the memorial wall, Steve Nelson was in attendance and takes that legacy very seriously. Steve was just 19 when he went to serve in Vietnam and Cambodia in 1969 and 1970. Twelve men from his unit, including his best friend, were killed.

Steve took a bullet in his back and his shoulder, but survived. Twenty-five years ago, he spent two nights sleeping in the shrubs near the memorial, where he was considering ending his life. A fellow veteran helped save him. He comes back to the wall to remember the people on it. "I live for these guys, because they didn't live," said Steve, as he pointed to the memorial.

We never know the stories of the people we are around each day and the things they may have suffered and survived. Pain and grief affects people in multiple ways. Someone once said, "Hurt people hurt people."

Remember that as you come across people in your path, speak words of kindness and healing whenever you can.

MIGHTY GOD, *only You understand the pain and evil some people have had to endure. Help me be mindful today of the hurting people I may encounter.*

# I BROUGHT YOU OUT

*Choose this day who you will serve.* — Joshua 24:15b

Joshua 24:1-7a—Then Joshua gathered all the tribes of Israel to Shechem, and summoned the elders, the heads, the judges, and the officers of Israel; and they presented themselves before God. And Joshua said to all the people, 'Thus said the Lord, the God of Israel: Long ago your ancestors—Terah and his sons Abraham and Nahor—lived beyond the Euphrates and served other gods. Then I took your father Abraham from beyond the river and led him through all the land of Canaan and made his offspring many. I gave him Isaac; and to Isaac I gave Jacob and Esau. I gave Esau the hill country of Seir to possess, but Jacob and his children went down to Egypt. Then I sent Moses and Aaron, and I plagued Egypt with what I did in its midst; and afterwards I brought you out.

When I brought your ancestors out of Egypt, you came to the sea; and the Egyptians pursued your ancestors with chariots and horsemen to the Red Sea. When they cried out to the Lord, he put darkness between you and the Egyptians, and made the sea come upon them and cover them; and your eyes saw what I did to Egypt.

Joshua was recounting Israel's history to them, centered around the God Who had constantly delivered them. Note the phrases such as, "led him through," "brought you out," and "your eyes saw what I did."

Take a few minutes to think through your personal history and thank God for the times He led you through as well. Today, choose to serve Him.

STRONG DELIVERER, *thank You for Your story in my life. As we write my history, may You be evident on every page.*

# THAT'S THEIR LEGACY

*But as for me and my household, we will serve the Lord.* —Joshua 24:15d

*Joshua 24:7b-14—Afterwards you lived in the wilderness for a long time. Then I brought you to the land of the Amorites, who lived on the other side of the Jordan; they fought with you, and I handed them over to you, and you took possession of their land, and I destroyed them before you. Then King Balak, son of Zippor of Moab, set out to fight against Israel. He sent and invited Balaam son of Beor to curse you, but I would not listen to Balaam; therefore he blessed you; so I rescued you out of his hand.*

*When you went over the Jordan and came to Jericho, the citizens of Jericho fought against you, and also the Amorites, the Perizzites, the Canaanites, the Hittites, the Girgashites, the Hivites, and the Jebusites; and I handed them over to you.*

*I sent the hornet ahead of you, which drove out before you the two kings of the Amorites; it was not by your sword or by your bow.*

*I gave you a land on which you had not labored, and towns that you had not built, and you live in them; you eat the fruit of vineyards and olive groves that you did not plant.*

*Now therefore revere the Lord, and serve him in sincerity and in faithfulness; put away the gods that your ancestors served beyond the river and in Egypt, and serve the Lord.*

Who would your family say that you serve? Your friends? Co-workers? We must all make the choice, and even to not make a choice, is to make one. Who will you serve with your life?

HOLY GOD, *change my heart day by day to love You more, to serve You more, and to walk with You, as You lead me.*

# I'D HAD ENOUGH

*For the Lord your God is God of gods and Lord of lords, the great God, mighty and awesome, who is not partial and takes no bribe, who executes justice for the orphan and the widow, and who loves the strangers, providing them with food and clothing.*
—*Deuteronomy 10:17-18*

When Zach Hudson of the Lake Mary Police Department made a call to a home and found two elderly women with no food or electricity and after having made numerous visits around town with discoveries such as this, he said, "I'd had enough. And that's when I started the Seniors Intervention Group."

Zach's organization has now tended to the basic needs of nearly 1,000 seniors in Seminole County, Fla. Utilizing hundreds of volunteers, the elderly are provided with food, transportation, home and vehicle maintenance, or help around the house.

"As cops and firefighters, we see people at their worst," Zach said. "And when you see seniors on a regular basis constantly being scammed or victimized, you start to ask yourself: 'Why? What can we do? I'm tired of walking away from this elderly person's house and not being able to fix the problem.'"

Once a month, the group schedules a large project where volunteers descend on a neighborhood to do a massive group endeavor. Hudson said this is often a great way to identify individuals who need more help.

"We need more organizations, businesses, churches, police departments, and fire departments to get on board, see the big picture, see the problem," said Zach, who hopes to see his nonprofit model replicated nationwide. "This is just the beginning."

Seeing needs and meeting them are two very different things. It is easy in our culture to criticize without taking action. Men like Zach Hudson change that paradigm by not only taking action, but mobilizing others to action.

Have you had enough of something? Why not join Zach and do something about it.

GREAT SHEPHERD, *help me to talk less and act more; to not criticize, but to capitalize on every opportunity to make a difference.*

# TO SUFFER SILENTLY

*The righteous know the rights of the poor; the wicked have no such understanding.*
—*PROVERBS 29:7*

Nickolaus Dent takes care of his mother who has been battling AIDS for as long as he can remember. He does the shopping, cooking, cleaning and the laundry. He also makes sure she takes her medication. Nickolaus also goes to school, because he is just 13 years old.

Since Nickolaus' father died two years ago, he has taken on the full-time job of caregiver, leaving him with little time and energy to study or socialize.

"Helping her out is a bigger priority than going to school, because I feel if I don't have her, I don't want to go to school. Whatever happens to her happens to me," Nickolaus said.

Twenty-two percent of high school dropouts in the U.S. quit school to care for a family member.

In Palm Beach County, Fla., the area where Nickolaus lives, Connie Siskowski founded the American Association of Caregiving Youth.

"No child should have to drop out of school because of care-giving. These children suffer silently behind closed doors," said Connie. "They don't have the help and the support and the recognition that they need. We can't change the health condition of the person (receiving care), but we can provide the skills, resources, and the value to the children, so that they can have a little more balance in their life. And also so that they know that they're not alone."

As our society becomes more isolated and people connect less and less, situations like Nickolaus and his mom can easily stay hidden.

Sometimes we can make a difference simply by paying attention and seeing those who need our help.

FAITHFUL ONE, *give me the eyes and ears to see and hear those around me who are silently suffering in some manner. Help me to provide help and care anywhere I can.*

# LIFE & DEATH

*Be strong and bold; have no fear or dread of them, because it is the Lord your God who goes with you; he will not fail you or forsake you.* — DEUTERONOMY 31:6

In her Chicago neighborhood surrounded by gang violence, Diane Latiker opens her home to young people who wish to choose a better path. She runs a community program called Kids Off the Block. Diane's non-profit has taught life skills and provided recreational activities to more than 1,500 young people so far.

Diane talks about her endeavor, "Our community is plagued by violence, hopelessness, and negativity. We're growing with so many kids. The work that I, and so many others, do can literally be the difference between life and death for a generation that seems to have lost all hope. Deciding eight years ago to open my life to others has enriched not only my life, but the lives of hundreds of young people. This proves to me that giving hope to others is the key to changing lives. For that I am grateful. I know I'm only one person, but I believe in the power of one. I really do. I believe that I can do things and I can change people. And it's been working. If I can make a change in a generation, then my community is going to get better, because they're going to be the ones that take it over."

What is it that, in a community with thousands of people, motivates one person to believe he/she, with little or no resources, can change things? It's an amazing thing to watch when someone steps up. And it works.

Be encouraged today to keep showing up and stepping up yourself—with God's strength.

SAVIOR, *Your Word is filled with people who took on insurmountable odds—and with You—won. Fight my fear and give me courage to go about my work with hope.*

# THAT'S MY JOB

*His divine power has given us everything needed for life and godliness, through the knowledge of him who called us by his own glory and goodness.* —2 Peter 1:3

Dr. Jeremy Kilburn, an Air Force pulmonologist who was also a trauma surgeon on a stint in Afghanistan, was hiking with a friend, Dan Grasso, in a rugged section of a state park near Big Bear Lake when he fell and broke his leg and injured his ankle. The California Highway Patrol sent two officers in a medevac helicopter to the area.

After landing, Paramedic Tony Stanley exited the helicopter and was struck in the back of the head by one of the blades. He immediately collapsed. "I knew that for Tony to have a chance of surviving, I would have to get Jeremy to him," Dan stated. Dan helped Jeremy hop 50 yards down the hill—on a broken leg—where he hooked Tony up to oxygen and put pressure on his wound.

"Thanks to the assistance they provided, Tony is alive today," CHP Commissioner Joe Farrow reported. "I cannot even imagine the pain Dr. Kilburn was in, unable to walk. Without regard to his own injuries and pain, Dr. Kilburn performed critical life-saving steps." They managed to control Tony's bleeding throughout the 40-mile-plus journey back to a hospital.

Jeremy doesn't see himself as a hero for keeping Tony alive. "That's my job. I do this every day," he said.

For those who serve and save, personal pain and sacrifice can somehow be set aside. It is an amazing gift from God. You may have this same gift, but if not, you have another that fits your life and passion. Discovering and cultivating your gift is one of the keys to a fulfilled life.

SAVIOR, thank *You that You created me with a unique personality, skill set, and gift. Help me to develop and excel in all that You have given me.*

# GOING TO GREAT LENGTHS

*I do not cease to give thanks for you as I remember you in my prayers.*
—EPHESIANS 1:16

Sixty years ago, Chicago Firefighter John Francis Minich saved 12 people from a burning building in a fire that had been set by an arsonist. One of the last people he carried from the building was a pregnant woman. After he got her to safety, he removed his crucifix necklace and put it in her hand.

Shortly after the rescue, Minich collapsed and died from a heart attack and smoke inhalation. He was 43.

His name was etched in granite at a local memorial and his badge was mounted on the Wall of Honor at the Quinn Fire Academy. But, somehow, his grave was never properly marked. Enter Debbie McCann, the child of the pregnant woman John saved.

Debbie found his gravesite at All Saints Cemetery. "She went to great lengths to contact our office," said Chicago Firefighters Union President Tom Ryan. "She originally planned to pay for the headstone on her own." He told Debbie that it would be taken care of, with no cost to her.

The Chicago Fire Department, along with the Firefighters Union Local 2, joined with Debbie to honor the anniversary of John Minich's death with a permanent grave marker. "This was something that had to be made right," said Tom Ryan. "He gave his life and made the ultimate sacrifice for the people he served and that needed to be recognized."

It is true in this life that no one owes us anything, so when someone expresses true gratitude, it is admirable. More than ever today, showing thankfulness is a reflection of God's heart and blessing.

DELIVERER, *may I avoid an attitude of entitlement and expectation and just be grateful for anything anyone does for me. And thank You.*

# LOVE LIFE

*Love is patient; love is kind; love is not envious or boastful or arrogant or rude. It does not insist on its own way; it is not irritable or resentful; it does not rejoice in wrongdoing, but rejoices in the truth. It bears all things, believes all things, hopes all things, endures all things.* —1 CORINTHIANS 13:4-7

These quotes from Mother Teresa are centered around the theme of love—God's love for us and the love He gives us for others. It was a constant theme of hers that we can all grow in and be challenged by.

*"I have found the paradox, that if you love until it hurts, there can be no more hurt, only more love."*

*"If you judge people, you have no time to love them."*

*"Do not think that love in order to be genuine has to be extraordinary.*

*What we need is to love without getting tired.*

*Be faithful in small things, because it is in them that your strength lies."*

*"I'm a little pencil in the hand of a writing God, who is sending a love letter to the world."*

*"A life not lived for others is not a life."*

HOLY FATHER, *thank You for the lives of those who left their mark, as well as their words, to challenge and inspire. May I learn from them and love like them.*

# PRAYER PROCLAMATION

*So we fasted and petitioned our God for this, and he listened to our entreaty.*
*—EZRA 8:23*

Below is an excerpt from Abraham Lincoln's Proclamation for a National Day of Prayer and Fasting.

And whereas it is the duty of nations as well as of men, to own their dependence upon the overruling power of God, to confess their sins and transgressions, in humble sorrow, yet with assured hope that genuine repentance will lead to mercy and pardon; and to recognize the sublime truth, announced in the Holy Scriptures and proven by all history, that those nations only are blessed whose God is the Lord. . . .

We have been the recipients of the choicest bounties of Heaven. We have been preserved, these many years, in peace and prosperity. We have grown in numbers, wealth and power, as no other nation has ever grown. But we have forgotten God. We have forgotten the gracious hand which preserved us in peace, and multiplied and enriched and strengthened us; and we have vainly imagined, in the deceitfulness of our hearts, that all these blessings were produced by some superior wisdom and virtue of our own.

Intoxicated with unbroken success, we have become too self-sufficient to feel the necessity of redeeming and preserving grace, too proud to pray to the God that made us!

It behooves us then, to humble ourselves before the offended Power, to confess our national sins, and to pray for clemency and forgiveness.

Remember to pray for your nation and all those in service to her, from the government to the military to those in civilian service to the army of volunteers across the land. There are still many in this land who make America great—every day.

HOLY FATHER, *bless this nation and all who call her home—in service or civilian.*

# LONE STAR SURVIVOR

*And one of you said to them, "Go in peace; keep warm and eat your fill," and yet you do not supply their bodily needs, what is the good of that?* —JAMES 2:16

Navy SEAL Marcus Luttrell received the Navy Cross medal in 2005 after surviving a battle with the Taliban after his team was discovered inside Afghanistan on a mission. Three of his fellow teammates were killed. After being discharged from duty, Marcus suffered from PTSD and morphine addiction.

Marcus met Texas Governor Rick Perry while the two were in California, and hit it off. After hearing what Marcus had gone through, the governor and his wife invited him to come back and live with the Perry family in their Austin home. The family was not currently living in the governor's mansion, due to the damage from an arsonist's fire.

Governor Perry also worked with Navy Secretary Ray Mabus to get Marcus the medical and psychological treatment he needed. Marcus ended up being a regular in the Perry home for about two years.

Marcus established the Lone Survivor Foundation that focuses effort on helping wounded veterans when they return home.

We are accustomed to politicians acknowledging our current military and veterans anytime the opportunity arises out of protocol. Quietly inviting a struggling veteran to live in your home for two years is far past a simple salute or handclap. It is a great example and encouragement to us all that reaching out, serving, and making a difference in one life can change the world when we all do our part—regardless of title or status.

GREAT SHEPHERD, *it is one thing to be concerned about someone's problems, but quite another to become a part of the answer. Help me to consider that I might be someone's answer.*

# STANDING BETWEEN GOOD & EVIL

*Very truly, I tell you, the one who believes in me will also do the works that I do and, in fact, will do greater works than these, because I am going to the Father.*
—*John 14:12*

Rapides Parish, La., Sheriff William Earl Hilton stresses the importance of first responders.

"They alone can make the difference between life and death. They are professionally trained to handle any rapidly changing situation from an automobile accident to an active shooter. As law enforcement first responders, when it comes to protecting and serving, the 'protection' usually comes the easiest. All law enforcement personnel have taken an oath to enforce all the laws of the land. They will go as far as putting their lives on the line to protect a total stranger, standing between good and evil.

"Whether responding to an overturned tanker truck which may turn out to be leaking, leading to the evacuation of a community, to a terrorist event involving a whole city, no matter what the call, the personnel have to be ready. Whatever the call, the first thing that happens is establishment of command, then sizing up the scene by doing a hazard/risk assessment, then communicating the severity of the situation to other responders. Next is establishing perimeters and securing the scene to prevent it from becoming worse.

"All this is done within seconds of the first responder arriving on scene. The scene then determines what is done next. From evacuation to sheltering in place, decisions must be made in seconds to protect life and property. All this [must be] done while trying not to become a casualty yourself." said Hilton.

As a first responder, you are among an elite group with a special calling. You also know the importance of faith—relying upon and expressing it for yourself and those you serve.

SAVIOR, *in every first responder setting, there is so much faith expressed; most of what is done makes no sense outside of You. Guide me, lead me, protect me today.*

# I LOVE THIS WORK

*To this end we always pray for you, asking that our God will make you worthy of his call and will fulfill by his power every good resolve and work of faith.*
—2 THESSALONIANS 1:11

Russell Glaeske served as an Emergency Medical Technician for 35 years in Montana.

As he aged, he made the difficult decision to retire. But he soon realized that emergency response was in his blood and he couldn't let it go as quickly as he thought.

Russell put in the many hours of training and continuing education classes to earn his first responder certificate and returned to volunteer emergency service. He was approved to volunteer as a first responder in all emergency situations.

"I started as an EMT because I was a police officer and I felt I needed first aid training so I could be more effective in my job," Russell stated. "I liked the work and I found it very rewarding to have the knowledge and abilities to help people out in accidents or other emergency situations."

As a first responder, Russell may be called to a variety of emergency situations, from vehicle accidents to natural disasters to health emergencies such as heart attacks or strokes.

"We are called any time for any kind of accident or emergency situation. I love this work, I love helping out and I enjoy working with people," he proudly added.

Once a passion is in your blood, taking away the title doesn't take away the desire. Public service fits that description. It is never just a job.

Work and routine will always get stale at times, but strive to keep your mind and heart fresh and alert, with service at the forefront of your calling.

EVERLASTING GOD, *Keep me fresh and strong in my spirit, heart, and mind to serve to my fullest and finest each day.*

# NUMBER 926

*But Jesus called for them and said, 'Let the little children come to me, and do not stop them; for it is to such as these that the kingdom of God belongs.* —LUKE 18:16

Trey Pons had wanted to be a firefighter for as long as he could remember. He knows facts about fire trucks and is constantly learning about firefighting.

But Trey will never be able to live out his dream. He has autism, is deaf in his left ear, and blind in one eye. But he is a determined young man.

Jim Podolske, with Fire Emergency Services, heard about Trey. Jim, along with Trey's parents, organized a surprise for the boy. They brought him to a military firefighters training facility.

Trey was given a personalized fire helmet and gear, which he wore throughout the training. He worked on a mock car accident, smashing the car's windows and using the Jaws of Life to pry open the door. "I've never

seen him concentrate on something for so long," said his mom.

Next, Trey got to ride in a fire truck and sound the sirens. Then, with the help of his instructors, he used an industrial fire hose to extinguish a structural fire in one of the simulation buildings.

"This has been a lifelong dream for me and you guys are doing a great job," Trey told the current fire trainees. "This has truly been the best day of my life."

Jim Podolske said, "Earlier today, there were 925 firefighters in the Air Force. Now there are 926."

Even physical limitations don't squelch the desire to serve. Keep your eyes open. There could be a Trey in your life and committing just one day can make a lifelong dream come true.

CREATOR GOD, *expand my vision to see those around me who I could invest in and reach out to. Lead me to my "Trey's."*

# I UNDERSTAND

*Does not wisdom call, and does not understanding raise her voice?*
—*PROVERBS 8:1*

Understanding is critical in not only your relationships, but in your role of service as well. Being able to gain a correct read on a situation, interpret what people are expressing, and properly respond is critical to your job. The Bible has much to say and much we can learn regarding understanding.

*My child, if you accept my words and treasure up my commandments within you, making your ear attentive to wisdom and inclining your heart to understanding;*

*if you indeed cry out for insight, and raise your voice for understanding;*

*if you seek it like silver, and search for it as for hidden treasures—then you will understand the fear of the Lord and find the knowledge of God.* —*Proverbs 2:1-5*

*Happy are those who find wisdom, and those who get understanding, for her income is better than silver, and her revenue better than gold.*

*She is more precious than jewels, and nothing you desire can compare with her. Long life is in her right hand; in her left hand are riches and honour.*

*Her ways are ways of pleasantness, and all her paths are peace. She is a tree of life to those who lay hold of her; those who hold her fast are called happy.* —*Proverbs 3:13-18*

An on-going relationship with God will produce understanding, wisdom, insight, and knowledge. He created both You and those qualities, so He can impart those to You as You live and learn.

WISE GOD, *I desire to grow in and increase my understanding that I may grow in my relationship with You and others.*

# SOMETHING TO BELIEVE IN

*He alone is my rock and my salvation, my fortress; I shall not be shaken. On God rests my deliverance and my honor; my mighty rock, my refuge is in God.*
—PSALM 62:6-7

Jonathon Bussard was in grade school on Sept. 11, 2001 and watched the attacks on the World Trade Center and the Pentagon on television. Even at such a young age, he felt the call to duty that day. "Seeing it happen and then seeing ground zero had a huge impact on me," said Jonathon, a California native. "Coming from a military family who always had something to fight for and believe in, that definitely impacted my decision."

Jonathon, 24, joined the Air Force right out of high school. His job as a security force specialist has been to protect the people, property, and resources of the U.S. government. He said he chose this profession out of a sense of duty to country and the desire to support a greater cause. Jonathon's father also served in the Air Force, so he wanted to keep the family tradition alive.

Stationed at Offutt Air Force Base, Nebraska, Jonathon was deployed to the 455th Expeditionary Security Force Squadron in Afghanistan, responsible for security of Bagram Airfield.

Jonathon said, "I needed to do something life changing, and this is the best place to do it. I'm very grateful for it. It's been the best decision I've ever made my entire life. I talk to my wife regularly. She's the one who puts that smile on my face and makes me realize who I'm fighting for."

The benefits of joining the military are strong in many areas—from the need for discipline to college money to job training. But the heart of enlistment always lies in the honor of serving the nation and protecting her people.

MIGHTY KING, *may my own honor increase, as I grow more into Your likeness and character.*

# BUT HE DID

*Be dressed for action and have your lamps lit.* —LUKE 12:35

Staff Sergeant Mitchell Corbin, an aerospace technician with the Texas Air National Guard, was on Sam Houston Parkway in Houston, when he saw an overturned vehicle with flames coming from the engine. He also realized a woman was trapped inside. That's when Mitchell's military training kicked in.

"I knew that none of the doors were opening, so I had to break the window," he said. Mitchell stood atop the vehicle and managed to strike the window until the glass folded in. By that time, the fire had tripled in size with smoke and heat billowing from the engine.

"I told her I needed her to lift her hands for me to help her," he said. An onlooker jumped up onto the car and they both pulled the woman out.

"It's like a dream," she said. "I don't remember any of it. I felt someone pulling me and I heard a soft voice say, 'watch out for the glass.'" Mitchell carried her a few yards away and administered aid. As paramedics arrived, Mitchell went back to his car and drove on. It took a while for his identity to be discovered for her to thank him.

"I admire and respect the military and their training. There were other people there who did not know what to do, but he did. His training helped, but it was his heart that made him stop to help me," the woman said.

The heart, the training, and the need all come together to save a life. It happens multiple times a day, and all who serve, never know the day it may come. Stay ready. Stay strong.

SAVIOR, *I want to respond to Your call and be where You want me to be, doing what You want me to be doing. Lead me today.*

# I FEEL LIKE I OWE THAT

*Then the Lord said to Moses, 'I am going to rain bread from heaven for you, and each day the people shall go out and gather enough for that day. In that way I will test them, whether they will follow my instruction or not.* —EXODUS 16:4

Six-year-old Muhamed Mehme-dovic spent much of his childhood escaping through the Bosnian woods with his father and other men during the war there. His hometown of Srebrenica was destroyed, as genocide was committed against the Muslim population.

Muhamed explained, "The United States helped us by providing air drops of food, supplies, and medical equipment constantly for three years. Ultimately, their actions saved my life. 8,000 people died, just in my town."

"I originally wanted to be a pilot." he said, "They gave so much to my family. I feel like I owe that to the U.S."

Muhamed and surviving family members were finally able to get to the U.S. through a sponsorship program. "I graduated from high school in May. I signed the [commitment] papers in June. I told my parents in July and I left in October," he said.

So today, Senior Airman Muhamed Mehmedovic, a 19th Logistics Readiness Squadron air transportation journeyman, has completed four years in the Air Force.

"The circle is being completed," he said. "This is where I want to be. I joined as air transportation. One of the biggest aerial delivery squadrons is here. This is where all the riggers receive their training on how to properly put the parachutes on, rig the food, and put it on aircraft for it to be dropped in a specific location." Just as was done for Muhamed as a child.

The United States' humanitarian commitment to Bosnia passed on a spirit of service and commitment to Muhamed that will be returned with a lifetime of loyalty.

The circle is complete.

MERCIFUL GOD, *help me to remember every statistic has a name and every victim had a life. Help me to be professional, yet keep my service personal, because it certainly is to You.*

# THE RESCUE COMMUNITY

*He reached from on high, he took me, he drew me out of mighty waters. He deliv-
ered me from my strong enemy, from those who hated me; for they were too mighty
for me. They came upon me in the day of my calamity, but the Lord was my stay.*
—2 SAMUEL 22:17-19

Staff Sergeant Justin Tite, an aerial gunner, was aboard the lead HH-60 helicopter in a two-aircraft flight. They were to rescue two downed Army aircraft crewmembers in enemy territory about 25 miles east of Bagram, Afghanistan.

Justin's crew reached the crash site at dawn and inserted the first para-rescue team. Just after inserting a second team, the second helicopter, was engaged by enemy fire that injured a crewmember and damaged the aircraft.

They were forced to return to base. Justin covered them, while supporting ground teams, as they became pinned down by enemy fire. On one pass, Justin spotted enemy units attacking and returned fire, killing at least one insurgent. As recovery attempts resumed, the helicopter immediately drew heavy fire, taking enough damage to also force them to return to base for a spare aircraft.

During this round trip, Army ground troops in the area joined the engagement. Justin's crew returned to battle, and while taking more fire and further damage, managed to complete the rescue.

Ultimately, Justin's actions during the six-hour-long battle resulted in the life-saving rescue of three soldiers from the field of battle.

He said, "I couldn't be happier in another field than I am with the rescue community. Our motto is 'that others may live' and I think that every individual in the rescue community truly lives by that motto."

Those who risk their lives to serve have an undeniable calling. If you are one of those, pray for your teammates today. If not, pray for those called to risk it all today "that others may live."

STRONG TOWER, *provide protection and strength for all those today going out to
serve who risk their lives. God, go with them.*

# THE BEST BIRTHDAY

*The righteous flourish like the palm tree, and grow like a cedar in Lebanon. They are planted in the house of the Lord; they flourish in the courts of our God. In old age they still produce fruit. —PSALM 92:12-14A*

Joseph Keenan had been a private practice doctor in his hometown for more than 30 years. "All four of my grandparents were immigrants," he said. "They came here because there was opportunity. I realized as I got older, how good life was to me."

So he decided to join the military.

Due to his age, his first application was unsuccessful, but eventually, "One of the colonels looked at my credentials and said, 'We're going to try everything possible to get this guy in,'" Dr. Keenan said.

A year later, he was sworn in on his 61st birthday. "It was one of the best birthday presents I could have received."

On his 64th birthday, Lieutenant Colonel Keenan, of the Air National Guard 131st Fighter Squadron, celebrated his third anniversary of military service.

Dr. Keenan was eventually deployed to Afghanistan. "I was at Bagram and Kandahar and saw firsthand the sacrifices that are being made by the troops over there," he reported. "It's one of the best decisions I've ever made to join the United States Air Force. I feel so fortunate to be able to serve my country. People are very happy that I'm here and doing what I'm doing. It's just been a win-win situation."

Lt. Col. Christopher Borchardt said of the doctor, "I can train someone to be a doctor, but I can't train enthusiasm."

Throughout history, few nations have inspired people the way the United States has.

Know today that you are a part of something much bigger than yourself, yet you have a special place in the life of this nation by your service to her, just like Lieutenant Colonel Keenan.

SOVEREIGN GOD, *thank You for such inspiring people in such an amazing nation. Thank You for my place and my service here.*

# THAT'S WHO WE ARE

*For the whole law is summed up in a single commandment, "You shall love your neighbour as yourself." —GALATIANS 5:14*

Philadelphia firefighter Fran Cheney's unit was called to a house fire. As they rolled up, a brother was out front saying his sister was still in the house.

Fran rushed in and began to search the home. He heard screaming and found Mary Jackson on the second floor.

"I couldn't see. I couldn't breathe, nothing," said Mary.

Fran said Mary was "just smoky, heaving, trying to catch her breath. I mean it was just, you could hear it, she was in distress. I took a quick breath, ripped my helmet off, gave her the mask—it's on positive pressure, which means it just blows smoke away from her—and I just say, 'Let's go.'"

Fran carried her down the stairs and outside to safety, risking his own life.

Questioned about breaking procedure by taking his mask off, Fran responded, "If I was worried about that, I wouldn't be here, and neither would any of these guys that I work with. That's what we do. That's who we are."

And if saving a life wasn't enough, Fran donated his overtime pay of $500 to Mary and her family to help them get back on their feet.

"I've realized how special they are for us, for everyone," Mary said. "He went out of his way to save me."

Giving can become who you are. Whether giving of your time, energy, money, or even the risk of death to save—seeing, hearing, and feeling that your life changed someone else's brings a feeling like no other. It's the feeling of knowing why you've been put on this Earth.

DEAR GOD, *when I give sacrificially, I know I am showing Your character. May I grow in giving, in every way, to become more and more like You.*

# THE GIRL KEPT GOING

*Do not withhold good from those to whom it is due, when it is in your power to do it. Do not say to your neighbour, "Go, and come again; tomorrow I will give it" — when you have it with you. —PROVERBS 3:27-28*

Minor league football's Indianapolis Tornados were playing the Kentucky Reapers when Tornados' coach Jerry Senter collapsed on the field after going into cardiac arrest.

Jessica Anderson, a cheerleader for the team, also just happened to be an emergency medical technician and a firefighter.

"She didn't even blink," team president Evan Triggs said. Jessica rushed to the sideline and began performing CPR and lifesaving measures for 15 minutes before an ambulance arrived.

"He had flat-lined at that point," Evan said. "Anderson's CPR was the only thing that saved him."

Officials said Senter was clinically dead for nearly five minutes. "The girl kept going when the crowd was saying, 'he's gone.'"

"Jessica kept going at it, no matter what," said cheerleading coach Gina Fosso.

When Senter was released from the hospital, he met up with Jessica to thank her for her persistence.

Jessica said she did what she was trained to do. "I do not consider myself a hero. I was in the right place at the right time," she said. "I'm just very grateful that I was there and I'm humbled by everybody's reaction."

How would you properly thank someone who keeps trying to save you when others have given up? Thank God for those like Jessica who won't accept death as an option. Persistence and drive are crucial for those who serve.

If you're struggling with motivation today, ask God to give you a renewed passion. Someone just might end up depending on you to "keep going when the crowd said 'he's gone.'"

FAITHFUL & TRUE, *thank You that You never give up, never grow weary, or never even sleep. Give me strength and energy today to keep on keeping on.*

# UNTIL I REACH IT

*And can any of you by worrying add a single hour to your span of life? If then you are not able to do so small a thing as that, why do you worry about the rest?*
—LUKE 12:25-26

One very rainy spring, Abraham Lincoln was traveling to a meeting with a group of men. They had crossed many small streams where the water was high and rushing fast. After a long day of nearly being washed away, they came to a lodge where they spent the night. As they sat around the fire talking, someone mentioned that they would reach Fox River the next day and that it would be nearly impossible to cross.

During their discussion, they noticed a Methodist preacher sitting nearby who traveled the territory often. One of Lincoln's group asked, "Preacher, you've been listening to us talk. Do you have any special way of getting across Fox River? Any thoughts that might help us?"

He answered, "I know it is mighty hard to get across sometimes, but I have solved the problem with just one rule."

"Then what's your secret? Is there a special place to cross?" they asked.

"No. I cross where everyone else does in the way everyone else does. My rule is simply this—I have learned never to cross Fox River until I reach it."

An old saying goes, "Worry is taking responsibility for something God never intended for you to."

What is the one thing in your life that you are dreading the most right now? What are you worrying about today? Take a moment and ask God to help you deal with the problem and give Him your worry. Trust Him to take care of you.

COMFORTER, *I can waste so much time worrying about things that never happen. Remind to trust You when I am tempted to take responsibility for something I shouldn't.*

# MAKES US BOTH STRONGER

*Pleasant words are like a honeycomb, sweetness to the soul and health to the body.*
—PROVERBS 16:24

Sheriff's Officer Troy Ugrich in Minnesota said his big sister, Darlene Troumbly, is his hero. She is a corrections officer. "I work to keep the streets safe as a Road Deputy and arrest the bad guys and she books them in for me," Troy said.

One morning she had to check on an inmate with a history of drug abuse and mental illness. "From the moment I opened that door, the look in his eyes was like no other. I've never seen that before." Darlene said.

The inmate lunged at her. First, she used verbal commands, but the prisoner didn't stop. Next, she fired her Taser. "Everybody drops, but he kept coming," she said.

A group of deputies ran to the cell. "He threw me against the shelf quite a few times. Tried to get me down on the ground," she explained.

Another officer fired a Taser. When he finally fell, Darlene remembers, "He mouthed to me that he was going to kill me."

She and her brother talk frequently about that day. "You just fight, fight, fight until you win, and that's what she did. But when things turn ugly, determination is paramount with one thought: 'This isn't going to happen to me.'"

"Her training and my training and us talking about the situation makes us both stronger," Troy said.

Being able to talk about the realities of public service is crucial to emotional survival. In your own service, be sure you are talking and processing what happens to you and how you feel. It's what family is for and can keep you healthy.

HEAVENLY FATHER, *help me to know when I need to open up and share and also when to listen to others, but help me remember to tell You everything.*

# THE PAINS OF POVERTY

*Since there will never cease to be some in need on the earth, I therefore command you, "Open your hand to the poor and needy neighbour in your land."*
—*DEUTERONOMY 15:11*

Sal Dimiceli's The Time Is Now To Help non-profit assists about 500 people a year with food, rent, utilities, and other necessities in the Wisconsin area where he lives.

Sal said, "In our great country, more than 50 million Americans are desperately suffering the pains of poverty. There are a lot of people in extreme desperate need. People who are homeless, we'll help them get shelter; people who are hungry, we're going to feed them; people who have utilities off, we're going to turn them on; people that need transportation, we'll help fix their cars.

"Every penny helps our fellow creations in dire need, and I'm going to do it as expeditiously as I can. We're going to utilize all of our several hundred volunteers to make sure we can end their pain and suffering and show them there are people that care. We want to give them hope and show them that we do have a love for all people. I can't wait."

Sal continued, "I grew up as a little boy watching our utilities being off, being evicted, of us having little food, and with the pride of not letting people know. I made a promise to God at 12 years old. I'm 60 now, and I'm going to keep that promise for as long as I can breathe."

It is said that in any organization 20% of the people do 80% of the work. That statistic likely holds true for a nation as well. Be sure that you are part of the 20%, just like Sal Dimiceli.

PROVIDER, *help me to stay consistent and strong, focusing on my own service and never getting distracted by those who choose otherwise. Bless the 20 percenters!*

# GUARDING THE DOORS

*Upon your walls, O Jerusalem, I have posted sentinels; all day and all night they shall never be silent. You who remind the Lord, take no rest.* —ISAIAH 62:6

At the Interstate I-15 checkpoint in Escondido, Calif., U.S. Border Patrol agents became suspicious of a man driving a 2000 Volkswagen Jetta.

He was acting extremely nervous upon his initial stop. So they referred him for a secondary inspection where a K-9 team inspected the vehicle. The dogs alerted the agents to the running board on the driver's side. Upon visual inspection, they discovered a makeshift compartment with 13 bundles of methamphetamine weighing 22 pounds valued at $441,000.

The suspected smuggler and the narcotics were turned over to the Drug Enforcement Administration for further investigation. The vehicle was seized and impounded by the U.S. Border Patrol.

The U.S. Border Patrol maintains a high level of awareness and caution on all major corridors around our nation's borders to stop the smuggling of drugs, illegal weapons, human trafficking, and any and all illegal contraband.

For these agents, as with all law enforcement officers, there really is no such thing as a routine day. Every person or vehicle alerted and caught results in fewer drugs and weapons being brought into our nation. And with the increase in human slave trafficking, agents can literally save people's lives.

Regardless of your role of service, don't allow the mundane aspects of the job or the routine of the day to decrease your capacity to stay vigilant. People are indeed depending on you to be at your absolute best.

GREAT SHEPHERD, *keep me focused on what matters today. Help me to stay watchful on duty as I serve.*

# EVERY STEP IS WORTH IT

*Our steps are made firm by the Lord, when he delights in our way.* —PSALM 37:23

Specialist Troy Yocum served time in Iraq. While there, he received several emails from veterans who were struggling financially. When he returned home to Louisville, Ky., he decided to take action in a big way.

Hike for Heroes was born.

His 7,800-mile walk took about him 16 months, zig-zagging across America. "I thought, 'What better way to spread the word than literally going from town to town,'" said Troy. His goal when he began was to raise $5 million for veterans, but in New York at 6400 miles logged, he had only raised $200,000.

Mitchell Modell, the chief executive officer of Modell's Sporting Goods, heard about Troy and raised another $260,000 for his cause. Mitchell then announced that his stores and a few other large retailers would begin a fund-raising effort by asking customers to donate $1 to his cause, estimating this endeavor would raise another $1 million.

Troy logged about 20 miles a day, staying in donated hotel rooms, host homes, and in his tent, along with his wife and their two dogs. He actually stopped on the doorsteps of some needy vets along the way to deliver some of the money he had raised.

Troy stated, "Every step is worth it, because when I arrive to help another family, it is the best feeling. It's been a dream come true. It's going to help so many families."

Putting our money "where our mouth is" is a great thing, but committing a year of life and all your resources to a cause is an amazing and inspiring act. What are you that passionate about? To what are you that committed?

THE WAY, *today I acknowledge the walk that You took for me and all mankind—the road to the cross. Thank You that You made that commitment and gave up Your life for me.*

# THE WAY OF WISDOM

*Know that wisdom is such to your soul; if you find it, you will find a future, and your hope will not be cut off.* —PROVERBS 24:14

In this grand age of information, knowledge is readily available on any subject. You can Google a topic and access thousands of periodicals. However, wisdom can only be attained in the same manner as it always has—working it into your life, one experience at a time.

A great spiritual exercise is to read a chapter from Proverbs each day, every month. By the first day of the month, start over. Pray and ask God to give You His wisdom as you read about wisdom.

Here are a few more verses of encouragement regarding the often elusive quality of wisdom.

*For the Lord gives wisdom; from his mouth come knowledge and understanding.* —PROVERBS 2:6

*Get wisdom; get insight: do not forget, nor turn away from the words of my mouth.* —PROVERBS 4:5

*The fear of the Lord is instruction in wisdom, and humility goes before honour.* —PROVERBS 15:33

*How much better to get wisdom than gold! To get understanding is to be chosen rather than silver.*
—PROVERBS 16:16

WISE GOD, *there is an amazing mix of spiritual, emotional, and mental blessings that only Your wisdom can bring. May I both take wisdom in and pour it out.*

# ULTIMATE PROFESSIONAL

*Does he not see my ways, and number all my steps?* —JOB 31:4

Second Class Petty Officer Matthew Gene Axelson entered boot camp in Great Lakes, Ill., in 2000. He went directly to Basic Underwater Demolition training, graduating with class 237.

After training, he attended Army Jump School, SEAL Qualification Training (SQT) and SEAL Delivery Vehicle (SDV) school. He checked aboard SEAL Delivery Vehicle Team ONE in 2002 and joined ALFA Platoon. He deployed to Afghanistan in March 2005 in support of Operation Enduring Freedom.

STG2 Matt Axelson's personal awards include the Silver Star, the Purple Heart, the Navy and Marine Corps Commendation Medal, and the Good Conduct Medal.

Axe, as was his nickname, was a sniper. He was the ultimate quiet professional with a calming presence about him. He had the ability to remove the stress from any situation.

Axe died at the age of 29 during Operation Red Wings in an ambush in Afghanistan. He was survived by his wife. He had a political science degree and was an avid golfer who dreamed of playing in the PGA, but he died in service to his country. His future and dreams will never be realized, yet his military career and legacy as a Navy SEAL will live on forever.

Our choices will matter as to how we live—and how we die. Will we leave a legacy or just be forgotten? Will our lives have counted and matter? We have an opportunity to be a part of something great and to be great, if we choose.

Today, if you are living a life dedicated to service, you are a part of something great and are leaving a legacy for others, just like Matt Axelson.

HEAVENLY FATHER, *guide my daily choices to be in Your will, so my weeks, months, years, and finally, my very life, will matter now and after I'm gone.*

# PRESIDENTIAL BLESSING

*O Lord, God of my salvation, when, at night, I cry out in your presence, let my prayer come before you; incline your ear to my cry.* —PSALM 88:1-2

The following is an excerpt from a speech by President Ronald Reagan, February 6, 1986.

*"To preserve our blessed land, we must look to God. It is time to realize that we need God more than He needs us. We also have His promise that we could take to heart with regard to our country, that 'If my people, which are called by my name shall humble themselves, and pray and seek my face, and turn from their wicked ways; then I will hear from heaven and will forgive their sin, and will heal their land.'*

*"Let us, young and old, join together, as did the First Continental Congress, in the first step, in humble heartfelt prayer. Let us do so for the love of God and His great goodness, in search of His guidance and the grace of repentance, in seek-ing His blessings, His peace, and the resting of His kind and holy hands on ourselves, our nation, our friends in the defense of freedom, and all mankind, now and always.*

*"The time has come to turn to God and reassert our trust in Him for the healing of America. Our country is in need of and ready for a spiritual renewal. Today, we utter no prayer more fervently than the ancient prayer for peace on Earth.*

*"If I had a prayer for you today, among those that have all been uttered, it is that one we're so familiar with: 'The Lord bless you and keep you; the Lord make His face to shine upon you and be gracious unto you; the Lord lift up His countenance upon you and give you peace.'"*

LORD, *I receive that blessing today. Help me to live blessed, graced, and peaceful in You, as I go.*

# THEY DIDN'T WAIVER

*And Joshua said to them, "Do not be afraid or dismayed; be strong and coura-*
*geous; for thus the Lord will do to all the enemies against whom you fight."*
—JOSHUA 10:25

Lance Corporal Jeffrey Cole from Woodstock, Ga., saw five of his fellow Marines drop around him from insurgent gunfire. Then he was hit as three rounds blew him five feet back. He was down, but the bullets were stopped by his body armor.

"The enemy was advancing toward us," Jeffrey recalled. "I took a machine gun and started firing. Then I shot from my hip in a sweeping motion, left to right—150 rounds —and as I did, two rounds went through my arm. It spun me around and threw me into the ditch."

The enemy was advancing and Jeffrey could hear the calls over the radio, "All channels, anywhere, anything around us that can receive us— we need help now!" He continued to provide suppressive fire on the enemy. Suddenly, the sound of attack helicopters broke through the gunfire. The Marines staggered toward the rescue helicopter in the midst of enemy fire and climbed aboard.

Jeffrey was awarded the Silver Star for valor. He said, "Nothing I did comes close to the Marines I was with. Pinned down in a ditch, wounded, they fought for an hour against an enemy that got within 30 meters. Not once did they waiver. This award isn't my award. It's their award and all the guys who we lost who can't wear it now."

You may be in the military and know well what Jeffrey has gone through, but regardless of your place in service, you can live a heroic life. You can serve and help others. If a hero is an admired and brave person, then be a hero!

MIGHTY KING, *build my character, so I can be admirable. Grow my courage, so I can be brave.*

# A GREATER PLAN

*As it is written, "He scatters abroad, he gives to the poor; his righteousness endures forever." He who supplies seed to the sower and bread for food will supply and multiply your seed for sowing and increase the harvest of your righteousness.*
—2 CORINTHIANS 9:9-10

A young couple that sensed a calling to go to Africa as missionaries reported in New York to go on their journey to their new assignment. But there they were informed that his wife's poor health would not be able to withstand the climate.

Heartbroken, they returned home and prayerfully determined to give every penny they could to spread the Gospel around the world.

His father, a dentist, had started making a non-alcoholic wine for church communion services.

His son, Charles Welch, helped his father, Thomas Welch, make that ministry into a business.

The result was the creation of Welch's Grape Juice Company, a company that gave hundreds of thousands of dollars to world missions.

Charles could have gone back home thinking he had tried to give himself to missions and had failed. Instead, as he gave his career and money to God, the work of many missionaries was supported.

Where he thought he would serve, he ended up supporting and serving many who would go throughout the world.

We can make our plans, but God orders our steps. We can become bitter, while God desires us to become better. We can have great goals to serve, while God will make our service fit into His great plan.

LORD OF *THE HARVEST, I confess that I may make great plans, but You guide my steps and guard my life.*

# IT'S VERY SIMPLE

*For the Son of Man came not to be served but to serve, and to give his life a ransom for many. —MARK 10:45*

Dr. Albert Schweitzer was a famous medical missionary to Africa. One day he was helping a crew build a road when a visitor approached him. Shocked to see him doing physical labor, the man asked, "Doctor Schweitzer, why are you doing that? How is it that you push a wheelbarrow?"

Dr. Schweitzer replied, "Oh, it's very simple. You just pick up a shovel, fill up the wheelbarrow with dirt, then take hold of the handle, and push."

Dr. Schweitzer may have been world renowned for his humanitarian work, but he knew that his true purpose was being a disciple of the greatest servant of all—Jesus Christ.

All Christ's followers are called to ministry and that will always require serving others. Our culture teaches that we should work hard to get to a position where we are served, but if we are following Jesus, we are to be servants to Him and to those around us, no matter the title we carry.

Keep your eyes open today for "wheelbarrows you may need to fill," regardless of how small or unimportant the task may seem.

SON OF *MAN, help me, no matter what circumstance I am in, to serve, even when I am leading.*

# THAT'S THE TICKET

*Commit your work to the Lord, and your plans will be established.*
— PROVERBS 16:3

Albert Einstein, the world-renowned physicist, was traveling by train from Princeton. The conductor came by to check the tickets of each passenger. When he got to Dr. Einstein, the famous physicist reached in his vest pocket. He couldn't find his ticket, so he looked through his trouser pockets. He looked in his briefcase, then in the seat beside him. No ticket.

The conductor said, "Dr. Einstein, I know who you are. We all know who you are. I'm sure you bought a ticket. Don't worry about it."

Einstein nodded appreciatively.

The conductor continued down the aisle checking tickets, and just as he was about to move to the next car, he looked back to see Dr. Einstein on his hands and knees, still looking for his ticket.

The conductor rushed back and said, "Dr. Einstein, please don't worry, I know who you are. You don't need a ticket."

Einstein looked up at him and said, "Young man, I too, know who I am. What I don't know is where I'm going!"

There are seasons in life when we don't know who we are, but we think we know where we're going. Then there are seasons when we know who we are, but don't know where we're going, like Dr. Einstein. There can also be seasons where we aren't sure of either!

Here's the good news: God knows who you are and He knows where you're going. Get to know Him through a personal relationship and He can make sure you find your ticket.

SOVEREIGN LORD, *I believe You know me and where You want to take me. Give me strength to comply with and obey You today.*

# SURROUNDED ON ALL SIDES

*Our heart has not turned back, nor have our steps departed from your way.*
—PSALM 44:18

Lieutenant Michael P. "Murph" Murphy graduated from Penn State with two degrees—political science and psychology. Although accepted to law school, he accepted an appointment to the Navy's Officer Candidate School at Pensacola, Fla.

Murph began Basic Underwater Demolition/SEAL training in 2001. Upon graduation, he attended the Army Jump School, SEAL Qualification Training, and SEAL Delivery Vehicle school.

After several deployments around the world, in 2005 Murph was sent to Afghanistan in support of Operation Enduring Freedom.

He was one of a four-man SEAL team called Operation Red Wings. A fierce gun battle ensued on the face of a mountain with a Taliban force. Murph moved into the open to gain a better position to transmit a distress call, exposing himself to enemy gunfire.

He provided his unit's location and the size of the enemy force. At one point he was shot in the back, causing him to drop the transmitter. He picked it up, completed the call, and continued firing at the enemy who was now closing in.

Severely wounded, Murph returned to his cover position with his men and fought on. By the end of the two-hour battle, Murph and two others of the four were dead. An estimated 35 Taliban were also killed. Murphy was 29.

Would Michael Murphy have ever been hailed a hero in American history had he chosen to be a lawyer? Possibly, but not likely.

We each have many sides to who we are. We must take what God has placed in us and develop it to the fullest potential. But He is always right there, guiding, helping, leading—right to the end.

HOLY FATHER, *though there are so many things I want to accomplish, I have but one life. Guide me to make it the life You desired when You created me.*

## MY FREQUENT PRAYER

*But truly God has listened; he has given heed to the words of my prayer. Blessed be God, because he has not rejected my prayer.* —PSALM 66:19-20A

The following are quotes regarding prayer from President Jimmy Carter.

"I would like to have my frequent prayer answered that God let my life be meaningful in the enhancement of His kingdom and that my life might be meaningful in the enhancement of the lives of my fellow human beings." —Excerpt regarding his prayers from his inaugural address, January 20, 1977

"I call upon all the people of our Nation to give thanks on that day for the blessings Almighty God has bestowed upon us, and to join the fervent prayer of George Washington who as president asked God to "impart all the blessings we possess, or ask for ourselves to the whole family of mankind." —Thanksgiving speech to the nation, November 27, 1980

President Carter's years as a Sunday school teacher at his home church are well documented, so faith was, and is, an important aspect of his life and service.

Faith is an important part of anyone's service—a faith in God, in people, in hope, in peace, and in love. The gift of service is itself an act of faith.

DEAR GOD, *grow my faith, my hope, my love for You and for people as I serve today.*

# WHEN DUTY CALLS

*The name of the Lord is a strong tower; the righteous run into it and are safe.*
—*Proverbs 18:10*

### A Firefighter's Prayer
AUTHOR UNKNOWN

*When duty calls me, oh Lord, wherever flames may rage,*
*Give me the strength to save some life, whatever be the age.*
*Help me embrace a little child, before it is too late*
*Or save an older person from the horror of that fate*
*Enable me to be alert, and oh Lord, guide my every move,*
*For life is so precious, please don't let us lose.*
*I want to fill my calling and to give the best in me,*
*To guard my every neighbor and protect their property.*
*And if according to thy will, that I must give my life,*
*Then with Thy protecting hand, my Lord,*
*I pray thee, protect my children and my wife. Amen*

Regardless of your position of service, this prayer can be prayed for strength, help, alertness, victory, calling, and protection. We must, in obedience, act upon and receive God's help, while at the same time, realizing we are totally dependent on God's intervention. Trust and obey—for there's no other way.

PROTECTOR, I *confess that my work, my life, and my family are in Your hands. Lead me as I obey You. Guard me as I serve You.*

# I'M GOING IN

*Be pleased, O Lord, to deliver me; O Lord, make haste to help me.* —PSALM 40:13

Donald Lubeck lived in a rural area of Massachusetts. A severe storm was moving through one night, when suddenly lightning flashed and the smoke alarms began to beep. He ran downstairs to find the basement on fire. As he went back to the second floor and dialed 911, he realized the phone was already out.

"I could hear the fire moving through the house," Donald said. Hundreds of yards away, the closest neighbor Jeremie Wentworth, realized that he was hearing a smoke alarm beep in the distance. He grabbed a phone and a flashlight and took off.

Seeing the black smoke, he dialed 911, then called out, "Is anyone there?" He heard, "Help me! I'm trapped!" coming from the balcony. The 911 dispatcher warned Jeremie not to enter the house. "But there was no way I was going to let Don die in that fire," he said. "I told the dispatcher, 'I'm sorry, but I'm going in.'"

"Inside the house I was yelling for Don. Then I had to run outside to catch my breath." There he saw Donald on the balcony. "I shined the flashlight around and noticed a ladder," said Jeremie. He managed to pull Donald down just as the second floor of the house collapsed.

Don still chokes up when he tells the story. "I was alone," he said. "Then I heard the most beautiful sound in my life. It was Jeremie."

Every day, first responders, and yes, even alert neighbors, create the most beautiful sounds to those threatened by danger or illness—a voice of rescue. Whatever life calls upon you to do today—be ready!

SAVIOR, *guide me today. Give me strength today. Help me to pay attention to life and live it to the full.*

# TWO MEN AT THEIR DOOR

*Learn to do good; seek justice, rescue the oppressed, defend the orphan, plead for the widow.* —ISAIAH 1:17

Taryn Davis was just 21 years old when her husband, Michael Davis, an Army corporal, was killed in Iraq.

When her Google search for "widow" turned up the result: "Do you mean window?" she knew she had to take action.

Just four months after Michael's death, she created the American Widow Project, a nonprofit organization helping young military widows find the emotional support they need. Since beginning, Taryn has connected to more than 900 of these military survivors through the Internet and weekend retreats.

Taryn said, "More than 3,000 widows had their lives changed with two men at their door. After they get that news, the real struggles start.

"Many of the wounds from those affected by these conflicts cannot be seen with the naked eye. And that's where the American Widow Project comes in. At our retreats, for example, we cover all costs for their time with us, so the only thing they need to worry about is healing and connecting with their sister widows."

She continued, "Most of those suffering from the most major of losses don't receive the support and compassion they so deeply deserve."

In a very real way, the spouse of a soldier is making an equal sacrifice for our nation. And when that spouse is killed, the ultimate sacrifice has been made.

Pay attention to the news in your area regarding those lives taken in battle across the globe, because a survivor may be left with little support system right where you are.

MIGHTY HEALER, *I pray today for all those who are serving our nation and all those left at home. Hold them up and keep them strong.*

# 100 CENTS, 25 TIMES

*Give liberally and be ungrudging when you do so, for on this account the Lord your God will bless you in all your work and in all that you undertake.*
—DEUTERONOMY 15:10

A man decided to try an experiment, knowing he would never see the outcome. He wrote a note across the top of a one-dollar bill that said, "Write what this bill was used for."

On the 25th transaction, someone listed and reported the results.

*Five times for wages*
*Five times for cigarettes*
*Three times for candy*
*Three times for a restaurant meal*
*Twice for clothes*
*Twice for haircut/salon*
*Twice for laundry*
*Once for groceries*
*Once for car repair*
*Once for a magazine*

An interesting observation the reporter made was that not once was the dollar used for charity, church, or any sort of giving.

Do you make it a regular practice to support your local church, charity, or the needy? Money may be a necessary evil to have to make and spend, but it can also be a tremendous blessing to give away to help others.

PROVIDER, I *recognize today that even though my money may flow from a person or an organization, ultimately, it comes from Your hand. May I bless You and others by generously giving.*

# PRAYER & CONFESSION

*Listen to the sound of my cry, my King and my God, for to you I pray.*
—*PSALM 5:2*

The Rev. Robert A. Crutchfield wrote "The First Responder's Prayer."

*Father in Heaven,*
*Please make me strong when others are weak,*
*Brave when others are afraid and vigilant*
*when others are distracted by the chaos.*
*Provide comfort and companionship to my family*
*when I must be away.*
*Serve beside me and protect me, as I seek to protect others.*

*Amen*

Psalm 91:14-16 is a valuable passage for confession and meditation.

*Those who love me, I will deliver; I will protect those who know my name.*
*When they call to me, I will answer them; I will be with them in trouble, I*
*will rescue them and honor them. With long life I will satisfy them, and show*
*them my salvation."*
*Faithful servant, may your hope and faith increase as you pray, confess, and*
*draw near to your Heavenly Protector.*

ALMIGHTY GOD, *I pray these prayers today . . .*

# THE GOOD WORK AHEAD

*Happy are the people to whom such blessings fall; happy are the people whose God is the Lord.* —PSALM 144:15

Following is an excerpt from President Bill Clinton's second Inaugural address, January 20, 1997.

*"May those generations whose faces we cannot yet see, whose names we may never know, say of us here that we led our beloved land into a new century with the American Dream alive for all her children; with the American promise of a more perfect union a reality for all her people; with America's bright flame of freedom spreading throughout all the world. From the height of this place and the summit of this century, let us go forth. May God strengthen our hands for the good work ahead and always, always, bless our America."*

Regardless of the political party in control of the White House or Congress, there has always been a recognition that the God of America is the God of Abraham, Isaac, and Jacob, the God of the Old and New Testament, the God Who sent His only Son to die for us. Ours is a rich heritage of freedom, promise, and hope—essential characteristics of Christianity. This faith is built into our DNA as a nation, the foundation of who we are.

Thank God today for your nation. Pray to be a good steward of all you have been given, because of that privilege.

LIGHT OF *THE WORLD,* thank You for the privilege of being a part of a nation whose God is the Lord. May I take my place in its history.

# FEAR GOD & SHUN EVIL

*The Lord said to Satan, "Have you considered my servant Job? There is no one like him on the earth, a blameless and upright man who fears God and turns away from evil." —JOB 1:8*

Job was a very wealthy and blessed man. But the greatest distinction to God was that he "was blameless and upright . . . feared God and turned away from evil."

It is a sobering moment in Scripture when Satan points out how God has blessed Job and essentially declares that the only reason Job loves God is because of the blessings.

So God tests Job. Satan attacks and Job loses everything. As he surveys the devastation and even the loss of his children, he proves God to be right about him. Scripture said in verse 22: "In all this Job did not sin or charge God with wrongdoing." And things just get worse as Satan then attacks Job's health. This culminates in Job's wife telling him, "Do you still persist in your integrity? Curse God,

and die." And even still, Job did not sin.

For 40 more chapters, the drama goes on between Job and three of his "friends," as God entered the picture and talked with Job. In the end, Job is blessed with far more than he lost and brought back to health.

This account in Scripture is difficult to understand in the spiritual realm, but the truth displayed over and over in Job's life is that obedience to God doesn't guarantee that nothing bad will ever happen, but it does mean He will bless and see you through anything.

Wouldn't it be wonderful—and such a great goal—to have the Lord look at you and speak the words of today's featured verse?

HOLY GOD, *remind me daily that priority one for me is obedience to You. If I do that, everything else will take care of itself.*

# STAND TOGETHER

*For you girded me with strength for the battle.* —PSALM 18:39A

Crowded together at an airport gate at Louis Armstrong International Airport in New Orleans, excited and anxious family members and friends stood ready to applaud, greet, and hug 30 local heroes returning home from supporting Operation Enduring Freedom in Afghanistan.

Louisiana National Guard's 236th Combat Communications Squadron were all returning home safely after a six-month deployment. As the soldiers filed off the plane, loud cheers and loving embraces were plentiful.

"These events are very important to us," said Major Harry "Chip" Trosclair, Jr., 236th CBCS detachment commander. "There are a lot of happy families here and happy families mean happy service members." "It was a huge surprise to see all of my family here," said Senior Airman Steven D. Bordelon. "It just feels so good to receive such a big, warm welcome."

As the War on Terror continues and people are made aware of the incredible sacrifices of our troops, anywhere our military appears in public, there is applause and heartfelt gratitude expressed—particularly in airports, as soldiers travel to and from their assignments.

If you are a deployed soldier, please know there are millions standing with you today. This same scene awaits you when you return home. For those of us in other service, may we continue to support those in the military until the last American returns home.

ABBA FATHER, *as a nation we ask Your blessings and protection on all those who serve in harm's way today. Cover them with Your mercy and grace. Surround them with Your presence.*

# 22 YEARS OF SECRECY

*You have set our iniquities before you, our secret sins in the light of your countenance.* —PSALM 90:8

Eric O'Neill worked as an investigative specialist with the FBI's Special Surveillance Group, and he played a major role in the capture of suspected double agent FBI agent Robert Hanssen. O'Neill was assigned to work as Hanssen's assistant and to learn all he could about the secret information Hanssen was passing on to the Soviet Union.

The ultimate goal was to get Hanssen to relax his rigid control of his Palm Pilot for a brief period, while O'Neill, under an intense time crunch, secretly copied its encrypted contents and then return it undetected. All went perfectly until O'Neill couldn't recall from which briefcase pocket he had taken the device. O'Neill knew that if Hanssen realized the Pilot was breached and suspected him, his life would be in danger.

But the plan worked, the evidence was gathered, and Hanssen was arrested at a park near his home in Virginia. He was charged with selling American secrets to Russia for $1.4 million in cash and diamonds over 22 years. On July 6, 2001, Hanssen pleaded guilty to 15 counts of espionage and was sentenced to life in prison. The FBI described Hanssen's treason as "possibly the worst intelligence disaster in US history."

There are those who only live for personal gain, holding no real loyalties. As long as they exist, there will have to be men like Eric O'Neill who are willing to risk all to stop them.

All those who work and serve America are a part of the solution, not only to keep her strong against terror and tyranny, but to preserve our way of life.

ALMIGHTY GOD, *bless and protect all those today who are working in secrecy to protect us. May evil be defeated.*

# I HAD TO GET HIM OUT

*Let mutual love continue. Do not neglect to show hospitality to strangers, for by doing that some have entertained angels without knowing it.* —HEBREWS 13:1-2

Benjamin Franklin Lane, 73, of Depew, Okla., was headed down Highway 16 when he witnessed a one-car crash in front of him. "I saw the vehicle in front of me veer off the highway, and then it was going over and over and then burst into flames," he said.

As Lane pulled over and hurried to the burning car, another man approached and the two forced the car door open. "I just knew I had to get him out," Benjamin reported. "The seats were on fire, the interior was on fire and everything." Both men were able to drag the driver to safety, away from the wreckage and burning grass.

"I was just doing what I had to do," Benjamin said. When emergency crews arrived, Benjamin said the other man quickly left the scene. "I don't know where he went, didn't get his name or nothing," Benjamin said.

"I'm just glad a young man showed up to help a 73-year-old get somebody out of a car." Benjamin said the mystery man basically swooped in to help him pull the man from the burning car and then just disappeared.

In a news release, the sheriff's office and the Twin Hills Fire Department said if not for the heroic actions of these men, "the life of the man in the wrecked vehicle would have surely been lost."

An important point of this hero story is that Benjamin also just happened to be a retired fire chief, after 20 years of service.

Two decades of service as a fire chief embeds the desire to save lives, even at 73 years old. And the unknown man who helped him? Only God knows. Regardless, the world is full of heroes. Be a hero today to all those you serve!

SAVIOR, **strengthen** me today to engage life, to love and serve people, and if called upon, to save as well.

# RISEN FROM THE ASHES

*He must increase, but I must decrease.* —JOHN 3:30

There are many amazing stories that have emerged from the aftermath of September 11, 2001. Stories of bravery, self-sacrifice, and service, above and beyond the call of duty, have risen from the ashes in New York City. As has been the custom of our nation throughout its history, we allowed triumph to come out of tragedy.

One of the many who lost their lives that September day was a Franciscan Friar, named Mychal F. Judge. He was 68 when he was killed by debris from the collapse of the towers.

When first responders pulled the Friar's body from the rubble, they found a small card in his pocket with words that have become known as Mychal's Prayer:

*Lord, take me where You want me to go*
*Let me meet who You want me to meet*
*Tell me what You want me to say and*
*Keep me out of Your way*

What better prayer could any of us pray on a daily basis? We need a prayer that both confesses submission and professes service to our Creator.

Your life is marked by a call of duty to your fellow human beings.

Today, as you live and serve, think on Jesus' words of allowing Him to become greater, while also whispering this prayer that was pulled from the rubble of 9-11.

LORD, *take me where You want me to go, let me meet who You want me to meet, tell me what You want me to say, and keep me out of Your way.*

# TO INSPIRE & TO CHANGE

*All who believed were together and had all things in common; they would sell their possessions and goods and distribute the proceeds to all, as any had need.*
*— ACTS 2:44-45*

"I saw the happiness, joy, and ability of Leti, a 17-year-old girl, who I gave her first wheelchair," said Richard St. Denis.

Since 2008, Richard and his non-profit organization, World Access Project, have provided hundreds of wheelchairs to people living with disabilities in rural Mexico. He and his group also teach recipients how to use their chairs and maximize their quality of life.

"There's a huge need for wheelchairs in Mexico, the plight of those who are stuck in their house because they can't move, and all the lives we are changing," said Richard. "I hope that people will realize that those who have so much (should) help those in desperate need, in whatever country. I hope new volunteers, individuals, or organizations will come to Mexico to give away a wheelchair, to encourage, to inspire and to change lives.

"When American volunteers participate in a wheelchair donation, they realize the huge difference they can make in another person's life and the unexplainable feeling of watching someone get up off the floor into their first wheelchair.

"The one who receives the wheelchair laughs and the mother cries tears of joy. I hope that not a single used wheelchair in the U.S. will ever be thrown into a dump and that every wheelchair that is sitting in a garage or basement will now be given to someone who desperately needs it."

For stories such as today's, it's not about recycling, but reinstating—getting items out of storage and into the right hands. What's in your attic, storage building, or barn that someone else might desperately need?

PROVIDER, *teach me to see my life as a source for those in need. To recycle, to reinstate, to revive the old into new for those in need.*

# I HAVE HEARD YOU

*Before him there was no king like him, who turned to the Lord with all his heart,*
*with all his soul, and with all his might, according to all the law of Moses; nor did*
*any like him arise after him.* —2 KINGS 23:25

Josiah became king of Israel at age 8. When he was 26, he ordered that the Temple of God be repaired. Through this "remodeling," the Book of the Law was discovered. When Josiah heard the words read from it, he immediately knew they were the words of God. He also knew that his forefathers "did not obey the words of this book." The priest then went to a prophetess who spoke these words:

"But as to the king of Judah, who sent you to inquire of the Lord, thus shall you say to him, Thus said the Lord, the God of Israel: 'Regarding the words that you have heard, because your heart was penitent, and you humbled yourself before the Lord, when you heard how I spoke against this place, and against its inhabitants, that they should become a desolation and a curse, and because you have torn your clothes and wept before me, I also have heard you,' said the Lord. 'Therefore, I will gather you to your ancestors, and you shall be gathered to your grave in peace; your eyes shall not see all the disaster that I will bring on this place.'"

It is clear in Scripture that God has a standard of holiness, but it is also clear that when His children obey, He is full of grace and mercy.

Regardless of your family history, your own background, or anything you have done in the past, God desires to forgive and restore. He sent His Only Son to bridge the gap between His holiness and your sin. You can turn to the Lord with all your heart, with all your soul, and with all your might today.

DEAR JESUS, *thank You that I can know You and not just know about You. Thank You that You forgive, restore, and offer me Your holiness.*

# DEFEATING STATISTICS

*Declare his glory among the nations, his marvelous works among all the peoples.*
—1 CHRONICLES 16:24

In Malawi, a nation in southeast Africa, risk of maternal death is 1 in 36, compared to that of American women at 1 in 2,100. Only 54 percent of deliveries in Malawi have a skilled medical professional present.

Enter Lauren Goodwin, a Peace Corps volunteer. "I arrived in Mangochi and met with the District Health Officer, Dr. Saulos Nyirenda. "Dr. Nyirenda and I initiated the TBA (Traditional Birth Attendants) mapping project to locate, interview, and collect GPS locations of each TBA. He mobilized his team. I trained them in GPS. The workers rode on motorcycles, bicycles, and walked in the far reaches of the district to locate the birth attendants.

"The data was then compiled to create Malawi's first TBA maps. Policies are in development which will provide courses for both trained and untrained TBAs.

"I had incredible experiences with mothers. I saw a delivery in the crowded district hospital and after an episiotomy repair. I also visited a traditional birth attendant home, arriving just after two women had delivered the most beautiful and perfect babies," said Lauren. "When I left Malawi, I felt inspired and proud of my impact and the footprint I hoped I had left behind to make '1 in 36' a statistic of the past."

It is an amazing truth that one person can literally change the mortality rate of a nation. In so many places around the world, a little goes a very long way. A trained and educated American can impact generations of people.

Stay on the cutting edge in your area of service, not only in education, but also in keeping your passion and drive alive.

ALMIGHTY GOD, *thank You for the education and training that I am so privileged to have. Motivate me to keep my skills current and my heart ready to serve.*

# THE RIGHTEOUS OF THE WORLD

*And by your offspring shall all the nations of the earth gain blessing for themselves, because you have obeyed my voice.* —GENESIS 22:18

During the Nazi domination of World War II, thousands of Poles, mostly Roman Catholics, risked their lives to save Jews. Any Pole caught aiding Jews was executed, sometimes entire families.

Once the war ended and communism took hold, for decades, the heroism was not discussed. The Jewish survivors would send letters and gifts of gratitude to their benefactors, but the Poles kept quiet, out of modesty, or fear of anti-Semitism. They worried that gift packages from the West might create jealousy from neighbors in a troubled economy.

But things have now changed. Gatherings of rescuers in Warsaw take place where Jewish representatives take turns praising them for their heroism. The rescuers deny that they are exceptional, but when they are alone, they often discuss the brutality that they witnessed, which still brings them to tears.

"We did what we had to do," said Halina Szaszkiewicz, 89. "There was nothing heroic about it." But the Jewish officials see it differently. "You, the righteous of the world, think your behavior was ordinary, but we all know it was something more than that. It was truly extraordinary," Stanlee Stahl, the executive vice president of the Jewish Foundation for the Righteous, proclaimed.

History bears the fact that humans can be horrifically cruel to one another, yet history also reveals that because of great sacrifice and risk some will endure to serve and save. There are still both kinds of people in the world. Thank God today that you can be one who serves, one who saves.

LORD OF *ALL, lead me to overcome evil and promote what is good and righteous, whether in a major moment or a minor detail.*

# RIDING FREE

*The Lord is a warrior; the Lord is His name.* —EXODUS 15:3

Warriors' Watch Riders is a nation-wide coalition of bikers—groups and individuals—dedicated to the support of our nation's warriors.

What they all have in common is an unwavering support of our troops and their families. They do not claim to be a veteran's group or a motorcycle club. They ride their motorcycles to draw public attention to the cause and the cause is American troops.

Warriors' Watch provides motorcycle escorts for military units returning from war, for units deploying, and for individual warriors coming home or shipping out. Warrior's Watch works very closely with other troop support groups to provide a motorcycle escort component to their good work when appropriate.

Warriors' Watch will attend, promote, and add excitement to fund-raisers, family-support events, and other related activities. The group's definition of "troops" includes veterans of all military branches, police and firefighters, and first responders.

Warrior's Watch is an all-volunteer army; they engage in no fund-raising activities and they receive no donations.

Their creed is "Above all, Warrior's Watch riders are free Americans and we will at all times and in all things conduct ourselves in such a way as to be worthy of the freedom that was purchased for us by the blood of our nation's warriors."

Patriotism is alive and well and living in groups such as Warrior's Watch—people standing together to be a part of the land of the brave and the free. Thank God today for your freedom and the responsibility you have been given in the liberty granted to you by almighty God.

HOLY GOD, *help me not to take my freedom for granted. May I live today as a good steward of all the liberties I have been granted by You.*

# NO STRANGER TO DANGER

*The evil do not understand justice, but those who seek the Lord understand it completely.* —*PROVERBS 28:5*

Illinois State Police Trooper Zachary Peters, a 12-year veteran, was on patrol when he saw a burning car. He called in the incident, then approached the vehicle to find a woman inside, bleeding and unresponsive. Unable to open the doors, Peters broke a window and struggled to pull her out, all the while inhaling wafts of black smoke.

"Her legs were stuck underneath her seat and there was a lot of blood. The airbags had deployed and she was not wearing her seat belt," Zachary reported. "Because of the extensive damage, she was wedged in." The trooper was able to pull her from the wreckage before first responders arrived.

State police Director Hiram Grau said, "This trooper is no stranger to placing his life in danger and his selfless actions speak volumes to the dedication of his police service." Zachary had saved another person in a car crash by applying direct pressure on a severe leg wound and, with another trooper, applied a tourniquet until paramedics arrived.

Zachary shared, "I just remember thinking that I had to get her out of there as quickly as I could or we were both going to burn up. I don't think I'm a hero. It's my job. That's what state troopers do."

In multiple locations on a daily basis, first responders pull people to safety and save lives, only to answer to the title of hero with, "I was just doing my job." We must continually be grateful that we are a part of a nation that values life, has an infrastructure to offer aid when trouble strikes, and people like Zachary Peters.

MERCIFUL GOD, *thank You for all the many blessings we have available. Help me to remain ever grateful and not take these gifts for granted. Lead me to bless others today.*

# EVERYDAY DANGERS

*You will know them by their fruits.* —MATTHEW 7:16A

In 1997, Fred Baker was a senior corrections officer at Bayside State Prison in New Jersey. An inmate ended his life by fatally stabbing him.

Fifteen years later, to the day, his family gathered around Acting Governor Kim Guadagno and Assemblyman Nelson Albano to sign a bill titled "Fred Baker's Law," making July 30 an annual recognition in New Jersey of Corrections Officer's Day.

"It is truly my honor to have some small part in making sure your son's honored yet again," said Governor Guadagno. "I do know the dangers corrections officers face and I wanted to thank them publicly, in a public hearing for their great sacrifices."

"I am so happy," said Fred Baker, Sr. "This is great for all the officers. It's not just for Freddy, but for everyone."

Since Baker's death, much has been done in his name to help protect corrections officers in New Jersey, such as to require that all must wear stab-proof vests on the job.

"You need to know the dangers that these men and women face every day," said Governor Guadagno. "You need to know that they are truly our unsung heroes." Guadagno knows firsthand what corrections officers do, as she oversaw operations at the county jail, when she was the sheriff of Monmouth County.

Senseless deaths happen daily to law enforcement officials, military personnel, and first responders. But all who know the fallen brothers or sisters also know they would be pleased that they brought a positive impact to the world. That is the point of sacrifice.

COUNSELOR, *bless and comfort all the families that have lost a loved one to the war abroad or the war on our own streets.*

# DRIVEN TO MY KNEES

*By day the Lord commands his steadfast love, and at night his song is with me, a prayer to the God of my life.* —PSALM 42:8

Abraham Lincoln was known by reputation to be a man of prayer. He once said, "I have been driven to my knees many times by the overwhelming conviction that I had no place else to go. My own wisdom, and that of all about me, seemed insufficient for the day."

Lincoln, speaking with a wounded General at Gettysburg, said, "When everyone seemed panic-stricken, I went to my room and got down on my knees before Almighty God and prayed. Soon a sweet comfort crept into my soul that God Almighty had taken the whole business into His own hands."

During the Civil War a friend of Abraham Lincoln was visiting the White House. He wrote, "One night I was restless and could not sleep. From the private room where the president slept, I heard low tones. Instinctively I wandered in and there I saw a sight which I have never forgotten. It was the president kneeling before an open Bible. His back was toward me. I shall never forget his prayer: 'Oh, Thou God that heard Solomon in the night when he prayed and cried for wisdom, hear me. . . . I cannot guide the affairs of this nation without Thy help. Hear me and save this nation.'"

What is going on in your life right now that feels like a private "civil war?" Do you have a burden? Concern? Stress? Get somewhere completely alone, with no concern of being overheard, and talk to God. Tell him exactly what is happening and how you feel. Ask for His help.

ALMIGHTY GOD, *thank You for being available to me 24/7 for any reason or any problem.*

# WEAPONS OF LOVE

*Whoever diligently seeks good seeks favour.* —Proverbs 11:27a

The U.S. military is obviously well known for their ability to fight and defend, but there is another side to each branch that works to bring much positive change to the world.

In the Air Force, for example, here are just a few samples of humanitarian work.

In Iraq, Airmen distributed school supplies and backpacks to children.

More than 120 Joint Task Force-Bravo personnel hiked two miles up steep terrain to deliver food to people living in an isolated village near Comayagua, Honduras. Their mission is to support joint, combined, and inter-agency exercises and operations in Central America.

A team of medically trained Airmen from around the U.S. traveled to the Dominican Republic to provide medical care to the people there. The exercise was designed to foster goodwill and improve relations between the United States and the governments of Colombia, Dominican Re-

public, and Jamaica. The locals called the team "miracle workers."

U.S. civil engineers and medical Airmen traveled to Quang Tri Province, Vietnam, to provide construction assistance and medical care to local communities. The trip was part of an operation that spanned the Asia-Pacific region.

Airmen took part in New Horizons Panama, a 12-week humanitarian assistance mission designed to improve critical infrastructure and provide medical care throughout Panama. The team distributed more than $4,000 worth of school supplies, toys, sports equipment, clothes, and food for Panamanian children.

Even when deployed to a war zone, once stabilized, American troops have been known historically as goodwill ambassadors, reaching out to children, the elderly, and friendly locals. When fighting evil, promoting good is a strong ally.

MERCIFUL GOD, *help me always to promote good, peace, and hope in all that I do and to be an ambassador of right, good—and You.*

# CREATIVE CARE

*But be doers of the word, and not merely hearers.* —JAMES 1:22A

Homefront Hugs USA is a grass-roots organization based in Michigan with a heart and passion to give unconditional support to our troops, their families, and veterans.

Homefront Hugs was founded after 9-11 by a wife and daughter of veterans. Beginning with a small group of volunteers, the organization has grown to over 50,000 members.

Volunteers write cards to our wounded troops and notes to the medical staff who care for them. Volunteers develop long-lasting relationships with deployed heroes, wounded veterans, or families dealing with a long deployment.

Homefront Hugs also encourages the start-up of kids' and teens' clubs in schools to support our heroes.

A counselor is available via email to deal with issues related to separation from children, preparations for a second or third deployment, coming home and adjusting to the family again, depression and behavior issues in children when the soldier is away, having to be mom and dad at the same time, and explaining the war and a soldier's purpose to children.

Volunteers try to make war more bearable for all, making sure no veterans or their families feel forgotten.

A wise person once said, "Don't just stand there, do something!" Groups such as Homefront Hugs USA are taking great needs, joining with a creative idea, and serving our troops—pro-active service to the greater good. So, are you standing there or are you doing something?

CREATOR GOD, *when I feel a burden or see a need, help me to respond with creativity, passion, and a pro-active response.*

# INSIDE ENEMY TERRITORY

*But I am not ashamed, for I know the one in whom I have put my trust, and I am
sure that he is able to guard until that day what I have entrusted to him.*
—2 TIMOTHY 1:12

In the summer of 2005, a four-man Navy SEAL team consisting of Lt. Michael Murphy and Petty Officers Danny Dietz, Matthew Axelson, and Marcus Luttrell headed out on a surveillance and reconnaissance mission near the Afghanistan-Pakistan border.

The goal was to disrupt activity in the region by Anti-Coalition Militia, with a primary target being Ahmad Shah, a terrorist leader with close ties to Bin Laden.

Not long after the team's insertion, the SEAL Team was ambushed by Shah and his group. Three of the four men were killed.

"Night Stalkers," a special operations unit of the United States Army that provides helicopter aviation support for Special Operations Forces, was sent in to rescue the team. One of Shah's men fired an RPG, striking the helicopter. Eight Navy SEALS and eight U.S. Army aviators were killed.

Marcus Luttrell was the only survivor. He was initially knocked unconscious and injured, but he managed to escape and was later rescued. The rescue operation was also able to recover the bodies of the fallen soldiers.

In April 2008, Shah was traveling with an Afghan refugee trader who he had kidnapped. When Shah failed to stop at a border checkpoint, he opened fire on the police and was killed in the exchange of gunfire.

None of us can know the time or the day our end will come, but we can know what will happen when that day comes. We can trust in our Savior to take care of us beyond death. Thank God today that you can know that you know Him!

SAVIOR, *thank You that even though life gives no guarantees, You give a guarantee after death, if we trust in You.*

# BLOOD:WATER

*And let the one who believes in me drink. As the scripture has said, "Out of the believer's heart shall flow rivers of living water." —JOHN 7:38*

The award-winning Christian band Jars of Clay wanted to respond to the HIV/AIDS crisis in Africa. They shared stories of creative, compassionate, hard-working Africans who were bringing health, hope, and healing into their respective communities.

Blood: Water Mission was born with a simple mission—to provide a clean blood supply and clean water to Africa.

To start, the band launched the 1,000 Wells Project to provide clean water and sanitation to 1,000 communities in sub-Saharan Africa. The effort was based on the equation that $1 provides one African with clean water for an entire year.

Millions of dollars have been raised by tens of thousands of individuals seeking to make a difference. To date, more than 1,000 communities in Africa now have life-saving water and health care. The effort has helped over 600,000 people in 13 different countries.

The work continues to provide clean water, sanitation and hygiene training. Funds are raised for health clinics, community health workers, and groups that help in the prevention and treatment of people affected by HIV/AIDS.

It's a new day in many areas where village leaders now have the resources and training to bring clean water, sanitation, and health care into their communities. Stomachaches, skin diseases and diarrhea have disappeared. Women and children no longer walk several miles a day to carry filthy water. Those with HIV are living longer, stronger lives.

We all have a God-given platform. Some are just bigger than others. But if we all take responsibility for our circle of influence, we can change lives forever and impact a lost and dying world.

GREAT PHYSICIAN, *thank You for both physical water and Living Water that You provide. May I take neither for granted as I seek to make a change in this world.*

# ABOVE & BEYOND

*You prepare a table before me in the presence of my enemies.* —PSALM 23:5A

The 2012 shooting rampage in Aurora, Colo., during the opening night of the movie "The Dark Knight Rises" that left 12 people dead and 58 wounded, proved once again that first responders are critical to saving lives.

As moviegoers began streaming out of the theatre, police and EMTs found it difficult to tell who was actually shot and who simply had blood on them from others.

Police, firefighters, paramedics, doctors, and other medical workers launched into a mass casualty response.

Aurora Mayor Steve Hogan told reporters, "We didn't lose more lives, because our first responders not only did their job, they went above and beyond."

The dispatch recordings and interviews with first responders depict a well-oiled team of law enforcement and medical personnel—no squabbling, no hysteria, despite the terror that confronted them. Victims had been struck in the head, neck, chest, and arms by shotgun, handgun, and high-velocity rifle ammunition.

Eric Hunter, a radiology technician, had been watching the Batman movie in the theater next to the shooting. He and an off-duty paramedic aided two terrified teenage girls, one of whom had been shot.

Dispatchers called in ambulances from all over the area, yet some were too badly injured to wait, so police began driving victims to hospitals. The Medical Center of Aurora soon teemed with five trauma surgeons, two neurosurgeons, two orthopedic surgeons, several ER doctors, nurses, and technicians.

Anytime evil lashes out, you will find those who represent good. The public servants in Aurora proved to be valiant and courageous.

Thank God today that you too can stand on the side of the right and the just.

ALMIGHTY GOD, *we never get accustomed to tragedy and are always surprised when it strikes. Ready me to serve in any situation You may call me to. May I be a force of good for You.*

# ON AMERICAN SOIL

*Be strong and of good courage, and act. Do not be afraid or dismayed; for the Lord God, my God, is with you.* —1 CHRONICLES 28:20

A massive wildfire called the White Draw fire was raging in South Dakota. The 145th Airlift Wing of the North Carolina Air National Guard, based in Charlotte, sent Modular Airborne Fire Fighting System (MAFFS) equipped C-130s to the area.

"The support of civil authorities during natural disasters is a key and unique mission of the National Guard," said Army Major General Gregory Lusk, the adjutant general of North Carolina National Guard. "The MAFFS mission represents interagency coordination between the guard, the U.S. Forest Service, the Department of Homeland Security, and Department of Defense organizations to suppress the fires."

MAFFS is a self-contained aerial firefighting system that can discharge 3,000 gallons of water or fire retardant in less than 5 seconds, covering an area one-quarter of a mile long by 100 feet wide. Retardant is discharged along the leading edge of a fire, while water is dropped directly on the flames. Once the load is discharged, it can be refilled in less than 12 minutes.

While fighting the White Draw fire, one C-130 crew of six seasoned airmen flew in to dump retardant, but the massive fires can cause havoc with flying conditions and the plane went down, killing four of the guardsmen.

Lieutenant Colonel Paul K. Mikeal, Major Joseph M. McCormick, Major Ryan S. David, and Senior Master Sergeant Robert S. Cannon died attempting to protect property and save the lives of American citizens on American soil.

Regardless of the agencies involved or the state-of-the-art equipment available, human courage and skill is always required, as well as incredible personal risk, in saving lives in natural disasters. Pray for courage. Hone your skill.

HOLY GOD, *thank You for my skills and my desire to serve. May I use the resources available to me wisely, and always remember that human life is the reason we serve.*

# SAVING SURVIVORS

*My mouth shall speak wisdom; the meditation of my heart shall be understanding.*
—PSALM 49:3

In 1992, the United States Congress created the National Fallen Firefighters Foundation to remember America's firefighters killed in the line of duty. The nonprofit organization has developed programs to honor our fallen fire heroes and assist their families and co-workers.

Each October, the foundation sponsors the official national tribute to all firefighters who died in the line of duty during the previous year. Thousands attend the weekend activities held at the National Fire Academy in Emmitsburg, Md. The weekend features special programs for survivors and co-workers along with moving public ceremonies.

The foundation provides travel, lodging, and meals for immediate survivors of fallen firefighters being honored. This allows survivors to participate in sessions conducted by trained grief counselors, and to participate in the private and public tributes.

When a firefighter dies in the line of duty, the foundation provides survivors emotional assistance through matching survivors with similar experiences. Spouses, children, and stepchildren of fallen firefighters are eligible for scholarships for education and job-training costs.

Under a Department of Justice grant, the foundation also offers counseling to fire departments after the death of one of their own.

For the families of firefighters and all first responders, the daily knowledge that loved ones might not come home is always there. When that becomes reality, a strong support system is vital.

Empathy is crucial for those who grieve. No one can help a fallen firefighter's spouse like another spouse who has faced the same loss. Understanding the loss and feelings are irreplaceable connections.

DIVINE HEALER, *help me to practice and connect empathy anywhere that my personal experience and loss can benefit another. May my actions and words bring healing anytime I have the opportunity.*

# BECAUSE PEOPLE PRAYED

*But as for me, my prayer is to you, O Lord. At an acceptable time, O God, in the abundance of your steadfast love, answer me with your faithful help.* —PSALM 69:13

General George Patton as told to Chief Chaplain of the Third Army, James O'Neill:

*"Chaplain, I am a strong believer in prayer. There are three ways that men get what they want; by planning, by working, and by praying. Any great military operation takes careful planning, or thinking. Then you must have well-trained troops to carry it out: that's working. But between the plan and the operation there is always an unknown. That unknown spells defeat or victory, success or failure. It is the reaction of the actors to the ordeal when it actually comes. Some people call that getting the breaks; I call it God. God has His part, or margin in everything. That's where prayer comes in.*

*"Up to now, in the Third Army, God has been very good to us. We have never retreated; we have suffered no defeats, no famine, no epidemics. This is because a lot of people back home are praying for us. We were lucky in Africa, in Sicily, and in Italy simply because people prayed.*

*"But we have to pray for ourselves, too. A good soldier is not made merely by making him think and work. There is something in every soldier that goes deeper than thinking or working—it's his guts. It is something that he has built in there: it is a world of truth and power that is higher than himself. Great living is not all output of thought and work. A man has to have intake as well. I don't know what you call it, but I call it religion, prayer, or God."*

General Patton called "getting a break," God's part. What do you call "it?"

DEAR GOD, *thank You for this reminder that there is an unknown throughout life that only You can affect. Between "my plans and my operation," may You work in my life.*

# COME INSIDE WITH US

*I truly understand that God shows no partiality, but in every nation anyone who fears him and does what is right is acceptable to him.* — ACTS 10:34-35

William Wallace Brown, Jr. was buried at age 68 in the garden at St. John's Episcopal Church, across from the White House. St. John's is called the "Church of Presidents," since nearly every U.S. leader from James Madison has worshiped there. Former members of Congress and prominent professionals attended the burial service.

Brown "really understood that the kingdom of God is for all of us," Rev. Luis Leon said. "It doesn't matter about ethnic background, race, or class—all the things that we allow to divide us. In God's eyes they're not really important."

But there was something unusual about this funeral. William Brown was a homeless man who had lived on the streets of Washington for 15 years.

In 1989, he spotted then-President George W. Bush entering the church and asked the president to pray for him. Bush answered, "Why don't you come inside with us and pray for yourself." William became a regular at the 8 a.m. service and always placed a crumpled dollar bill in the silver collection plate. Church member Dolph Hatfield had become William's best friend, inviting him for a meal or taking him grocery shopping after church. Dolph stated that in the eyes of God "the homeless and the most important are one and the same."

God has a place for each of us—a place of significance here on earth and in Heaven—regardless of whether we're a president, a pauper or in between.

CARING GOD, *help me as I serve to treat all people as Your loved ones and family. Guide me to serve unconditionally.*

# THE STRENGTH OF 10,000

*For who is God except the Lord? And who is a rock besides our God? —the God who girded me with strength, and made my way safe.* —PSALM 18:31-33

At the Aurora movie theatre on the night of the Batman movie premiere where the horrific shootings took place, 17-year-old Stephanie Rodriguez's brother had talked her into going with him and his friends.

As the 2012 shootings began, Stephanie prayed: "Dear God, please help us. Let all of us get out." When the gunman briefly stopped, she rushed toward the exit.

As she made it safely outside, Stephanie saw a man lying on the pavement, screaming, "My leg! Help me!" as others were rushing past him.

She knelt down and pushed her hands on his thigh, trying to stop the blood like she had seen doctors do on television. She took off her new belt and tied it around his leg. Then Stephanie held his leg, while her brother and two strangers dragged him to a grassy spot, safe from the fleeing cars.

Through it all, she was calm, even with a stranger's blood covering her hands and clothing.

"She had the strength of 10,000 men," said Todd Peckham, who was also helping victims. "She didn't flinch when she put pressure on a gunshot wound with her bare hands."

"It was adrenaline," Stephanie said. "My first reaction was to help him."

The next day, Stephanie walked into the man's hospital room and when his mother asked how old she was—"I told his mom I just turned 17 and she just burst into tears."

They say character is proven when no one is looking, but in Stephanie's case, it was when someone was in trouble. Thank God for the Stephanies of the world.

HEAVENLY RESCUER, *while the world runs past all kinds of hurting people every day, help me to see and hear them, and like Stephanie, to stop and do something about it.*

# FOR THE FIRST TIME

*There is therefore now no condemnation for those who are in Christ Jesus. For the law of the Spirit of life in Christ Jesus has set you free from the law of sin and of death.* —ROMANS 8:1-2

Michael Kelly was serving three 40-year prison terms for murder, assault, and robbery. He had been abandoned by his parents as a child and grew up on the streets, eventually becoming a gang member. Kelly had spent all his adult life in prison.

Kairos prison ministry put on a retreat for the worst of prisoners and the warden ordered Kelly to go.

On the second day of the retreat they were giving out goody bags of cookies. Kelly got one and found a note inside from an 11-year-old girl. Kelly read the note. Then he read it again. Then one more time. It said, "I don't care if you're in prison for killing someone like me. I still want you to know I love you and Jesus loves you too."

"I knew it was real," Kelly shared. "I knew for the first time that someone loved me, that God loved me. I could accept it or turn away and go back to my life. But I wasn't going back. I was going to Jesus."

After 17 years Kelly was paroled and now holds three chapel services a day sharing the hope and grace he has found in Christ. He said, "I want to help change lives. I want people to know what I know."

There is no one who sins more than Christ can save, no one passes His grace. The worst sinner may come to Him and be changed forever.

What about you? Have you experienced what Michael Kelly did? Have you come to the point of realizing you need a Savior?

LORD JESUS, *I receive You today to save me, forgive my sins, and give me a new heart and life. Lead me to the life You created me to have.*

# GOD IS NIGH

*How long must I see the standard, and hear the sound of the trumpet?*
—JEREMIAH 4:21

Everyone knows "Taps"—the haunting tune played at military funerals. The song, as we know it today, came from the Union Army Brigadier General Daniel Butterfield during the Civil War.

But Captain John C. Tidball started the custom of playing taps at a military funeral.

It was in early July, 1862 at Harrison's Landing, that a corporal in Tidball's Artillery, died. They wanted to bury him with full military honors, but could not allow the traditional firing of three guns over his grave, due to the close proximity of the enemy. Tidball later wrote, "The thought suggested itself to me to sound Taps instead, which I did. The idea was taken up by others, until in a short time, it was adopted by the entire army."

It became a standard component to U.S. military funerals in 1891. Here are three verses of the song:

Day is done, gone the sun, from the hills, from the lake,

From the skies, all is well, safely rest, God is nigh.

Go to sleep, peaceful sleep, May the soldier or sailor, God keep.

On the land or the deep, safe in sleep.

Thanks and praise, for our days, neath the sun, neath the stars,

Neath the sky, as we go, this we know, God is nigh.

So much of our tradition and history as a nation has spiritual roots and recognition of God—even the words to Taps refer to God's presence.

Be sure in your own life that you include your faith in all that you do and daily live knowing that "God is nigh."

ALPHA & OMEGA, *it is obvious that You are woven throughout the fabric of our nation. May I represent well a thread of Who You are as I serve.*

# THE ARMS OF DIVINE GUIDANCE

*Gird your sword on your thigh, O mighty one, in your glory and majesty. In your majesty ride on victoriously for the cause of truth and to defend the right.*

—PSALM 45:3-4A

Douglas MacArthur was one of the most respected generals in American history. Here are just a few quotes from his exceptional career.

*There is no security on this earth; there is only opportunity.*

*Old soldiers never die; they just fade away. And like the old soldier in that ballad, I now close my military career and just fade away, an old soldier who tried to do his duty as God gave him the sight to see that duty.*

*The soldier, above all other men, is required to perform the highest act of religious teaching— sacrifice.*

*In war, when a commander becomes so bereft of reason and perspective that he fails to understand the dependence of arms on Divine guidance, he no longer deserves victory.*

*Believe me, sir, never a night goes by, be I ever so tired, but I read the Word of God before I go to bed.*

There is a clear connection between many great Americans and faith in God. The promise that we are living for more than ourselves and that a loving, engaged God is guiding us brings a responsibility and hope to all that we do.

EVER PRESENT GOD, *thank You that I can have purpose and hope in how I live and how I serve. Lead me on to even greater things as I follow You.*

# WATCHMEN IN THE WATER

*He himself is before all things, and in him all things hold together.*
—COLOSSIANS 1:17

In 1790, the United States Coast Guard was formed to protect the vast coastline of the United States when Congress consolidated two existing agencies to form an all-in-one maritime service. The previous agencies were the Life Saving Service and the Revenue Cutter Service.

Currently, the U.S. Coast Guard not only secures the shores of the United States, doing search-and-rescue missions, but has cutters and offshore ships deployed all around the world.

In addition to rescuing people from the oceans, the Coast Guard has stopped billions of dollars of illegal drugs from entering the U.S.

Each year, the Coast Guard responds to well over 200,000 search-and-rescue incidents, saves about 4,000 lives, and prevents around 200,000 pounds of cocaine and literally tons of heroin and marijuana from entering the United States.

These maritime heroes are the silent guardians of our nation's water boundaries and only rarely make the news. Today, be aware of those who are watching, protecting, and risking for our way of life to continue.

An intricate network is held in constant balance inside our nation, around our borders, and around the world. Thousands upon thousands of public servants do their jobs with excellence and dedication each and every day. Stand proud as you take your place among them.

OUR SUSTAINER, *You are the glue that holds our nation together and sustains our many systems and processes. Bless our nation and its servants today!*

# HIS WORD IS SURE

*Those of steadfast mind you keep in peace—in peace because they trust in you.*
*—ISAIAH 26:3*

William Carey is considered one of the greatest pioneering missionaries of all time.

In the late 1700s, an attitude pervaded the church that discouraged missionary work. Carey asserted that Jesus' Great Commission applied to all Christians of all times.

"Multitudes sit at ease and give themselves no concern about the far greater part of their fellow sinners, who to this day, are lost in ignorance and idolatry," said Carey.

In 1792, he organized a missionary society and preached a sermon with the now-famous words, "Expect great things from God; attempt great things for God!" Within the year, Carey and his family were headed for India.

Illness plagued the family and loneliness set in: He wrote, "I am in a strange land. No Christian friend, a large family, and nothing to supply their wants. Well, I have God and His Word is sure."

In December 1800, after seven years of missionary labor, Carey baptized his first convert, Krishna Pal, and two months later, he published his first Bengali New Testament.

Over the next 28 years, he and his helpers translated the entire Bible into India's six major languages and parts of 209 other languages and dialects. By the time Carey died, he had spent 41 years in India. His mission could count only some 700 converts in a nation of millions, but he had laid the foundation of Bible translations, education, and social reform for generations to come.

Today, take heart and be encouraged in your own journey. You follow in the steps of many great humanitarians. So—"Expect great things from God; attempt great things for God."

SOVEREIGN GOD, *though a life of service can be lonely and even misunderstood, help me to stay steadfast and relying on You for my peace.*

# PRESIDENTS' PASTOR

*For God shows no partiality.* —ROMANS 2:11

Every U.S. president since World War II has met with Billy Graham. Both Johnson and Nixon offered him high positions in government, but Graham quickly and graciously refused.

There was a religious side to Lyndon Johnson that people did not know. Billy was probably closer to Johnson than to any other president. He spent more than twenty nights at the White House during Johnson's administration. Every time Billy would say to him, "Let's have a prayer," the president would get on his knees to pray.

In a letter to Graham, Johnson wrote, "My mind went back to those lonely occasions at the White House when your friendship helped to sustain a president in an hour of trial."

Billy met Ronald Reagan a year after he married Nancy. The two remained close friends. "I remember when Reagan was president of the Screen Actors Guild, a union leader, and a very strong Democrat," Billy said.

On March 30, 1981, after the assassination attempt on President Reagan's life, Billy flew immediately to Washington, D.C., to comfort and pray with Mrs. Reagan, and do anything he could for the president.

Reagan said of Graham, "It was through Billy Graham that I found myself praying even more than on a daily basis, and that in the position I held, that my prayers more and more were to give me the wisdom to make decisions that would serve and be pleasing to God."

Remember, that to God, every person is equally valuable. And some of those—only You can reach. The same Spirit in Billy Graham can work through You too.

HEAVENLY GUIDE, *help me to realize that there are people that you want to reach through me. I want to be available to you, for them.*

# I'LL REMEMBER THIS FOREVER

*For the rendering of this ministry not only supplies the needs of the saints but also overflows with many thanksgivings to God.* —2 CORINTHIANS 9:12

As devastating wildfires spread through Colorado and Wyoming, 21 firefighters from Maryland volunteered to go help fight the blaze.

Squad Boss Bert Wagner said, "It was the highest fire in the nation—one of the highest places in the nation. We came from about 43 feet above sea level and went to 11,900 feet. You have to walk five to eight miles to get to the fire up very steep rocky terrain."

Wildfire Specialist Kevin Massey said, "We would get up in the mornings and it would be in the low 30s with ice on our tent and we were hailed on. We had one crewmember who had to be hospitalized for altitude sickness. Working 15 to 16 hours a day, while gasping for air was one of the biggest challenges. Your heart's racing and you're carrying a load, carrying 50 to 60 pounds of gear with us." Kevin continued, "To see someone picking through what was left of their home, everything they had, it was pretty devastating."

But after all this work and risk, what did the firefighters say they would recall of this trip? "We had a cafeteria set up in the middle school in Laramie and the walls were covered with posters and letters from the children. For me, this is what I'll take and I'll remember forever."

It is amazing how simple, heartfelt gratitude can often erase sacrifice and hardship for first responders. It is a reminder of the reason for this service in the first place—helping others.

SAVIOR, *thank You for the many ways You have taken care of, saved me, provided for me, and helped me. May my life reflect gratitude to You as well as all those who help me in so many ways.*

# LONG AFTER WE LEAVE

*He leads the humble in what is right, and teaches the humble his way.*
—PSALM 25:9

Navy Seabees of Naval Mobile Construction Battalion 40, along with four containers of tools and equipment, arrived in Vietnam to support Pacific Partnership—a humanitarian and civic assistance mission in the Asia Pacific region.

"Our mission was to construct a four-room health clinic in one of the most impoverished communities in the country and renovate two other clinic buildings," said Senior Chief Builder Todd Bernashe, assistant officer-in-charge.

This was the first deployment for many team members.

"After all was said and done, there were 22 Seabees to conduct a mission originally intended for 25," he said. "After our departure flight was pushed back for the third time, there were 29 days to complete what was originally planned for 34."

The Seabees worked seven days a week for long hours, working in over 100 degree weather with high humidity while wearing long-sleeve shirts and pants to prevent against insect-borne illnesses.

"It's hot out here, but to be a part of something that will help the members in this community long after we leave means something," said Builder 1st Class David Garcia.

"The work of the Fighting Forty in Hung Lam and Hung Tam will serve the communities for many years to come. The finished product of our efforts will be part of our legacy," said Engineering Aide Third Class Kyle Jeffreys.

What kind of teammate are you? Do you work toward the common good of the group? Do you put the others before yourself? God's spirit can provide the ability and strength to step back, look up, and reach out.

HOLY ONE, *when I want my way, draw me to give way to Yours. When I put me first, nudge me to step behind my team.*

# MODERN DAY WARRIORS

*I will look with favor on the faithful in the land, so that they may live with me;*
*whoever walks in the way that is blameless shall minister to me.* —PSALM 101:6

First responders are placed in so many challenging situations that impact their faith. The National Center for Chaplain Development, a nonprofit organization, provides support and emotional assistance.

Ken Schlenker, founder of the center, explains, "What we are trying to do is equip people to come alongside our first-responder community. They are our modern day warriors, the heroes of today. We are trying to be first responders to the first responders."

Larry Grihalva with the California State Firefighters Association said, "I wish I had this 20 years ago. How do you tell someone their loved one has died? It's a very difficult thing and we're not really trained what to say and what not to say. That not only helps us in our patient care, but it makes ourselves healthy when we go home to our families, so we don't take the stress home with us."

"Other people don't understand what we go through. So, I thought if I have something to offer, I need to use that to help the others, and that was really my motivation," stated Tricia Higgins of the Chino Valley Fire District.

Ken Schlenker added, "We need to get in the situation as soon as we possibly can, as close to the scene as it happens, with brief and simple interventions that can provide hope to the person, to give them the ability to decompress."

Receiving spiritual help, as well as giving it when needed, is an important part of service. Stay open to both, so you can continue to grow and to give.

LORD GOD, *as You pour into me, I can pour out to others. Help me to constantly look to You and to those who spiritually support me, as I also look for places to help others.*

# STEPPING UP TO THE PLATE

*With God are wisdom and strength; he has counsel and understanding.*
—JOB 12:13

Oftentimes, National Guardsmen have to trade in their rifles for the necessary tools needed in a crisis.

Fifty-seven Alaska National Guardsmen with shovels arrived in Cordova for "Operation Deep Dig" following a major snowstorm.

Alaska Army National Guard Captain Chad Ausel said, "As soon as we got here, we identified a priority list for safety and familiarization training with Cordova. We asked for a subject-matter expert on how they've cleared snow here safely and then completed training on harnesses, ropes, and knots to make sure the guardsmen are trained to do the mission safely."

As soon as training was completed, Captain Ausel said, "The city officials identified three locations this morning and we're going to stay in squads to clear those areas."

Mayor Jim Kallander commented, "I can't say enough about how impressed I am with the Homeland Security response, the governor's office response, and now the National Guard is stepping up to the plate. It's exactly what we needed."

As the first military responder in all domestic emergencies, the guard focuses on doing everything it can to help communities. Captain Ausel added, "Guardsmen will stay as long as they're needed. We hope to leave Cordova in a better situation. This is why they signed up to serve in the National Guard."

The National Guard has met crucial needs in countless situations, utilizing any means required for the job. In so many areas of service, a whatever-it-takes, jack-of-all-trades kind of ingenuity is needed to take care of people. God's wisdom, coupled with personal experience, is a great source for meeting any need.

CREATOR GOD, *You give knowledge, understanding, and especially wisdom. Grant me what I need, as I need it, and help me to rely on You for it all.*

# WITHOUT SECOND THOUGHTS

*I hold my life in my hand continually, but I do not forget your law.*
—PSALM 119:109

Police in Rancho Santa Margarita received a call that a teenage boy was on a bridge, about 40 feet above California 241 Toll Road. He was preparing to jump.

Within two minutes, motorcycle patrol officer Deputy Tim Africano arrived.

The boy was on a ledge just a few inches wide. The deputy managed to climb up, balance himself, and grab him with one hand before he jumped.

Tim was able to hold on until two other officers arrived. As the officers grabbed onto the boy, he refused to help or cooperate, so Tim had to pull the boy to safety by his waistband, as the other officers helped. The entire rescue took place before firefighters could shut the freeway down.

"I'm just glad I was there to help," Tim said. "I was just doing my job."

"This teenager would have jumped from the overpass if it hadn't been for the quick actions of Deputy Africano and responding deputies," Lieutenant Brian Schmutz said. "Their bravery and concern for this troubled young man saved his life and spared his family from tragedy and loss."

One witness stated, "They quickly came to the young man's aid without second thoughts of their own safety. One officer risked his own life. It was not an easy rescue."

One of the great stresses of all first responders is what a day will hold. Will it be an uneventful day or one of crisis?

Will I save a life or be too late? Will I be called upon to risk my life, and if so, what will happen? That's why each day is best left in the hands of God.

DELIVERER, *my days are Yours. My life is in Your hands. Help me to make each day count.*

# CAN YOU SEE ME?

*The Lord looks down from heaven; he sees all humankind. From where he sits enthroned he watches all the inhabitants of the earth—he who fashions the hearts of them all, and observes all their deeds.* —PSALM 33:13-15

Sergeant Adam Burke was a combat veteran and Purple Heart recipient after being wounded in battle during a 15-month tour in Iraq. Collapsed and riddled with shrapnel, he recalls praying, "Lord, can you see me? If you get me home, I promise I'll make my life worth saving."

Fast forward to one day in the food court of the mall, Adam was stunned to see a young vet asking if he could have people's food scraps. He knew that day he must find some way to help wounded veterans coming back home.

From that incident, Veterans Farm was born. Burke explains, "Our mission is to help disabled combat veterans reintegrate back into society through the use of horticulture therapy, while working together in a relaxed, open environment. Veterans will work as a team to develop solutions that will enable them to overcome physical and mental barriers. We're partnering with organizations like Farmers Veterans Coalition to assist disabled veterans in obtaining the resources to start their own farm or to work with larger farming organizations."

Veterans Farm helps disabled veterans reintegrate into society through sustainable agriculture training. They also cooperate with the Veterans Affairs work therapy program.

Many people's lives have been defined by a single moment, just like Adam Burke.

We never know when God will speak in a dramatic, yet profoundly simple way or answer a simple prayer whispered on a battlefield. Watch closely and listen always for where God may be showing you His plan.

GOOD SHEPHERD, *whether it be a life changing moment for me or a time where You use me in someone else's life, help me to watch and listen for You.*

# THE KIND OF GUY HE WAS

*For the Lord God is a sun and shield; he bestows favour and honour. No good thing does the Lord withhold from those who walk uprightly.* —PSALM 84:11

In 1942, Japan invaded the Philippines and marched 10,000 Americans 100 miles to a work camp in the jungle in what became known as the Bataan Death March. Only 4,000 survived the brutality of their Japanese captors. One of those survivors was Abie Abraham.

After the war, and after surviving the horror of Japanese captivity and torture, he could have come home. He could also have been angry and bitter. Instead, he gave the next 30 months to help find the bodies of his fellow soldiers.

Abie would go on to write two books about the Bataan Death March and volunteer at the Butler, Pa., Veteran's Administration. He died at age 98.

A friend said, "He gave two-and-a-half years of his freedom to make sure those men were properly identified, that their bodies were taken care of. That's just the kind of guy Abie was." Another shared, "I never saw or heard him say anything bad about anybody."

"I was never one of those guys, hero guys wearing medals and all that," Abie once said.

Honor and loyalty, particularly to this level, are rare human traits. Constantly challenge yourself toward a higher level of personal honor. Keep inspiration in your life to excel in loyalty and integrity. If you do, your life will not only matter here and now, but even years after you are gone— just like Abie Abraham.

LIGHT OF THE WORLD, *You are the source of all good things. Grow me, mold me, shape me in Your qualities for my life to make a difference.*

# THE RISK OF "IF"

*For he stands at the right hand of the needy, to save them from those who would condemn them to death.* —PSALM 109:31

Marine Lance Corporal Winder Perez was wounded in a Taliban attack in southern Afghanistan. But there were some extenuating circumstances to his wound. A 12-inch live remnant from an RPG—rocket propelled grenade—was lodged in his leg.

A crew of four New Mexico National Guardsmen agreed to take the risk of flying Perez by medevac helicopter to get medical care.

"Each of us on the aircraft had to agree to take the patient on," Specialist Mark Edens said. "There was quite a bit of alarm among the crew at the time, as you can imagine," Captain Kevin Doo added. "If the RPG exploded, you know Specialist Edens and Sergeant Hardesty are working on the patient directly over him, shrapnel alone would have been devastating. And about 18 inches behind where the patient is lying is over 300

gallons of jet aviation fuel, and it would have been catastrophic."

So they flew the 65 miles to the nearest field hospital, cautiously trying to keep Perez's condition stable.

When the helicopter landed, the team stayed outside the facility. Navy Lieutenant Commander James Gennari and Army Staff Sergeant Ben Summerfield, an explosives expert, began removing the RPG section from his leg.

Wearing full combat gear and a flak jacket, Summerfield finally pulled the RPG from Perez's leg, so that medical teams could treat his injuries. The soldier recovered from the wound.

Whether you have never been in a crisis such as this, or your job requires this level of risk almost daily, it is once again a reminder that our lives are not in our own hands and not under our control.

HEAVENLY CARETAKER, *today I recognize that You are in control of my life. Guide me in the simple, daily choices, and the hard calls.*

# THE WOMEN OF WAR

*Charm is deceitful, and beauty is vain, but a woman who fears the Lord is to be praised.* —PROVERBS 31:30

In October, 1997, the "Women in Military Service for America Memorial" was dedicated at Arlington National Cemetery. It is a national memorial honoring the women who have served in our nation's defense in all branches of the service.

Today, over 400,000 women serve as active duty, Guard, or Reserve. Here are a few historical facts about women in service.

During World War I, over 12,000 women were the first to enlist in the Navy and Marines and all served stateside.

In World War II, approximately 400,000 American military women served stateside and overseas in the Army, Navy, Marines, Coast Guard, and in the Women Air Force Service Pilots. They served in every theater of the war. Eighty-eight female military nurses were held prisoners of war, while more than 460 lost their lives.

Seven thousand American military women served in Southeast Asia during the Vietnam War. The majority were military nurses assigned to military hospitals, air evacuation, hospital ships, and field units. The eight women who died are memorialized on the wall at the Vietnam Veterans' Memorial.

The first female fighter pilot to deliver a payload of missiles and laser-guided bombs in combat was in the first wave of strikes against Iraq in Operation Desert Fox. After 9-11, when Operation Enduring Freedom was launched, women were among the first deployed troops.

In an ever-increasing manner, women have taken on critical roles of military service for our nation. We all owe deep respect to all of the women who daily serve our country.

LORD OF ALL, *please bless today each woman who is serving our nation and their families as they are away. Guide them, guard them, and give to each, as they need.*

# A KICK IN THE HEAD

*Even though you intended to do harm to me, God intended it for good, in order to preserve a numerous people, as he is doing today.* —GENESIS 50:20

Many years ago, a horse kicked Stan Brock in the head, nearly killing him. There was no doctor nearby—in the Amazon Rain Forest. He had to recover on his own.

"It kind of jarred my thinking into, 'Hey, let's bring these doctors a little bit closer than 26 days on foot,'" Stan said.

He got his pilot's license and a small plane to bring medical care to the people with whom he worked.

"Instead of taking weeks and weeks, the airplane could get there in just a few hours," he said. "[If] somebody was badly hurt or injured, we could put them in the back of the airplane and take them somewhere for care."

In 1985, Stan started a nonprofit, Remote Area Medical. Since then, the all-volunteer group has offered more than 660 medical clinics worldwide, providing free health care to half a million people. Stan said, "The patients are so grateful for what we're able to do for them."

Though he started as an overseas venture, Stan soon got so busy in the United States that he had to cut back on foreign commitments.

More than 70,000 people, many of them full-time doctors and nurses, have donated their time and expertise to Stan's cause over the years.

"It always has been a volunteer effort," Stan said. "All these people, they're buying their own hotel and paying their own travel expenses to get here."

For Stan Brock, that kick in the head prompted health care for over half a million people.

How about you? What does God want to use in your life to help others?

MIGHTY GOD, *help me to see any and all opportunities You place around me every day. Don't let me miss anything that You have for me.*

# SENSE OF SECURITY

*I lift up my eyes to the hills—from where will my help come? My help comes from
the Lord, who made heaven and earth.* —PSALM 121:1-2

When Iraq War veteran James McQuoid returned home from his second tour, his mind was still in the war zone.

When a child cried, he heard kids screaming in Fallujah. Jingling coins reminded him of ammunition.

James has post-traumatic stress disorder (PTSD) and suffers from flashbacks, nightmares, and a heightened sense of alertness. He was having nightmares every night.

Paranoid, he isolated himself, even from his wife. "I'd stay in my house all the time," said James. "Windows were blacked out. I had cameras on the outside, so I could monitor the area."

Then, through veteran Mary Cortani's non-profit called Operation Freedom Paws, James was introduced to a service dog named Iggie. She explains, "They have an injury that people don't understand. They have to find a way to balance what they're feeling, what they've experienced, with everyday life. Service dogs are but one tool in the healing process for our veterans."

Iggie wakes James from nightmares, turns off lights, creates space for him in public places, and helps when anxiety strikes. Mary adds, "When a veteran trains their own service dog, they have a mission and a purpose again. It gives them something to focus on and to complete, a sense of security and safety. They've always got their buddy at the end of the leash. My life is blessed every day that I get to spend time with these amazing men and women who've served our country."

A life committed to service is meeting practical needs. Protect and nurture your own service by making sure you are always connect to people and stay on the front lines of love in action.

PRINCE OF *PEACE, lead me to stay connected to people and acting on Your behalf to meet needs. I pray today for peace and healing for our men and women with PTSD.*

# COME, FOLLOW ME

*But those who do what is true come to the light, so that it may be clearly seen that their deeds have been done in God.* —JOHN 3:21

One day a young man walked up to Jesus and asked, "Teacher, what good deed must I do to have eternal life?" And he said to him, "Why do you ask me about what is good? There is only one who is good. If you wish to enter into life, keep the commandments."

He said to him, "Which ones?" And Jesus said, "You shall not murder; You shall not commit adultery; You shall not steal; You shall not bear false witness; Honour your father and mother; also, You shall love your neighbor as yourself."

The young man said to him, "I have kept all these; what do I still lack?"

Jesus said to him, "If you wish to be perfect, go, sell your possessions, and give the money to the poor, and you will have treasure in heaven; then come, follow me."

When the young man heard this word, he went away grieving, for he had many possessions (Matthew 19:16-22).

Jesus was explaining to this young man that the life God offers has two sides—the first is obeying His commands. But the second is about actively loving people in His name. God knows we can't be perfect and keep all the Law—that's why He sent Jesus to die in our place and offer us a relationship with Him.

Be certain today that your service to people is an expression of Your love for God, not an attempt to gain God's approval. No amount of good deeds can get us into Heaven. That is only through a relationship with Christ. Serving people is simply an expression of our love for God.

AUTHOR OF *LOVE*, thank You that I don't have to work for Your approval, but You accept me through Christ, as I accept Christ and desire to serve Him.

# IN THE NAME OF LOVE

*He has told you, O mortal, what is good; and what does the Lord require of you*
*but to do justice, and to love kindness, and to walk humbly with your God?*
—MICAH 6:8

Bono, the iconic lead singer and front man for the legendary rock band U2, once said, "Celebrity is currency, so I wanted to use mine effectively."

The rock star has two different types of fans. The obvious ones who love his music; the second are those who respect and appreciate all he has done with his platform to serve people. He has proactively fought poverty and hunger since the mid-1980s. When he meets with world leaders, he doesn't talk about fame and hit records, but about getting funds to needy people and making effective change for good.

In 1986, Bono was taken to Ethiopia with World Vision for a first-hand look at third world poverty. There, Bono and his wife developed an education program to spread information on health, hygiene, and other issues. He followed that trip with visits to Nicaragua and El Salvador to draw attention to those conflicts and to help the children there.

Bono has helped to create the ONE, DATA, RED, and EDUN campaigns. He was on Forbes' Generous Celebrity List for his work to fight the spread of AIDS and for debt relief in Africa. He donated $50,000 to One in Four Ireland, a charity that helps survivors of sexual abuse, and has received three nominations for the Nobel Peace Prize. His humanitarian work led to his being knighted by the Queen of England in 2007.

Bono shared, "A wise man told me, 'Stop asking God to bless what you're doing. Get involved in what God is doing, because it's already blessed.'"

That's a great word. So—get involved in what God is already doing—today.

LORD OF ALL, *lead me into what You are doing and blessing. And help me to use my life and influence effectively for good too.*

# UNITED EFFORT

*Make every effort to maintain the unity of the Spirit in the bond of peace.*
—EPHESIANS 4:3

When most people think of the United States military, they think of soldiers on bases throughout the world, and troops stationed in Afghanistan. But the U.S. Armed Forces are also our nation's strongest first responder team, on American soil and overseas, present in times of disasters such as:—Earthquakes—Floods—Hurricanes—Snowstorms—Tornadoes—Tsunamis—Wildfires.

Lieutenant General Ken Keen, U.S. Army Commander, Joint Task Force states, "When an international humanitarian crisis occurs, the U.S. military is often called upon to be a first responder with its capacity to provide robust logistics, manpower resources, and life saving aid."

In any given year, the U.S. military conducts humanitarian projects in nearly 100 nations. Some examples from recent years are: —Operation African Lion—a group from all service branches that provided medical care to five villages in Morocco. —Operation Balikatan—a joint effort by the U.S. Army surgeons and the Armed Forces of the Philippines Nurse Corps to provide medical care in the Philippines. —Mission Dire Dawa—a military effort to eliminate parasite infestation in Ethiopia.

Marine Corps Major General Timothy Ghormley said, "We're waging peace, and we're waging it as hard as we can."

The United States has long been an example to the world of cooperation, unity, and righteousness. You are a crucial cog in that wheel. Be a force of good in the world today.

SOVEREIGN GOD, *thank You for our rich history of service to the world. Guide me, lead me, to be a force of Your work today.*

# FACE TO FACE

*In the beginning when God created the heavens and the earth.* —GENESIS 1:1

Lord Kelvin, the British inventor who formulated the second law of thermodynamics, said, "The commencement of life upon Earth certainly did not take place by any action of chemistry or electricity or crystalline grouping of molecules. We must pause, face to face, with the mystery and miracle of the creation of living creatures."

Dr. Robert Millikan, American nuclear physicist and Nobel Peace Prize winner, stated, "Just as behind this watch there had to be a watchmaker, so behind the intricate precision and timing of this great Universe, there had to be a Great Creator or Designer!"

British scientist Sir Isaac Newton, who formulated the laws of gravitation and motion, stated, "There are more sure marks of authenticity in the Bible than in any profane history. All my discoveries have been made in answer to prayer. I can take my telescope and look millions of miles into space; but, I can go away to my room and in prayer get nearer to God and Heaven than I can when assisted by all the telescopes of Earth."

Scientists have long been known more for questioning God and creation than supporting it. However, many scientists have come to the conclusion that the Scriptures are accurate.

Our personal belief of where we come from strongly affects our self-esteem.

CREATOR GOD, *I believe You created me with purpose and for a purpose. Thank You for life and breath. May I use both well today as I serve in Your name.*

# VOTE EVERY DAY

*We have gifts that differ according to the grace given to us: prophecy, in proportion to faith; ministry, in ministering; the teacher, in teaching; the exhorter, in exhortation; the giver, in generosity; the leader, in diligence; the compassionate, in cheerfulness.* —ROMANS 12:6-8

---

*Volunteers don't just do the work. They make it work.*
—CAROL PETTIT

*Volunteers are not paid, not because they are worthless, but because they are priceless.*
—UNKNOWN

*I always wondered why somebody didn't do something about that. Then I realized I was somebody.*
—LILY TOMLIN

*Volunteers do not necessarily have the time; they just have the heart.*
— ELIZABETH ANDREW

*One of the greatest diseases is to be nobody to anybody.*
—MOTHER TERESA

*Volunteering is the ultimate exercise in democracy. You vote in elections once a year, but when you volunteer, you vote every day about the kind of community you want to live in.*
—UNKNOWN

---

There is literally an army of volunteers in our country. Recent studies report that 62.8 million adults volunteer 8.1 billion hours in local and national organizations, valued at almost $173 billion, if paid for.

Whether your area of service is paid, underpaid, or volunteer, you are being somebody to everybody, to turn Mother Teresa's phrase. Even when you work alone or feel alone, know that you matter and your work is making a difference for many.

HEAVENLY FATHER, *I want to keep making a difference in my community, making it a better and safer place in which to live. Lead me, guide me, empower me.*

# NO REGRETS

*If you are pure and upright, surely then he will rouse himself for you and restore to you your rightful place. Though your beginning was small, your latter days will be very great.* —JOB 8:6-7

Doyle "Bodie" Glennon, Jr. was awarded EMT of the Year for the State of Louisiana, as well as the Robert E. Motley EMT of the Year Award, given by the National Association of Emergency Medical Technicians at the EMS Expo.

Working as an EMT for over 10 years, he said, "As silly or naïve as this may sound, I know that something I do makes a difference."

Here's the irony of Bodie's dedication to EMS: he earns $7.35 an hour and receives no benefits. He works 48 hours on duty, followed by 48 hours off duty. Every other weekend, he works 72 hours straight.

The ambulance service he works for has been seriously affected by Medicare changes and a large number of people living in the area have incomes well below the poverty line.

The company operates two ambulances and runs approximately 15 calls a day.

With a wife and two children to take care of, he said, "You learn to cut a lot of corners. My wife is quite frugal and good at managing money." When asked if he's ever regretted getting into EMS, Bodie answers, "No. Never. I like the idea of being able to help. It is what I was put on this earth to do."

The decision that taking care of people and saving lives is worth more than acquiring things is an honorable and respectable choice.

Be encouraged that you rank among the best this nation has to offer. Be proud of that place, while humbled by your fellow service members.

FAITHFUL ONE, *thank You that I stand beside amazing men and women in this nation who put others before themselves. I commit my place in this circle to You.*

# BRACE FOR IMPACT

*The Lord is my light and my salvation; whom shall I fear? The Lord is the stronghold of my life; of whom shall I be afraid?* —PSALM 27:1

Captain Chesley "Sully" Sullenberger and First Officer Jeff Skiles had just taken off from LaGuardia Airport on Flight 1549 when they struck a flock of large birds and lost power in both engines.

"It was the worst sickening, pit-of-your-stomach, falling-through-the-floor feeling I've ever felt in my life," Sully said. "I knew immediately it was very bad."

As he took over the controls from Skiles, his mind raced with the moment he saw the birds enter his screen, the noises they made on impact, the distance to reach an airport, and of course, the river below. The flight attendants, along with the 150 passengers were told to "brace for impact" as the jetliner angled down toward the Hudson River, relying only on gravity and Sully's skills.

He miraculously managed to glide the aircraft safely onto the water. Within minutes, the crew helped their passengers out on the aircraft's wings and first responders from New York City arrived quickly to rescue passengers and crew as the plane began to sink into the freezing water.

Regarding the first responders, Sully said, "Thank you seems totally inadequate. I have a debt of gratitude that I fear I may never be able to repay."

There were two great dangers in this harrowing incident. The first was the possibility of a fatal crash. The second was people drowning inside or outside the plane. Sully avoided the first and first responders avoided the second.

All 155 lives were saved through quick response, skill, and providential grace.

Today, in your area of service, work and train hard, but always pray harder.

SAVIOR, keep *my mind alert, my heart refreshed, my skills sharp, and my knees bowed.*

# LORD, IS THAT YOU?

*[Jesus said] "Let anyone with ears to hear listen"* —MARK 4:23

Mary Phillips, a patient-care supervisor for 15 years at a St. Louis hospice, tells how her first responder was a dog.

"My friend, Pat, dropped by my office with Jacques Pierre, her Maltipoo. He kept his distance from me. I grumbled, 'Is this really a good place for a dog?' Pat answered, 'Jacques Pierre has a special way with people when they're sick.'

"I went outside and called my daughter. Suddenly, I felt a tremendous pain in my right temple. I heard my daughter say, 'Mom, what's the matter?' I staggered inside and while lying on the floor of my office, was praying for relief.

"The door flew open. It was Pat with Jacques Pierre. 'What's going on?' she asked. The dog ran up and started licking me in one spot—my right temple. 'Does Jacques Pierre know something I don't?' I wondered. 'Lord, are you trying to warn me?'

"I told Pat, 'Take me to the emergency room.'

"The ER doctor reported, 'You have a brain aneurysm near your right temple. We have to operate right now.'

"Two months later, I went back to work. Pat was there with Jacques Pierre. At first, I was disappointed that he didn't lick my hand the way he always did others. Then it occurred to me: If Jacques Pierre was back to keeping his distance from me, it must mean my crisis was over. I could get back to being me."

God can use many unique methods to inform and warn us—even a dog. Listen. Watch. Be alert. He will speak to You today.

FAITHFUL ONE, *I want to learn to hear Your voice—in my own heart and in unique ways, such as today's story. Help me to have ears to hear You.*

# A PASSIONATE CALLING

*I am grateful to Christ Jesus our Lord, who has strengthened me, because he judged me faithful and appointed me to his service.* —1 TIMOTHY 1:12

Inspirational speaker and writer Karen McCracken penned "The Paramedic."

*Skilled ready hands, sirens blaring fierce*
*A willing heart to serve, sounds of tragedy pierce*
*Twenty-four with no rest, who else would they send*
*Exhausted he returns still and back yet again*
*Sharpening his blade, educating his brain*
*For when the tones command, objectivity must remain*
*There's no turning back, though fears never fade*
*With life or with loss, the call has been made*
*Precise decisions come forth, made with lightning speed*
*No time for second-guessing, the calls has its needs*
*Axe and hammer aside, air tank strapped*
*These mere tools of the trade don't define the real craft*
*For stamina and strength, willfullness and heart*
*Sureness and speed are the utter most parts*
*When a call comes forth, no time for a toss*
*The first responder is made at his very first loss*
*The man who acts brave, but denies real pain*
*Is a coward inside and toils in vain*
*For as years quickly run, every face he will see*
*Pronounced guilt and pain will never flee*
*His soul sinks so deep and the veil deftly falls*
*Across the eyes to mask hurt from each tragic call*
*Resonating far too long, each tragedy that came*
*Yet again he musters up to do twenty-four yet again*
*A hero they call him, but to him he's just a man*
*With a passionate calling to save lives, if he can*

DELIVERER, *give me courage when I fear. Peace when I fret. Hope when I doubt. And love when I don't know what to do.*

# STOPPING A SILENT KILLER

*A bad messenger brings trouble, but a faithful envoy, healing.* —PROVERBS 13:17

Do you know the leading cause of death in Africa among children? Malaria. And a child asleep in his bed at night has no way of fending off the silent deliverers of the disease. That is, until Nothing But Nets was launched.

Nothing But Nets is a global, grassroots campaign to raise awareness and funding to fight malaria.

A column by Rick Reilly about malaria in Sports Illustrated led to the creation of the campaign in 2006. In just a few years, it has engaged hundreds of thousands of people to try to end malaria deaths on the continent.

With a diverse group of partners from the United Methodist Church to the Boy Scouts of America to VH1, the success of Nothing But Nets is a testament to the power of passionate people coming together to make the world a better, healthier place. Anyone can make a difference by providing a long-lasting, insecticide-treated bed net, distributing it, and educating communities on its use.

With partners in the field such as UNICEF, the UN Refugee Agency, and the World Health Organization able to transport the nets to Africa, distribute them to families, and educate them on proper use, lives are literally being saved.

A constant theme in this book is how easy it is to make a difference in the world. We hope you will find new places to give and serve, while you receive encouragement and strength for where you already give and serve.

HEALER, it *is amazing the many avenues that You have shown me where a small gift or a simple effort can literally save and heal. Thank You that You allow me to be Your hands and feet to the world.*

# UNDER GOD

*But incline our hearts to him, to walk in all his ways, and to keep his commandments, his statutes, and his ordinances, which he commanded our ancestors.*
—1 KINGS 8:58

Dwight D. Eisenhower will forever be known as a great general and a great president.

He was the first president to officially join a church while in office. On February 1, 1953, a few weeks after his first inauguration, he was baptized and became a member of the National Presbyterian Church in Washington, D.C.

The words "under God" were added to the Pledge of Allegiance during the Eisenhower administration. He said in a speech on Flag Day, June 14, 1954, after signing a bill authorizing the added words, "In this way we are reaffirming the transcendence of religious faith in America's heritage and future; in this way we shall constantly strengthen those spiritual weapons which forever will be our country's most powerful resource in peace and war. These words will remind Americans that, despite our great physical strength, we must remain humble. They will help us to keep constantly in our minds and hearts the spiritual and moral principles which alone give dignity to man, and upon which, our way of life is founded."

The presence and importance of God and faith has been quietly leaving the political realm, as our culture moves toward more secular values. Yet, throughout history, God has never conquered nations through politics, but rather by gathering the hearts of His children—one at a time. Keep your heart focused on Him.

MERCIFUL GOD, *help me to stay encouraged to follow You, no matter who does or doesn't. May I be one who leads others toward You—by words and actions.*

# LIVING MEMORIALS

*Remember for my good, O my God, all that I have done for this people.*
—NEHEMIAH 5:19

On any Memorial Day, there is a group of former Navy Seals who won't be cooking out or hanging out at the lake. They'll be on a journey.

Carry The Load (CTL) is a 1,700-mile, 27-day relay from West Point, New York to Dallas, Texas. The non-profit organization, founded by Clint Bruce, supports organizations that help veteran families.

Clint is a U.S. Naval Academy graduate and former SEAL. CTL's mission is to bring back the true meaning of the holiday—honoring men and women who gave their lives for our nation.

The organization invites veterans, surviving families, and all others to join the relay. Individuals, businesses, and organizations sponsor segments of the relay to help families of fallen heroes.

Along the way, participants also collect stories of American soldiers, police officers, fire fighters, first responders, and other service men and women who have lost their lives in the line of duty.

When asked about how the 1,700-mile trek symbolized CTL, Bruce responded, "At mile 20, when you don't have any more and you start walking for someone else, the pain kind of goes away. You start thinking about the person who was willing to do these things for you."

When any of our troops lose their lives, it is important that we all work to keep their memory alive and support their families by all means possible. We must all remember that their deaths afford our lives in a free land by and through the grace of God.

COMFORTER, thank *You for the freedom that I can so easily take for granted. May I be a good steward of my time, energy, and service today.*

# UNDER THE RADAR

*Let every person be subject to the governing authorities; for there is no authority except from God, and those authorities that exist have been instituted by God.*
—ROMANS 13:1

A police officer had found the perfect hiding place for watching for speeders on a long, straight stretch of road. After several successful, busy days of writing tickets, he noticed that everyone passing by was at or under the speed limit.

Growing suspicious, he asked another officer to drive the stretch of road to check things out. Soon, the officer pulled up and informed his partner that he had found two grade school age boys that had taken advantage of the speed trap.

The first boy was standing a hundred yards down the road on the shoulder, holding a sign that read "SPEED TRAP AHEAD." Then about a hundred yards past the officer was his accomplice, holding a second sign that read "TIPS HERE." There was a bucket beside him full of ones, fives, and tens from grateful drivers. The officers quickly broke up the boys' "ring" and informed their parents.

Badges, police cars, weapons, and uniforms are the items that a city, county, or state gives a man or woman to display the fact that they are law enforcement officers. But there is another invisible quality given to these officers—authority.

Authority stands behind the badge, the gun, the car, or the uniform. It creates the grace to handle a mischievous boy or the power to apprehend a threatening criminal. As respect for authority erodes in our culture, let us uphold honor and valor in our area of service. Today's story is humorous, but may we be known as those who uphold respect for all—particularly those in authority over us.

LORD GOD, *You are my ultimate authority. I know You have placed all authorities. Help me to respect, whether I support or disagree.*

# WHAT IF IT BECAME A HABIT?

*If I give away all my possessions, and if I hand over my body so that I may boast, but do not have love, I gain nothing.* —1 CORINTHIANS 13:3

Doug Eaton wanted to celebrate his 65th birthday in a big way, so he asked his friends for ideas. "One of my friends said, 'Why don't you do 65 random acts of kindness?'"

So Doug spent 65 minutes standing on a busy intersection in Oklahoma City, handing out $375 in $5 bills to people passing by. Many people said, "I can't believe this" or "bless you" as he handed them the cash. Others were reluctant to take his money, as he told them, "It's okay, it's just a blessing," then he explained about his birthday.

Doug said, "Some people who don't take the money just say, 'Man, I love what you are doing. I won't take it, but give it to someone who needs it.'"

During the same day, Doug paid $50 for his $12 haircut and $10 for his $1.09 cup of coffee, bought lunch for several people at a local restaurant, and gave bus fare to a stranger. "This day has been one of the biggest blessings of my life," he said. "I don't know if I can wait until another birthday to do this again.

But what if it became a habit? Or what if a lot of people did their birthday number of random acts of kindness on their birthday? How good would that be?"

As amazing as this idea is, God intends to use us every day to show His love and kindness to the world. He loves us, then we share that love with others. It really is that simple. As you serve today, watch for your "random" moments.

AUTHOR OF LOVE, *the money, time, energy, and care that You want me to share— show me where You want it to go. Help me be faithful to listen and obey.*

# A BIBLE AND A COIN

*So faith by itself, if it has no works, is dead. But someone will say, "You have faith and I have works." Show me your faith without works, and I by my works will show you my faith.* —JAMES 2:17-18

George Muller was known as a man of prayer and action.

He incorporated both by operating an orphanage in England on faith. Here is one such account: "The children are dressed and ready for school, but there is no food," the housemother informed him. George asked her to seat the 300 children in the dining room. He thanked God for the food and waited. Within minutes, a baker knocked on the door. "Mr. Mueller," he said, "last night I could not sleep. Somehow I knew that you would need bread this morning. I got up and baked three batches for you. I will bring it in."

Soon, a milkman knocked at the door. His cart had broken down out front. The milk would spoil by the time the wheel was fixed. He asked George if he could use some free milk. George smiled as the milkman brought in ten large containers.

More than 10,000 children lived in the orphanage over the years. When each child was old enough to leave, George would pray with him and put a Bible in his right hand and a coin in his left. He explained to the young person that if he held onto what was in his right hand, God would always make sure there was something in his left hand also.

The balance between faith and work will always be delicate, but the Christian life requires both. God asks us to trust Him for His part, while we do ours. Today's story about George Muller shows what amazing things can happen when we find the balance.

PROVIDER, *help me to balance my faith and action. Lead me to grow in both. Teach me to rely upon You, as I step out in faith.*

# RAPID RESPONSE

*For it was you who formed my inward parts; you knit me together in my mother's womb. I praise you, for I am fearfully and wonderfully made. Wonderful are your works; that I know very well.* —PSALM 139:13-14

A routine traffic stop quickly changed to crisis as Officer Humberto Franco noticed that one of the occupants of the car he'd stopped was concealing a weapon.

Radioing for help, Van Nuys Area Gang Impact Team Officers Thomas Appleby and Isaac Moreno arrived on the scene and ordered the passengers out.

One passenger ran from the car, into traffic, pulling a handgun from his pants, and firing several shots at the officers.

Franco apprehended the other suspects while Appleby and Moreno chased the shooter who attempted to take a hostage. With the help of a security guard, the officers finally captured the suspect, after he continuously fired his weapon even after being wounded.

The entire episode occurred within two minutes and put more than one hundred people at risk. All the officers were required to make numerous split-second decisions both to protect bystanders and decide when to fire on the suspect.

It is always amazing to hear how law enforcement officers, firefighters, and military troops can couple trained skill with momentary decisions that simultaneously save lives and stops evil. God is involved when the body, brain, and spirit harmoniously take care of business.

MIGHTY GOD, *Your creation is amazing, but none so much as the human mind, body, and spirit. Thank You for how You enable us to connect them to do our jobs with excellence.*

# BE A GAME CHANGER

*Go also the second mile.* —MATTHEW 5:41b

During the economic recession of the past few years, firefighters have battled blazes in foreclosed and abandoned homes.

Often a home is fully ablaze and threatening other homes or structures before anyone realizes it.

The city of Detroit has had a particularly difficult bout with these blazes, creating a heavier workload. But this hasn't hindered the first responder's desire to save property and lives.

One Detroit man escaped from his home when a fire broke out.

As firemen arrived, the man realized his two dogs were trapped inside. He frantically urged the firemen to go in and rescue his dogs.

Moments later, firefighters brought out two dogs. "You're going to have to stand back, sir," the men told the animals' owner.

The man, emotional, pets them trying to see any sign of life, but they do not respond.

Then, one of the firefighters kneels down and takes off his air supply and puts it over the snout of the animals, one at a time. Within a few minutes, both dogs begin to respond, open their eyes, and breathe again on their own. The dogs' owner stretches out his hand to the firefighter, thanking him for saving the lives of his beloved friends.

This level of attention and care is what makes firefighters—as all first responders—heroes. The fireman in this story cared about the man's life and his loss. His actions changed the outcome of the story. He was a game changer.

What story will God use you to change today? Pay attention—and care. It's always worth it.

FAITHFUL ONE, *there are stories out there that I will be able to change how they end. Guide me, lead me, to watch and stay ready to be where You want, to do what You want.*

# PREPARED TO GO

*You have given me the shield of your salvation, and your help has made me great.*
*You have made me stride freely, and my feet do not slip.* —2 Samuel 22:36-37

"Dr. Livingstone, I presume?" has long been a catchphrase since journalist and explorer H. M. Stanley found missionary David Livingstone in the jungles of Africa as the only white person within several hundred miles, after Livingstone was presumed to be "missing."

Livingstone was well known for his exploration of Africa and his humanitarian work. He inspired abolitionists of the slave trade, explorers, and missionaries. He opened up Central Africa to missionaries who established education and health care for Africans, as well as opened up trade with the British. Livingstone was held in high regard by many African chiefs and tribes.

Attempts to navigate a certain African river prompted another famous quote, "I am prepared to go anywhere, provided it be forward."

Livingstone's faith is evident in his journal, where one entry reads: "I place no value on anything I have or may possess, except in relation to the kingdom of Christ. If anything will advance the interests of the kingdom, it shall be given away or kept, only as by giving or keeping it I shall promote the glory of Him to whom I owe all my hopes in time and eternity."

It has been said that there are two types of people in the world—pioneers and settlers. Pioneers go into uncharted territory and blaze new trails for others to follow, while settlers follow the proven trails and work the land.

As you serve, pioneer new trails in your area of service. "Promote the glory of Him to whom [you] owe all [your] hopes in time and eternity."

IMMANUEL, take *me where You want me to go, as long as You are with me. May Your Spirit guide me to blaze new trails in my lifetime.*

# 500 ROUNDS

*O Lord, my Lord, my strong deliverer, you have covered my head in the day of battle. Do not grant, O Lord, the desires of the wicked; do not further their evil plot.* —PSALM 140:7-8

Los Angeles police officers Trevor Jackson and Rich Ramos were on patrol on a foggy night when, at 3 a.m., they heard a call that a police cruiser was in pursuit of an apparent drunk driver. The pair joined the chase.

And then, through the fog, shots were fired.

A recent controversial case had caused the department to issue a policy that officers could not fire at a vehicle without proof of threat and permission.

The car did a U-turn and opened fire on the line of patrol cars. Again and again the shooter drives by and fires, but no officer shot back.

What the police didn't yet know was that the 20-year-old driver had a plan to die. He told his friends to watch the news, because he was "going out like Scarface." He had 500 rounds of ammunition in his car.

Finally, Officer Jackson lowered his window and aimed his shotgun. As he saw muzzle flashes, he fired, blowing out the windows. Ramos then fired 17 shots, while Jackson emptied two magazines from his Glock.

The vehicle careened out of control and smashed through a wrought-iron fence, stopping in a parking lot. Both men inside were still shooting. Sixteen more officers eventually assumed positions and opened fire.

By the end of the shoot-out, the passenger was dead and the driver was still alive, but with 22 gunshot wounds.

This became the third largest gun battle in the history of the Los Angeles Police Department, but not one officer was hurt.

Situations such as this are why every law enforcement officer deserves our respect and needs our prayers.

MIGHTY GOD, *first responders are also often front liners who place themselves between the innocent and harm's way. Protect those who protect and save those who serve.*

# WATER-TIGHT WAYS

*For the word of the Lord is upright, and all his work is done in faithfulness.*
—PSALM 33:4

Ten principles from Noah and the ark:

1. Remember that we are all in the same boat.
2. Plan ahead. It wasn't raining when Noah was building the ark.
3. Stay fit. When you're 600 years old, someone may ask you to do something big.
4. Don't listen to critics; just get on with the job that you need to do.
5. Build your future on high ground.
6. For safety's sake, travel in pairs.
7. Speed isn't always an advantage. The snails were on board with the cheetahs.
8. When you are stressed, just float for a while.
9. Remember that the ark was built by an amateur; the Titanic by professionals.
10. No matter how bad the storm, when God is with you, there's always a rainbow coming.

There is much practical wisdom to be found in each of the Bible's stories and Noah is no exception. It is a great thing to consistently read the Bible, but an even better practice to regularly study God's Word. As you dig into it, God will increase your understanding.

AUTHOR OF LIFE, *thank You for the gift and truth of Your Word. Give me understanding by Your Spirit as I read and study what You say to me.*

# DIVING DEEP

*"You shall love the Lord your God with all your heart, and with all your soul, and with all your mind." This is the greatest and first commandment. And a second is like it: "You shall love your neighbor as yourself." —MATTHEW 22:37-39*

Master Deputy Kenneth Kay of the Wake County, N.C., Sheriff's Department received a call to respond where two children, a 10-year-old girl and a 7-year-old boy, were fishing with family members at a dam in the Neuse River. They waded into what looked like still water, but were pulled under.

Kenneth and two Raleigh police officers arrived and jumped into the water, despite the dangerous currents. Deputy Kay said, "Going underneath, we could not see anything." He said that currents were so strong underneath the surface, another officer had to push him down to get to the bottom.

Jeff Hammerstein of the Wake County Emergency Medical Services, said, "The currents can easily pull a person under and hold them under."

Fishermen say the rushing water near the dam is too dangerous to enter.

Though the water appeared still where the children went in, currents whipped up by the dam, churned by objects underneath, make the area especially unpredictable. The children's bodies were found four hours later.

"I have a little girl at home and I kind of look at it the same way, if my kid is in there, I'm going to stay in there," Deputy Kay said.

What drives first responders to take every circumstance they encounter as one they can save? The deputy's last quote said it all. They have to put themselves in a "what-would-I-want-done-for-me-and-my-family" position. Every time they do, though, it brings a physical, mental, and emotional risk. This has to come from a place deep in the soul accompanied by God-given strength.

STRONG TOWER, *grow my heart in my love and care for people. Deepen my soul to put others before myself, no matter the risk.*

# HARVESTING CHANGE

*And these are the ones sown on the good soil: they hear the word and accept it and bear fruit, thirty and sixty and a hundredfold.* —MARK 4:20

In the 1980s, a trend became popular for music artists to play for benefit concerts that raise money and awareness for various world causes. Most were one-time events.

But in 1985, when Willie Nelson, Neil Young, and John Mellencamp put together their first Farm Aid event, little did they know that over 25 years later, they would still be at it and would have formed a non-profit to help farmers year-round.

To date, Farm Aid has raised and distributed over $40 million dollars toward preserving American agriculture and saving the family farm.

In 2001, Dave Matthews added his name and voice to the cause.

Farm Aid has four focal areas.

1. To promote Americans buying locally grown food from farmers. TV, radio, web, and print media are all utilized to promote this aspect.

2. To open up new markets for the family farmer—providing more opportunities for farmers to sell and consumers to purchase.

3. To provide assistance to any family farm that needs help. A 1-800-FARM-AID number is staffed to help farmers who call.

4. To bring governmental change and to rally citizen support of the American family farm.

We can learn from these artists about longevity to an area of service. It's the difference in looking at the world through a windshield and a telescope. God wants to help us focus and commit to our personal passion, so that years down the road, we not only are still taking action, but we are making effective change, because we have aimed straight. So—focus, take aim, and pray for your passion.

GREAT SHEPHERD, *there is much to be said for staying power. Help me to focus on and be committed to where You want my energy placed.*

# TAKE A 180

*The human mind may devise many plans, but it is the purpose of the Lord that will be established.* —PROVERBS 19:21

At the Aurora movie theatre on the night of the Batman movie premiere where the horrific shootings took place in 2012, Jarell Brooks, an 18-year-old pastor's son, started to crawl toward the exit when he bumped into a young mother, holding her 4-year-old daughter and 4-month-old son, too scared to move.

"It's just me and my kids," she said. She and her fiancé had become separated in the confusion.

"When I saw her, I kind of had to take a 180. You have to help this woman. You can't live with yourself knowing a family was hurt or killed," he said.

Jarell crawled alongside the woman and children, shielding them from the gunman. He guided her toward the door and when the mother began to stand so did Jarell. Immediately, he was hit in his left leg.

Shrapnel also struck the woman in her right leg. Jarell kept moving them along, but now he kept a hand on his wound.

Once outside the theater, they were separated.

Jarell was losing a lot of blood when paramedics rushed him to the Denver Health Medical Center.

On the Sunday after the shooting, the young family attended services at the church where Jarell's father serves as pastor. During a prayer time, the family came forward.

"God had a plan in putting Jarell where he did," his dad said.

We never know who we truly are until we're tested and God does have a plan in putting us where we are.

SAVIOR, *it is comforting to know that You ordain my days and see every moment. I want to cooperate with You to be where You need me to be, to serve.*

# LIVING LIFE HEAD-ON

*Seek the Lord and his strength, seek his presence continually.*
—1 CHRONICLES 16:11

Maine State Police Trooper Douglas Cropper spotted an 88-year-old man in a Toyota Corolla driving north in the southbound lane on I-295. He knew the elderly man, obviously confused, was endangering many lives, including his own. It was a matter of time before a head-on collision occurred. It would just depend on how many cars and people were involved.

Douglas first attempted to flag down the man, but when he did not stop, the state trooper jumped into his cruiser and drove onto the interstate. He managed to catch up to the vehicle, driving parallel to him and then pulling ahead. As he reached a crossover median lane, he turned his car into the oncoming lane, just in time to cause the man to crash into the driver's side of his cruiser. Trooper Cropper managed to stop the car with no one hurt, including the elderly man and himself.

The trooper's dash camera recorded the entire incident. A certain tragedy was once again averted by quick thinking, bravery, and skill.

When any first responder is heading into a volatile situation, the risk is understood, but must be taken to serve and save lives. It is wired into the DNA of one who protects and defends.

If your passion or motivation has been struggling lately or you have been questioning if the work is worth it, know there is a world out there that needs one such as you. Your life has a calling larger than any doubt or fear. Live out who you are today!

ALMIGHTY GOD, *give me courage larger than my fears, strength bigger than my doubts, and inspiration to live my life out loud today!*

# GOD'S BEST GIFT

*I cry to you; save me, that I may observe your decrees. I rise before dawn and cry for help; I put my hope in your words. My eyes are awake before each watch of the night, that I may meditate on your promise.* —PSALM 119:146-148

Abraham Lincoln, 16th president of the United States: "I believe the Bible is the best gift God has ever given to man. All the good from the Savior of the world is communicated to us through this book. I am profitably engaged in reading the Bible. Take all of this Book that you can by reason, and the balance by faith, and you will live and die a better man."

Theodore Roosevelt, 26th president of the United States: "A thorough knowledge of the Bible is worth more than a college education. Almost every man who has by his lifework added to the sum of human achievement has based his lifework largely upon the teachings of the Bible."

Woodrow Wilson, 28th president of the United States: "A man has deprived himself of the best there is in the World who has deprived himself of a knowledge of the Bible."

Herbert Hoover, 31st president of the United States: "There is no other book so various as the Bible, nor one so full of concentrated wisdom. Whether it be of law, business, morals, etc., he who seeks for guidance may look inside its covers and find illumination."

For every commandment and precept God gave in Scripture, He also gave us practical principles of why and how we are to follow His law. For example, we are not to murder, because we are to love and respect life. Then God sent His only Son to show us what His life looks like. The instruction manual of life is God's Word.

ALPHA & OMEGA, *thank You for giving us Your Word and then allowing us to see Your Word lived out. Guide me as I read Your Word. Lead me as I follow Your life.*

# VETERANS DAY

*The Lord goes forth like a soldier, like a warrior he stirs up his fury; he cries out, he shouts aloud, he shows himself mighty against his foes. —Isaiah 42:13*

What originally began as Armistice Day, on November 11, 1919 by President Woodrow Wilson, was officially changed by law to Veterans Day by President Dwight Eisenhower and Congress in 1954. Our nation has honored the service of all her veterans—past and current—on this day ever since.

In 1945, World War II veteran Raymond Weeks from Birmingham, Ala., had the idea to expand Armistice Day to celebrate all veterans, not just those who died in World War I. Raymond led a delegation to General Dwight Eisenhower, who supported the idea of a national Veterans Day. Weeks led the first national celebration in 1947 in Alabama and annually until his death in 1985. President Reagan honored Raymond at the White House with the Presidential Citizenship Medal in 1982 as the driving force for the national holiday. Elizabeth Dole, who prepared the briefing for President Reagan, determined Raymond as the "Father of Veterans Day."

It is estimated that there are approximately 23 million living veterans and approximately 1.5 million in current service to our nation spread over 150 countries. Today, if you are current military, you are a part of a vast portion of our population, as well as our rich history. All are grateful for your sacrifice and service to our country.

If you are a veteran or a surviving family member, all Americans are grateful for your service and salute you today. May God bless and protect all of the United States' veterans and current military today and every day.

ALMIGHTY GOD, *thank You for all those who have served, and are serving, faithfully in our military. For those who are on the front lines today, comfort and protect each one and their families.*

# THE FIRST ONE THERE

*And there are varieties of services, but the same Lord.* —1 CORINTHIANS 12:5

Andrew Hayes is an officer at Little Sandy Correctional Complex in Kentucky. Most people might think that corrections officers are only guards that keep inmates from escaping or hurting someone. But, there is much more to the job.

Andrew was the first responder to a medical emergency call for an aging inmate in the recreational area.

He didn't know if the man had a heart attack, seizure, or another health problem, but he administered CPR until the man could be sent to a hospital.

Not long afterwards, the scene was repeated when another inmate had a heart problem in a different recreational area. Andrew said, "I never dreamed it was happening again. You just react. The training they give us here helps a lot."

In both situations, Andrew commended those who helped and the quick reaction to both medical emergencies.

"I just happened to be the first one there," he said.

Andrew said his greatest reward came when he was visiting the second inmate in the hospital. "When I walked into the room, his face kind of lit up. He smiled and said, 'Thanks for saving my life.' That was probably one of the best feelings that I've gotten," he said, adding he shared a Christian message with the inmate before leaving.

There are so many facets to any first-responder role. As in Andrew's case, saving an inmate's life becomes a part of the protection a correctional officer provides. It's about serving and saving human life, regardless of the person and his/her past.

LORD OF ALL, *help me to continually broaden and expand my skills, never to stop growing professionally and personally.*

# WHEN I AM THIRSTY

*Rejoice always, pray without ceasing, give thanks in all circumstances; for this is the will of God in Christ Jesus for you.* —1 Thessalonians 5:16-18

A fellow Christian was talking to General Stonewall Jackson about the concept of continual prayer, referencing 1 Thessalonians 5:17.

"But how," said the man, "can one always be praying?"

General Jackson responded: "When we take our meals, there is the grace. When I take a draught of water, I always pause, as my palate receives the refreshment, to lift up my heart to God in thanks and prayer for the water of life. Whenever I drop a letter into the box at the post office, I send a petition along with it, for God's blessing upon its mission and upon the person to whom it is sent. When I break the seal of a letter just received, I stop to pray to God to prepare me for its contents, and make it a messenger of good. When I go to my classroom and await the arrangement of the cadets in their places, that is my time to intercede with God for them. And so of every other familiar act of the day."

'But," said the man, "do you not often forget these seasons, coming so frequently?"

"No," answered Jackson, "I have made the practice habitual to me; and I can no more forget it, than forget to drink when I am thirsty."

A concentrated and focused time of prayer is a needed daily practice to have a strong relationship with God. But being able to whisper prayers all throughout the day keeps an on-going dialogue with God and helps us constantly give things over to Him. God's help and counsel 24/7.

LIVING WATER, *teach me to pray throughout the day. Speak to me, as I learn to take every concern to You. Help me to give You all and every concern.*

# A WIN-WIN SITUATION

*The Father loves the Son and shows him all that he himself is doing; and he will show him greater works than these, so that you will be astonished.* —JOHN 5:20

When a devastating earthquake hit Haiti, former U.S. Marine Jake Wood posted this message on Facebook, "I'm going to Haiti. Who's in?"

The images on TV reminded him of his tours of duty in Iraq and Afghanistan. The skills he had acquired in the service—adapt to difficult conditions, work with limited resources, and maintain security in a dangerous environment—were all needed.

"Those are just lessons that you work at every single day in Fallujah," said Jake.

Three days later, Jake and seven others were heading into Haiti with medicine and equipment. Over the next three weeks, more than 60 volunteers from medical and military backgrounds set up triage centers in camps, treating whoever they could, and transporting people to hospitals.

Today, Jake's non-profit, Team Rubicon, has conducted 14 missions in the U.S., Chile, Pakistan, Sudan, and Myanmar.

"We realized we were more effective than many organizations that were down there with us," said Jake. "We also realized that most organizations weren't engaging vets. So we said, 'Let's try to improve this.'" He now has an army of more than 1,400 volunteers—80% of them military veterans.

"There's no limit to what veterans can do. They've already proven that they want to serve. And when they come home, a lot of them still want to do it," he said. "It's a win-win situation."

Resourceful would be a great description of Jake Wood. Connecting trained people and necessary resources to dire need time and again. Maximizing little to accomplish much is a biblical model and mandate.

PROVIDER, *it is easy to think I don't have what I need to accomplish great things, when, the truth is, if I have You and a heart to serve, I can do anything.*

# CRISIS TO CRUSADE

*But you, O Lord, are a shield around me, my glory, and the one who lifts up my head.* —PSALM 3:3

Eliot Jackson was born with both Hydrocephalus and a large cyst in the middle of his brain. Inside his first year, he had eight brain surgeries and now has two shunts that keep his head at normal pressure and drain fluid down into his abdomen. Eliot and his parents, Jeff and Elizabeth, went through a lot in a short time.

As they learned more about their son's condition, they also discovered that children born with the condition in third world environments, such as Africa, often die, because 90% of Hydrocephalus cases are fatal without proper surgery and treatment.

This led to the Jacksons' discovery of CURE International and their work in Uganda. Working with doctors in the U.S., CURE has taken alternative treatments to Africa to help the children who suffer from this condition there.

Since 2000, over 5,000 lives have been saved, ten surgeons have been trained, and groundbreaking research has been shared. Their goals are to train more surgeons, build more hospitals, and save more children. As an evangelical ministry, they also provide spiritual and emotional support.

The Jacksons' experience with Eliot's Hydrocephalus and CURE fueled such a passion to help other children and their parents that Jeff is now in a full-time position with CURE International.

Eliot is now a medical miracle and his dad is sharing Eliot's story with those in need across the world. Yet another story of how personal crisis is turned to a public crusade, when we choose to allow God to have complete control.

DIVINE HEALER, *teach me to be grateful for life, rather than complain away my days. Teach me to turn my problems into prayers, so You have the freedom to work as You will.*

# ADAPT AND OVERCOME

*He shall judge between the nations, and shall arbitrate for many peoples; they shall beat their swords into ploughshares, and their spears into pruning-hooks; nation shall not lift up sword against nation, neither shall they learn war any more.* —ISAIAH 2:4

The United States military is one of the few places where members are asked to "work yourself out of a job."

A six-member Joint Medical Operations Cell of advisers and mentors is working to transfer responsibilities at the Afghan National Army Hospital and the Afghan National Police Regional Training Center.

U.S. Navy Commander Janice Roach said, "Our team has had a sincere desire to help the Afghans achieve their mission and sustain their medical operations far into the future. They're ready to take over."

Petty Officer 2nd Class Joseph Nededog, biomedical equipment adviser, said, "One of our biggest challenges is the lack of resources available here. We have to adapt, overcome, and find a way to get it done and ensure what equipment we do have continues to operate."

"We are really appreciative of all the help, training, and documents the U.S. has given us," said Afghan National Army Major Gull Fada, Herat Regional Hospital deputy assistant. "The mentorship means so much to us and we are thankful for their assistance in these efforts. I hope people realize we have a good system in place now. One day we look forward to solving all our problems and have a safe and peaceful country."

Our nation has poured billions of dollars and hours into other nations over generations. Why? Because we continue on in the principles this nation was founded upon. Thank God today that we are a nation that serves the world and you are on the right team!

PRINCE OF PEACE, *thank You for the strong heritage and lineage I am privileged to be a part of and the service I am honored to give to the world through my nation.*

# FOR THE HUMAN SIDE

*The Lord is good to all, and his compassion is over all that he has made.*
—*PSALM 145:9*

Captain (Dr.) James Small was a high school physics and chemistry teacher almost a decade ago when he decided to serve his country as a U.S. Air Force physician. Now he lives in a remote, mountainous region of Peru 13,500 feet above sea level.

Captain Small and his fellow medical professionals from the 633rd Medical Group from Joint Base Langley-Eustis, Va., are taking part in New Horizons, a U.S. Southern Command-sponsored annual joint and combined training and humanitarian assistance exercise that takes place throughout Latin America and the Caribbean.

In cooperation with the Peruvian government, they have erected a 22-room, 6,300 square-foot, network of medical tents.

Captain Small said, "I think it makes me a better person to see the world from a different perspective. It makes me a better doctor, gives me a compassion and understanding for the human side of medicine."

As word passed through the community, people began lining up for appointments to receive care in one of the five specialties: pediatrics, internal medicine, family medicine, gynecology, and dental.

Captain Small added, "The 30 minutes you spend with one patient might be the most important time they've spent with a person in years. You're connecting with them, reassuring them that they are healthy, and they are so grateful for the care."

As people, we have a deep, innate need for purpose and meaning, to sense a reason for our own existence. There is also a strong desire to help and improve others' lives. It's simple—when we help others, we feel good about ourselves. That is both a God-given sense and privilege—all rolled into one.

CREATOR GOD, *help me to find satisfaction in You by serving others.*

# PROVIDE FOR THOSE WHO PROTECT

*Like cold water to a thirsty soul, so is good news from a far country.*
—PROVERBS 25:25

Since 9-11, the U.S. has activated approximately 850,000 members of the Guard and Reserve. But over a decade later, more than 776,000 have come back—three-quarters of a million Guard and Reserve members who've now returned to civilian life and gone back to work or are looking for a job.

Staff Sergeant Mike Fitzpatrick talks about giving his manager his Guard schedule a year in advance, but explains, "Then it would be a very contentious conversation with my manager and he'd be like, 'Well, do you really have to go?' And it's like, 'Well, there could be a warrant out for my arrest if I don't show up for the drill this weekend.'"

Senator Patty Murray of Washington State is the chair of the Senate Veterans' Affairs Committee. She has proposed a bill to toughen up the laws protecting veterans from labor discrimination.

Senator Murray said, "We have a policy in this country that we've had for a very long time. If we have men and women who are willing to protect all of us, we will provide them the support of this country, of our businesses, of our families, of our communities, to make sure they're not lost when they come home. So you're an employer in the United States? This is part of your responsibility."

Supporting the military—current or veteran, law enforcement, firefighters, or any first responders—by any means we can or inside our area of influence, is the right thing to do. Pray today for those who have served our country and are now looking for work in the private sector.

PROVIDER, *bless all those who have served and are serving our nation. Meet their needs, provide for them. Lead me to see any opportunity I have to be an answer to this prayer.*

# ONE SIMPLE MESSAGE

*For God so loved the world that he gave his only Son, so that everyone who believes in him may not perish but may have eternal life.* —JOHN 3:16

Billy Graham said, "Whether the story of Christ is told in a huge stadium, across the desk of a powerful leader, or shared with a golfing companion, it satisfies a common hunger. All over the world, whenever I meet people face-to-face, I am made aware of this personal need among the famous and successful, as well as the lonely and obscure."

In 1950, a congressman called Billy and asked, "Would you like to meet the President?" Without any briefing on protocol, he agreed and went in with three colleagues to speak with President Truman. Before he left, the two prayed together.

Graham said, "Eisenhower was the first president that really asked my counsel in depth when he was sending troops into Little Rock."

Just before Eisenhower died, Billy was invited to see him at Walter Reed Hospital. After talking again about assurance of salvation, the two men prayed. Eisenhower then said he was ready to die. Eisenhower said of Graham, "Billy Graham is one of the best ambassadors our country has but he told me, 'I am an ambassador of Heaven.'"

Billy Graham's estimated accumulated audience is over two billion people with over 3 million responding to his invitation to receive the Gospel of Christ. Over the years, Billy has never changed his simple message: "Accept Jesus Christ as your personal Savior." Below is Billy Graham's own recommended prayer for salvation.

LORD JESUS CHRIST, *I am sorry for the things I have done wrong in my life. I ask your forgiveness and now turn from everything that I know is wrong. Thank you for dying on the cross for me to set me free from my sins. Please come into my life and fill me with your Holy Spirit and be with me forever. Thank you, Lord Jesus, Amen.*

# FOR THE LOVE OF THE TRUTH

*No, the word is very near to you; it is in your mouth and in your heart for you to observe.* —DEUTERONOMY 30:14

George Washington, first president of the United States: "It is impossible to rightly govern the World without God and the Bible."

John Adams, second president of the United States: "The Bible contains more philosophy than all the libraries that I have ever seen and such parts as I cannot reconcile with my little philosophy, I postpone for future investigation."

Thomas Jefferson, third president of the United States: "I have always said that a studious perusal of the Sacred Volume will make you better citizens, better fathers, and better husbands."

John Quincy Adams, sixth president of the United States: "The first and almost only book deserving of universal attention is the Bible.

I speak as a man of the world. So great is my veneration for the Bible, that the earlier my children begin to read it, the more confident will be my hope that they will prove useful citizens of their country and respectable members of society. I have for many years made it a practice to read through the Bible once every year."

Zachary Taylor, twelfth president of the United States: "It was for the love of the truths of this great and good Book that our fathers abandoned their native shores for the wilderness."

Deciding to read the Bible on a daily basis, whether it be a verse a day or a chapter, will not only put you in the company of great men and women in history, but regularly put you in the company of God Almighty.

HOLY GOD, *draw me to read Your Word, to live by what I take in, and to love by how it teaches me to give.*

—324—

# CHILD'S PLAY

*Little children, let us love, not in word or speech, but in truth and action.*
—*1 JOHN 3:18*

*At that time the disciples came to Jesus and asked, "Who is the greatest in the kingdom of heaven?" He called a child, whom he put among them, and said, "Truly I tell you, unless you change and become like children, you will never enter the kingdom of heaven. Whoever becomes humble like this child is the greatest in the kingdom of heaven. Whoever welcomes one such child in my name welcomes me."*
—*MATTHEW 18:1-5*

People were bringing even infants to him that he might touch them; and when the disciples saw it, they sternly ordered them not to do it. But Jesus called for them and said, "Let the little children come to me, and do not stop them; for it is to such as these that the kingdom of God belongs. Truly I tell you, whoever does not receive the kingdom of God as a little child will never enter it." (Luke 18:15-17)

Jesus was always clear on His love for children. As we see crimes against kids growing, especially at the hands of their own parents, and as our culture continues to devalue children, we need to remind ourselves of two important truths.

First, our own hearts are to maintain a childlike quality, as Jesus taught, so that our faith and love can remain fresh and alert. Second, we must pay attention to and show value to all children. Regardless of your role of service, stoop down and look into the eyes of the kids in your life daily. They'll keep you close to God.

HEAVENLY ONE, *help me notice the children around me, to value them, and keep my heart humble, as they are.*

# GIVING LIVING

*Each of you must give as you have made up your mind, not reluctantly or under compulsion, for God loves a cheerful giver.* —2 CORINTHIANS 9:7

Millions of Americans regularly buy and sell their stuff on eBay. When eBay founder Pierre Omidyar went public with his brainchild in 1998, he became, as he called it, "ridiculously rich."

He promised then that he would give away most of his money in his lifetime. He even signed the Bill Gates and Warren Buffett Giving Pledge.

He and his wife started the Omidyar Network, a philanthropic investment firm. Pierre and Pam have given away more than $1 billion to programs spanning a wide range of causes, from poverty alleviation to human rights to disaster relief.

The French-born Iranian moved to the U.S. with his family at age six. He wrote code for his site "Auction Web"

at age 28 and then later renamed it eBay. The first item ever sold on his mega-site was his own broken laser pointer. The winning bid was $14.83.

When the majority of people hear stories of incredibly wealthy people giving away money, the common response is, "Sure, it's easy to give when you have that much." But actually, those at or below poverty level are consistently the biggest givers in the U.S. percentage-wise, at almost double that of middle-class. This proves once again that giving is a character quality, not a sign of disposable income.

Serving is giving and giving is serving. If you believe that "God loves a cheerful giver," then how happy has He made you?

ALL IN ALL, *thank You that my life can be given in service, but help me to grow in giving. Make me a cheerful giver.*

# FOR GOD'S HOLY SERVICE

*For with you is the fountain of life; in your light we see light. O continue your steadfast love to those who know you, and your salvation to the upright of heart!*
—PSALM 36:9-10

Christopher Columbus has always been an important character in American history and Columbus Day is now a federal holiday.

His four voyages across the Atlantic began the exploration and eventual colonization of America. Columbus viewed his journeys as also spreading Christianity.

Columbus stated, "It was the Lord who put into my mind (I could feel His hand upon me) the fact that it would be possible to sail from here to the Indies. All who heard of my project rejected it with laughter, ridiculing me. There is no question that the inspiration was from the Holy Spirit, because He comforted me with rays of marvelous inspiration from the Holy Scriptures."

Columbus offered some practical advice:

"You can never cross the ocean, unless you have the courage to lose sight of the shore."

"Riches don't make a man rich, they only make him busier."

"No one should fear to undertake any task in the name of our Savior, if it is just and if the intention is purely for His holy service."

Today, we don't have the opportunity to discover new lands or sail in search of treasure and fortune. However, God still leads His children to new works, new places of service, and to reach into places and hearts that need Him. There are still places of adventure and new places to discover as we follow Him. That's why He calls it the abundant life!

MIGHTY LORD, *lead me to discover all that You have for me. I don't want to miss anything You have planned.*

# HEART OF HEALTHCARE

*She opens her hand to the poor, and reaches out her hands to the needy.*
—*PROVERBS 31:20*

Great nurses gain great reputations and we all know what a vast difference they can make when we are celebrating a birth or anticipating a death, and any illness in between. Here are some great quotes regarding these angels of the first-responder team.

---

*"Nurses are the heart of healthcare."*
—DONNA WILK CARDILLO

*"Constant attention by a good nurse may be just as important as a major operation by a surgeon."*
—DAG HAMMARSKJOD

*"The trained nurse has become one of the great blessings of humanity, taking a place beside the physician and the priest."*
—WILLIAM OSLER

*"Nurses: one of the few blessings of being ill."*
—SARA MOSS-WOLFE

*"To do what nobody else will do, a way that nobody else can do, in spite of all we go through, is to be a nurse."*
—RAWSI WILLIAMS

*"Panic plays no part in the training of a nurse."*
—ELIZABETH KENNY

---

You can't serve people to the degree that most nurses do and not display a number of Heavenly qualities. We can all learn from these servants and be challenged by their level of commitment and care.

GENTLE HEALER, *give me strength today for my own service and teach me to care as You do.*

# MYSTERY OF MYSTERIES

*So we have the prophetic message more fully confirmed. You will do well to be attentive to this as to a lamp shining in a dark place, until the day dawns and the morning star rises in your hearts.* —2 PETER 1:19

Sir Walter Scott, the Scottish writer and poet wrote this of the Bible:

*"Within this ample Volume lies
The mystery of mysteries
Happiest they of human race
To whom their God has given grace
To read, to fear, to hope, to pray
To lift the latch, to force the way
But better had they ne'er been born
That read to doubt or read to scorn."*

Leo Tolstoy, Russian author and philosopher, wrote of Scripture:

*"To understand the whole work of the Master is not in my power;
but to do His will, written in my conscience, that is in my power,*
*and that I know without a doubt.
And when I do this, then undoubtedly I am at peace."*

Ralph Waldo Emerson, American author and philosopher wrote:

*"All I have seen teaches me to trust the Creator for all I have not seen."*

Let these brilliant writers and philosophers of history encourage you in your own faith journey to see that, just as intelligence and creativity can lead you away from God, it can also lead you closer to Him and more convinced than ever of His presence in your life daily.

MASTER, CREATOR, GOD, *thank You for the disciples in the past who have left testimonies of their faith in You. I want to leave my mark on Your history as well.*

# TO THE END OF THE AGE

*Better is the end of a thing than its beginning; the patient in spirit are better than the proud in spirit.* —ECCLESIASTES 7:8

Adoniram Judson was rejected entrance into India to preach the Gospel to the Hindus, yet after trying many times, he finally found an open door in Rangoon, Burma.

There was not one known Christian in that population of millions. At just eight months old, the Judson's first child died, as thousands of lives were claimed by cholera. The unusual spiritual beliefs of the locals discouraged the missionary couple, as there were no converts.

Six long, heart-breaking years passed until, on June 27, 1819, Judson baptized Moung Nau as the first Burman believer.

Judson wrote in his journal, "Oh, may it prove to be the beginning of a series of baptisms in the Burman empire which shall continue in uninterrupted success to the end of the age."

Opposition came and Judson was imprisoned and condemned to die as a British spy. However, in answer to prayer and the constant intervention of his wife to officials, his life was spared and finally, after 21 months, the British government was able to free him from prison.

Miraculously, his work began to take hold and the Gospel spread, until, at the age of 62, he died. Except for a few months away, Judson had spent 38 years in Burma. After his death, a government survey recorded 210,000 Christians—one out of every 58 Burmans!

Persistence is a difficult quality to acquire, but we must both wait and persist in order to accomplish all that God has for us. Take both inspiration and courage today from Judson's life. It's not always about how long it takes, but that we get there!

SOVEREIGN GOD, *You see our entire journey, when we can't even see around the next corner. Give me strength and grace to keep moving, pressing on to the goal.*

# ADRENALINE & INSTINCT

*Let your hand be ready to help me, for I have chosen your precepts.*
—*PROVERBS 119:173*

At the Aurora, Colo., movie theatre on the night of the 2012 Batman movie premiere where the horrific shootings took place, Dr. Comilla Sasson and Dr. Barbara Blok were the ER doctors on duty at the University of Colorado Hospital.

Dr. Sasson had dealt with gunshot patients before, but as police cruiser after police cruiser pulled up to the doors, they soon had 23 victims along with the usual room of people waiting for care.

As Aurora police cars kept rolling in, Dr. Sasson thought, "These people are badly injured and I've got two minutes to figure it out before the next one comes in.

"It was the longest night of my life," she said. "The first 9 to 10 patients were all in the resuscitation area. More than five could not tell us their names."

Dr. Sasson was surrounded by trauma surgeons, charge nurses, orthopedic specialists, radiology techs, cleanup crews, as well as first-year residents, just three weeks out of medical school.

One patient did die, but Dr. Sasson credits everyone in the ER, the operating rooms, hallways, pharmacy, at the theater, and at dispatch for saving 22. By the 7 a.m. shift change, Sasson said, "You're running on adrenaline, instinct, and flat-out guts."

For so many jobs, when things get hectic or critical, it doesn't mean a life or death situation, but for a first responder, it most often does.

Spiritual preparation is vitally important to each day to be ready for a potentially busy day. As you pray for yourself, pray also for those you will be dealing with today.

CARING GOD, *prepare me today for what is ahead, whether it be uneventful or traumatic. I pray also for those I will encounter today. Give me wisdom and strength.*

# NO STATUS QUO

*There is nothing better for mortals than to eat and drink, and find enjoyment in their toil. This also, I saw, is from the hand of God; for apart from him who can eat or who can have enjoyment? For to the one who pleases him God gives wisdom and knowledge and joy.* —ECCLESIASTES 2:24-26a

Ken Sheldon, Ph.D., associate professor in the department of psychological sciences at the University of Missouri-Columbia, said that all of us are born with a particular "set range" for happiness, which can be fine-tuned by various life circumstances.

"All of life is a process of becoming," said author Dr. David G. Myers. "From womb to tomb, we're developing. So we can, at any time, reshape our future."

Happy individuals have certain personal traits that set them apart from people with clouds hovering over their heads.

Dr. Sheldon's research shows happiness is associated with characteristics like autonomy, competence, close relationships, and high self-esteem.

While some people have convinced themselves that a new Lexus or a relocation to a beach house in California will bring lasting happiness, Dr. Sheldon warns that while these kinds of changes might work for a while, new possessions or living arrangements will eventually become part of your status quo and their power to deliver happiness will fade.

"The route to sustained happiness is not to change the static circumstances of your life, but rather to change the activities that you're involved in," said the professor. "This could mean committing to a new vocational plan, pursuing a new set of goals, or joining a new organization."

Living a life dedicated to service and giving of your particular skill set to better the world brings lasting contentment. Each situation and person with whom you connect provides a new challenge. Giving brings living. Serving brings satisfaction.

PRINCE OF PEACE, *thank You that You bring a new challenge and adventure every day through my place of service. Help me to be content with who I am, right where I am.*

# A BIGGER BACKPACK

*Those who try to make their life secure will lose it, but those who lose their life will keep it.* —LUKE 17:33

As a medical student, Benjamin LaBrot traveled to remote areas of Africa to treat people with all the supplies he could stuff in his backpack.

One day in Tanzania, his supplies ran out. "Having felt like I had just done so little, I cried for 20 minutes," Benjamin said. "I decided that I was going to come back and I would bring a bigger backpack." Today, he carries 20,000 pounds of medical supplies.

Benjamin began Floating Doctors, a nautical medical group that provides free health care for people in remote coastal regions. His team of volunteers travels on "The Southern Wind," a 76-foot-long refurbished ship. He explains, "On a ship, you can generate your own water, your own power. And those power sources can be from renewable energy sources."

"Most of these communities have fallen through the cracks, because they're too small, too far away, too hard to get to," said Benjamin. "The result is that you end up in a community which may never have been visited by modern health care providers."

Since the project began, 180 volunteers from nine countries have joined the effort, including medical residents, nursing students, and retired physicians. They have treated 13,000 patients in Haiti, Honduras, and Panama.

"I don't have a home. I had to give up a lot," he said. "But I gained everything."

God offers each of us an opportunity to serve Him by His life and power. It is the essence of where true life is found—and where you gain everything.

SON OF MAN, *You said that You had no place to lay Your head, yet You created the world. Remind me throughout this day that real security is found only in You.*

# PLENTY OF HEROES

*Discipline yourselves; keep alert. Like a roaring lion your adversary, the devil, prowls around, looking for someone to devour.* —1 PETER 5:8

A mom was at home with her young son when a man began breaking into her home. The woman grabbed up her child and her phone, ran into a bedroom closet, and called 911.

Two Harris County, Texas, deputies arrived as the burglar was putting two TVs into the woman's car.

As the deputies approached, the man drove the vehicle straight toward the officers. After resisting their orders to stop, the officers drew their guns and fired, wounding the man. The burglar drove the car about a block, then attempted to run into a home, where they were able to apprehend him.

Harris County Sheriff Adrian Garcia said, "We work hard to communicate to the public what they need to do under these very difficult and terrible circumstances, and she did exactly what we instruct folks to do. Get a phone (to call 911), have a safe place, take care of your family. Do not try to be a hero. The sheriff's office has plenty of heroes and we'll take care of the tough job."

"We are very, very grateful that the good guys and the good citizens were not injured," the sheriff added.

A major aspect of all first-response positions is education and training to help people avoid a crisis, or a crisis becoming worse.

In today's story, had the woman frozen in fear or attempted to stop the man, the outcome may have been much different. Stay fresh in training techniques and education for your role of service. As the saying goes: the best offense is a good defense.

STRONG TOWER, *help me to stay fresh and motivated in my place of service—for my safety and protection, as well as the best for those I serve and protect.*

# SOBERING MOMENT

*If we confess our sins, he who is faithful and just will forgive us our sins and cleanse us from all unrighteousness.* —1 JOHN 1:9

A man goes with his co-workers after hours to a bar and has too much to drink.

On his way home, a policeman pulls him over, and asks him to step out of the car. Just as the inebriated man starts to walk a straight line, the police radio calls for backup at a robbery just around the corner. He tells the man not to move, then the officer runs around the corner to assist his partners.

The man grows tired of waiting and drives home. When he arrives, he tells his wife that if anyone comes to the door, to just tell them he has been home sick all day.

Soon, the police are at his door and ask to see the man. The wife, as told, said that her husband is sick and has been there all day.

The police show her the husband's driver's license that the officer still had from the traffic stop. They then tell her they need to look in the garage. As the wife raises the garage door, there is the policeman's car with the red and blue lights still flashing. The drunken man had obviously driven the wrong car home!

If ever there was a story proving your sins will find you out, this is it. However, we can become quite good at hiding anything from lust to bitterness to greed inside us.

God knows it is there and it is poisoning us. Today would be a good day to open up your heart and allow God in to do what only He can do—forgive, restore, and renew.

REDEEMER, *please forgive me for* _____. *I want to be clean before You. Restore and renew me today by Your grace.*

# HIDDEN BEAUTIES

*For we walk by faith, not by sight.* —2 CORINTHIANS 5:7

A young man, on a new spiritual journey and desperate to "find God," sought out the wisdom of an elderly man whom he knew to be a godly man.

"Sir, how can I see God?"

The old man thought for a few minutes, then responded quietly, "Well, young man, I am not sure that I can help you. I have a very different problem. I cannot not see God."

Pastor and seminary professor Gerhard Frost wrote, "If one accepts each day as a gift from the Father's hand, one may sometimes hear a voice saying 'Open it. I invite you to share with me in these little appointments as we try to unwrap the hidden beauties in an ordinary day.'"

Perspective is the way we view something, while our perception is how we process what we see. That is why three different people can witness a crime or an accident and report three different stories.

There is an old saying that goes, "Perception is reality." This simply means what someone believes they see is real to the person.

The more faith we apply to our perspective, the more our perception of God's activity in the world will grow. This is why you cannot talk anyone into a relationship with God. Faith has to change both their perspective and perception.

How is your faith doing? How big is God in your reality? Keep praying and reading to grow your faith. The truth is we all need the reality of God in our lives.

FAITHFUL ONE, *thank You that You have always believed in me, even when I didn't believe in You. Thank You that I am in Your hand. Help me to stay focused on that reality.*

# JUST ONE LIFE

*Hatred stirs up strife, but love covers all offences.* —PROVERBS 10:12

Years ago a Johns Hopkins professor gave a group of graduate students the assignment to find 200 inner-city boys between the ages of 12 and 16. They were to investigate the boys' background and document their environment. They were then assigned to write a forecast on their chances for the future.

The students interviewed 200 boys and concluded that 90 percent of the boys had little chance of success and many would likely spend time in jail.

Twenty-five years later, another group of graduate students was assigned to follow up on the boys and evaluate the forecast of the other group.

Amazingly, the students located 180 of the original 200. They found that only four of the group had ever spent time in jail and the forecast was far off target.

What had happened? The students continually heard the same comment from the men: "Well, there was this teacher . . ." They then realized that "this teacher" was one woman.

After finding her in a retirement home, they asked, "What did you do?"

She smiled and said, "Well, I loved those boys."

Who has God placed in your life? Who might you help change the course of his/her life? There are people that God has planned for you to reach. Pay close attention and watch for where He is leading.

LIGHT OF THE WORLD, *I want to have that kind of impact on others. Open my eyes to see, my ears to hear, where You want me to invest my life.*

# LIFE'S BLOOD

*Like living stones, let yourselves be built into a spiritual house, to be a holy priest-hood, to offer spiritual sacrifices acceptable to God through Jesus Christ.* —1 PETER 2:5

The American Red Cross responds to 70,000 disasters every year from single house fires to large-scale emergencies. Ninety-five percent of this amazing work is accomplished through volunteers with the other 5 percent being done by just 35,000 employees.

An average of more than 9 million people annually receive Red Cross training in first aid, water safety, and other skills that help save lives.

Some four million people give blood through the Red Cross, making it the largest supplier of blood and blood products in the United States. The Red Cross also helps thousands of U.S. military troops, separated from their families, to stay connected.

Since its inception in 1881 by Clara Barton, the American Red Cross has been the nation's primary emergency-response organization, offering humanitarian care to victims of war and natural disasters. The goal is always the same: to prevent and relieve suffering.

Not connected to any government agency, an average of 91 cents of every dollar the Red Cross spends is invested in humanitarian services and programs.

Someone in the U.S. needs blood every two seconds. That need requires more than 38,000 blood donations every day, making the American Red Cross' indispensable role abundantly clear.

Much of our civilization is maintained through service, and in particular, volunteerism. If everyone who volunteers decided he or she was too busy or had better things to do, the world would be in dire trouble. You are a link in this vast chain of humanity. Your role is vital.

CREATOR GOD, *the network of people throughout the world that connects us to each other and vital needs is an amazing work and only You could be at the center of it all.*

# IT FINDS ME WHERE I AM

*I wait for the Lord, my soul waits, and in his word I hope.* —PSALM 130:5

Abraham Lincoln, 16th president of the United States: "I am busily engaged in the study of the Bible. I believe it is God's word, because it finds me where I am."

Ulysses S. Grant, 18th president of the United States: "To the influence of the Book we are indebted for the progress made in civilisation and to this we must look as our guide in the future. The Bible is the sheet-anchor of our liberties."

Woodrow Wilson, 28th president of the United States: "When you have read the Bible, you know it is the word of God, because it is the key to your heart, your own happiness, and your own duty."

Franklin Roosevelt, 32nd president of the United States: "The influence of the Scriptures in the early days of the Republic is plainly revealed in the writing and thinking of the men who made the nation possible. They found in the Scriptures that which shaped their course and determined their cause."

Dwight Eisenhower, 34th president of the United States: "To read the Bible is to take a trip to a fair land where the spirit is strengthened and faith renewed."

Paul stated in 2 Timothy 3:16-17, "All scripture is inspired by God and is useful for teaching, for reproof, for correction, and for training in righteousness, so that everyone who belongs to God may be proficient, equipped for every good work."

Allow God's Word to be your teacher, corrector, trainer, and equipper to lead you as you serve today and every day.

LORD GOD, *teach me, correct me, train me, equip me to serve You and neighbors across the street and around the world.*

# KEEPING YOUR EDGE

*Remind them to be subject to rulers and authorities, to be obedient, to be ready for every good work.* —TITUS 3:1

John Campbell was sailing in San Diego Bay when he spotted a capsized sailboat and saw a number of people fighting to survive in the cold water. He immediately dove in and tied a line between his boat and the overturned boat.

John then proceeded to pull people, one by one, onto his own boat, including a mentally challenged teenager and an elderly man who had been trying to hold onto their capsized sailboat. He continued to assist and encourage those in the water, including a mother and child.

He stayed in the water until all ten people were pulled from the ocean. He then assisted San Diego Harbor Police move survivors onto a police boat, where he stayed until everyone was safely back on land.

The Coast Guard presented John with their Certificate of Valor in Los Angeles, acknowledging that he singlehandedly rescued half of the people.

We can all say what we might do in a life or death situation, but we don't actually know until faced with that reality. If you are a first responder or member of the military, you may have been placed in this situation countless times. Regardless, a life committed to service is a life of preparedness and staying alert. "Keeping your edge" is an important part of this responsibility.

Are you there or do you need some fresh inspiration? Be mindful of who challenges you in this way and stay connected. Maintaining accountability can keep you ready for anything.

MIGHTY GOD, *inspire me to stay connected to those who challenge me and keep me strong. Help me to keep my edge to serve and protect.*

# MY LIFE PREPARED ME

*For surely I know the plans I have for you, said the Lord, plans for your welfare and not for harm, to give you a future with hope.* —JEREMIAH 29:11

At the Aurora movie theatre on the night of the 2012 Batman movie premiere where the horrific shootings took place, Chris Lakota's, a mixed martial artist, first reaction wasn't fear, but anger. He was at another movie when the evacuation began.

As Chris saw the people running out of theater 9, he realized someone was shooting in there; so he ran in. His initial thought was to find the shooter. But then he saw 18-year-old Bonnie Kate, limping from a gunshot wound to her leg.

Chris carried her out of the theater. Outside, he put a sweatshirt under her head and wrapped another one around her knee. He gave her some water and yelled for an ambulance.

"It was just pandemonium," he said. "People were screaming [and] running for their cars."

Chris and two others carried Bonnie to the front seat of a patrol car. "Think about positive things," he told her. "Think about your summer." He told her not to look at her leg, which at first was spouting blood. "Just keep your eyes up."

He stayed with her the whole time.

"I wanted to do something good," said Chris. "If you see bad, and you don't do anything, I feel it's just as bad as the evil itself. It felt like everything in my life prepared me to go in there."

Chris feels like he was meant to go that night. "I wouldn't change it for anything," he said.

If we believe in God and that He has a purpose for our lives, then there are no coincidences. The sooner we view life that way, the more impact we can have by living intentional lives, like Chris Lakota.

SOVEREIGN GOD, *I believe You have a plan for me and a purpose for every day. Lead me to live an intentional life!*

# PROVIDENTIAL PROMISES

*Into your hand I commit my spirit; you have redeemed me, O Lord, faithful God.*
—PSALM 31:5

Daniel Rodriguez kept his promise, playing as number 83 for the Clemson Tigers.

Daniel served as an Army infantryman in both Iraq and Afghanistan. During his second tour of duty, he was involved in the battle of Kamdesh where an estimated 400 Taliban insurgents attacked a remote American base.

Eight troops were killed and 22 were wounded in one of the bloodiest days in Afghanistan. Daniel took shrapnel in his legs and neck, as well as a bullet fragment in his shoulder. He was awarded a Bronze Star of Valor and Purple Heart.

One of the troops killed was Daniel's friend, Private First Class Kevin Thompson. Just a few days earlier, the two had discussed their futures and Daniel had promised Kevin that he would follow his dream of playing college football.

"I am very happy for Daniel," said Clemson coach Dabo Swinney. "I have no doubt that he will become a great leader for us. His background and story is an inspiration to us all."

Daniel said. "I'm just a cog on the wheel that's going to play my role and better the team from an individual standpoint. If I can help mold some of these guys in the locker room to have the same perspective on life I have, that's a benefit."

We will never understand on this side of Heaven why God calls some home, while He gives others second chances, but that is why He is God.

We are only called to trust and to take every opportunity with every day He gives us—just like Daniel.

HEAVENLY CREATOR, *turn my unanswered questions to trust and my fears into faith. Help me not to waste time, but maximize my days.*

# OUR LITTLEST HEROES

*All your children shall be taught by the Lord, and great shall be the prosperity of your children.* —ISAIAH 54:13

At Joint Base Langley-Eustis, Virginia, children were busy running excitedly from station to station and various events. Operation Hero has been helping and educating children on the deployment process for over a decade.

"We focus on trying to get the kids to understand the deployment process so it isn't scary for them anymore," said U.S. Air Force Master Sergeant Dawn Chapman, Airman & Family Readiness Center noncommissioned officer in charge of readiness.

"We want to make them feel like they are part of the process. The event gives them a hands-on view of the different career fields in the Air Force. They are also able to process through a mock-deployment line to experience what their parents go through every time they deploy."

"It puts it all in perspective in a fun, kid-friendly way," said Master Sergeant Julie Dandaneau, 633rd Surgical Operations Squadron flight chief of surgical services. "They see this and understand that we don't just pack our bags and leave when we deploy."

"Seeing the kids' faces light up when they do the different activities is its own reward," said Sergeant Chapman. "They are so happy knowing they can participate and be a part of something their parents are involved in."

Being a child of a military parent or first responder has definite blessings, but that role also comes with some unique circumstances and sacrifices. Parents who allow for their feelings ensure that they will see the benefits of a life of service and want to follow in dad's or mom's footsteps.

If you are a parent, be sure you pray regularly for—and with—your kids.

ABBA FATHER, *bless the children today of all those who serve. Show them the value of a life committed to others' lives. (Parent: Please bless, protect, comfort, and lead my child today.)*

# COMING FULL CIRCLE

*I cry to God Most High, to God who fulfills his purpose for me.* —*PSALM* 57:2

Marine Corporal Duy Nguyen grew up in Vietnam. When he was 14, he moved to the U.S., leaving behind everyone and everything he knew. At 19 years old, he joined the Marines. His reason? He said, "To make a difference. To accept the challenge of life as a Marine." He adds, "I'm thankful for my parents raising me to be the person I am today. My father is proud of who I have become."

Duy's worlds came together when he had the opportunity to participate in Pacific Partnership—in Vietnam with the Marine Corps Air Wing Support Squadron 171—as a motor transport operator.

One of only nine Marines chosen from 200,000, Duy said, "The opportunity to come back home after all of these years is hard to explain. For me, this is as much home as being back in the states. Just the other day I saw a child here in Vietnam that reminded me of myself when I was a child. It was like looking into a mirror of the past. It reminded me of just how fortunate I have been. I was fortunate to have chosen the life of a Marine. And now, on this mission, it is like everything has come full circle and I am able to realize that maybe things happen for a reason."

Life does often come back around, completing full circles, and things do, indeed, happen for a reason. Today, know that whatever you are going through, God is at work and cares deeply for your well-being. God is there and listening to you.

ALPHA & OMEGA, BEGINNING & THE END, *when life is good, may I be grateful. When life is tough and I may not understand, help me to trust You.*

# ROLL CALL OF HEROES

*You have made my days a few handbreadths, and my lifetime is as nothing in your sight. Surely everyone stands as a mere breath.* —PSALM 39:5

Twenty-six-year Navy veteran Jonathan Blunk, who served three tours in the Middle East over six years, dreamed of re-enlisting to become a Navy SEAL. That dream was stopped short by a crazed gunman's bullet in a movie theatre in Aurora, Colorado.

Law enforcement officials said there are indications Blunk tried to stand up to the heavily armed gunman and stop him. He died after throwing himself in front of a friend during the shooting. Kyle Dawson, his shipmate in the Navy, said Blunk matched the description of a man who went after the suspect.

"Law enforcement is leaning toward a theory that he was trying to get the (suspect's) gun to save people's lives," said Roland Lackey, an Air Force veteran who officiated at the funeral service. "He was a hero and I salute him."

Jonathan was a certified firefighter and EMT who spent much of his time in the Navy aboard the USS Nimitz. He received a full military burial, including a gun salute and the playing of Taps. Amy DeGuzman, his supervisor in the Navy and a pallbearer, conducted a ceremonial roll call of shipmates that included Jonathan's name. When there was no answer, a shipmate responded, "Jonathan Blunk gave his life saving another." Jonathan was survived by his wife and two young children.

Poet Linda Ellis once said, "On our tombstone is our birth year and year of death, but it's the dash that counts." That said, we have no way of knowing how long our dash will be. Today, love God, love your family, love your friends, serve with all you have, and make this one count!

GREAT SHEPHERD, *there is no better legacy to leave than one of service and bravery. Help me to make my "dash" count—today and every day I'm given.*

# DIFFUSING PAIN

*Relieve the troubles of my heart, and bring me out of my distress. Consider my affliction and my trouble.* —PSALM 25:17-18a

Mark Burleson was a Marine Staff Sergeant in Afghanistan when a bomb blast left him with severe burns, shattered bones, and a brain injury. Mark's right arm was gone below the elbow and his left arm was paralyzed.

"All the nerves were ripped from my spinal cord at the root," he said. "It felt like someone was lighting my arm on fire with a cutting torch."

Seeking relief, Mark signed up for dangerous surgery.

Neurosurgeon Dr. Allan Belzberg agreed to try a high-risk surgery.

"We only use it when we've exhausted all other options. If you're the slightest bit off, you paralyze his leg," the doctor said.

Using a microscope and a tiny electrode, Dr. Belzberg made 140 burns in damaged nerves dangling from Mark's spinal cord; the nerves intermixed with healthy connections to his lower limbs.

The surgery went smoothly and one week later, Mark said he felt as if he was given a new start on life, although he remained hospitalized for a year.

Mark struggled to find the words to thank the doctor, saying, "I love the man. I would do anything for him."

"This is a guy who is so tough he diffuses bombs for a living," said Dr. Belzberg. "He's the real hero."

The lifelong sacrifices that so many of our veterans and their families have undergone are unimaginable.

Pray today for all those veterans and current military who are hurt, disabled, and living with chronic pain. Ask God for comfort, strength, and relief in their bodies, minds, and spirits.

DIVINE HEALER, *comfort, strengthen, and bring miraculous relief to all those who have served our country and suffer today. Touch them and their families.*

# ENGAGING EMPATHY

*For wisdom will come into your heart, and knowledge will be pleasant to your soul; prudence will watch over you; and understanding will guard you.*
—*PROVERBS 2:10-12*

Marine Michael J. Zacchea, program director of the University of Connecticut Entrepreneur Boot Camp, helps disabled veterans find jobs.

"We are not producing enough jobs to absorb the veteran population," said Michael.

Asked about the biggest problems faced by returning vets, Michael answered, "One is mental health care and the other is employment. The rate of traumatic brain injury and PTSD is just about equal to the rate of unemployment among veterans—about 30 percent. And it is difficult to get the mental health care, because of the stigma attached.

"It's very satisfying to take a veteran from when he or she has the beginning of an idea to when they open the doors and start the business. They are very proud of what they have accomplished. I also work with corporate hiring managers to place veterans when they graduate.

A Purple Heart recipient, Michael said, "I went through what these veterans are experiencing today. I was in physical rehab and I accessed the health care industry for post-traumatic stress and traumatic brain injury. I've experienced all this and can guide them in their quest both to get the help they need and find gainful employment.

"My day is pretty full. It's not really a job, it's a calling," Michael added.

Pursuing a call to help veterans re-enter society and the work world is a valiant and much-needed mission. What better life can we lead than pouring into people's lives to better them? In your own service, put people first—always. God did. God does. God will. You should.

OUR PROVIDER, *lead me to be a lifeline to all those around me. Guide me to be a supply line for people. I want You to be able to count on me to help Your children.*

# STEPS TO CHANGE

*In the morning, while it was still very dark, he got up and went out to a deserted place, and there he prayed.* —MARK 1:35

Did you know that Alcoholics Anonymous recommends spending time alone with God, as you are now doing with this book.

As a result of this worldwide program, hundreds of thousands of people mired in despair and addiction are today leading happy, productive lives.

Even though they represent no specific religion, Step 2 of their "12 Steps" to recovery states, "We came to believe that a power greater than ourselves could restore us to sanity."

Step 11 declares, "We sought through prayer and meditation to improve our conscious contact with God as we understood God, praying only for knowledge of God's will for us and the power to carry that out."

If hopeless addicts have used spending time alone with God as a means out of their devastation, then we too can accomplish much with the same discipline.

Jesus Himself set aside time to be alone with His Father. He needed to talk with Him and listen to Him. So how much more do we?

You may not be a recovering addict, but you are a human addicted to sin. We all are. Even when you miss a day now and then, the lifelong habit of spending daily time with God will change your life.

STRONG HEALER, *I know spending this time with You gives me strength and guidance that I otherwise do not have. May this time with You not only change my day, but my life.*

# 25,000 WISH GRANTORS

*A desire realized is sweet to the soul.* —PROVERBS 13:19a

Ella, 7, has leukemia and her dream was to meet actor/singer Selena Gomez. On one special afternoon in West Hollywood, Ella got her wish. And that night she attended Selena's concert as her special guest.

Noah, 14, has to undergo chemotherapy, but he dreamed of attending the NBA All-star game. He not only got to attend the game, he was invited to meet all the players.

Robin, 10, has a brain tumor and is fascinated with Alice in Wonderland. Thanks to some highly committed people, she "visited" her dream story.

Connor, 13 wanted to see "Wheel of Fortune" and meet Vanna White. He got to attend two tapings and also get his picture made with the world-famous letter-turner.

Make-a-Wish Foundation began in 1980 with one little boy who had leukemia and wanted to be a police officer.

The foundation has now reached 250,000 children. Some 25,000 volunteers enable Make-a-Wish to grant the wishes of children with life-threatening medical conditions. Volunteers serve as wish granters, fundraisers, and special-event assistants. Some volunteers work for a year to bring wishes to reality.

When just one organization has 25,000 volunteers, you get a glimpse of the vast army of people who give of their time and energy every day to support amazing causes. With all the bad news today, a fact like this raises our hopes and helps us believe that there is good in the world.

LORD OF ALL, *thank You for the gift of children and the opportunity to give to them through organizations like Make-a-Wish. Thank You that we live in a nation where volunteerism and sacrifice are a part of our fabric.*

# HE'S A PATRIOT

*The Lord is my rock, my fortress, and my deliverer, my God, my rock in whom I take refuge, my shield, and the horn of my salvation, my stronghold.* —PSALM 18:2

What does the resume´ of an American hero look like? Consider Thomas Boyle, 62, of Barrington Hill, Ill. —U.S. Marine—two tours of duty in Vietnam right out of high school. —Recipient of the Cross of Gallantry. —Thirty years on the Chicago Police Force. —After retirement, trained police forces in war-torn Kosovo and Iraq. —He had begun to train Afghan police when an insurgent's bullet took his life.

Police highlight: Larry and Tyrone Strickland had shot to death Wheeling Police Officer Kenneth Dawson and fled in a stolen car, but Thomas hunted them down and recovered the murder weapon that was used to convict them.

"Thomas Boyle will always have a special place in the Wheeling Police Department," Wheeling Police Chief William Benson said.

Thomas' wife of 35 years, Pauline, said her husband was always driven to serve his country in the best possible way. When she learned of her husband's death, Pauline had gone to the post office to send a doll and stuffed animal to a little girl in Afghanistan who had touched her husband's heart.

Pauline said the safety and welfare of children was always a top priority for her husband, who would frequently give presents to local kids. "He's just a good American," said Pauline. "He's a patriot who loved this country."

Be inspired today by the story of a true hero, who lived his life in service and protection of others—at home and abroad. It's a reminder to make every day count—starting with today.

IMMANUEL, *thank You for men like Thomas Boyle who remind me not to take this life for granted and to not waste a single day. May my life count as his did.*

# CREATING COMMUNITY

*You do well if you really fulfill the royal law according to the scripture, "You shall love your neighbor as yourself." —JAMES 2:8*

For three decades, National Night Out (NNO) has become a mainstay event in many communities throughout the United States.

NNO is a unique crime and drug prevention event sponsored by the National Association of Town Watch. Typically the events are scheduled in late summer or early fall, around the beginning of the school year.

These campaigns involve citizens, law enforcement agencies, civic groups, businesses, neighborhood organizations, and local officials from over 15,000 communities in all 50 states, U.S. territories, Canadian cities, and military bases worldwide. Over 35 million people participate each year and the numbers keep growing.

The missions of National Night Out are to: —heighten crime and drug prevention awareness. —generate support for, and participation in, local anti-crime programs. —strengthen neighborhood spirit and police-community partnerships. —send a message to criminals letting them know that neighborhoods are organized and fighting back.

Often communities recognize NNO with block parties, cookouts, visits from local police and sheriff departments, parades, exhibits, flashlight walks, contests, and youth programs. NNO is an effective, inexpensive and enjoyable program to promote neighborhood spirit and police-community partnerships in our fight for a safer nation. The benefits of NNO help strengthen each community well beyond the one night.

Communities and neighborhoods connecting their citizens to each other and local law enforcement create goodwill, security, and partnership. Fostering true community is a biblical concept that our nation needs to strengthen and relationships are the driving force of our lives on every front.

CORNERSTONE, *You made it clear that our neighbors weren't just the people next door, but all those we encounter. Help me to love my neighbors.*

# RESTORATION NATION

*When the righteous are in authority, the people rejoice.* — PROVERBS 29:2a

Project 365, in association with National Night Out, is a call to action for a community to target a "problem area" and work towards improving and changing it over the course of a year.

Many communities work toward taking back a certain block or neighborhood from gangs, crime, and drugs. Often these projects are announced at National Night Out and/or their progress from the past year's project is reported.

Communities launching a Project 365 are encouraged to start small with a reasonable project that can see success in the first year, then build from there. Here are a few examples: —Clean up areas with trash-filled lots, abandoned cars, and graffiti. —Expand the number of Neighborhood Watch groups. —Target neighborhoods that have been traditionally tough to organize. —Reduce residential burglaries. —Initiate an auto theft protection program. —Reduce business robberies.

The end goal of a Project 365 is to make your community, neighborhood, or block a safer, more desirable place to live.

Working together for good can bring a community together in a unique way. Making a positive difference corporately will improve the strength of a population, as well as individuals and their relationships. America was built on a people coming together to improve quality of life for each other and she is still about that today.

LIGHT OF THE WORLD, *thank You for all those in this nation who work for her good. Strengthen us as a people to stay focused on our foundation of the common good for all.*

# ADDITION, NOT DIVISION

*For I am not ashamed of the gospel; it is the power of God for salvation to everyone who has faith.* —ROMANS 1:16a

Every U.S. President since World War II through Barack Obama has met with Billy Graham.

Billy said he found President George H.W. Bush easy to talk to about spiritual issues.

"He said straight out that he has received Christ as his Savior and that he is a born-again believer," said Billy.

Billy was with President and Barbara Bush at the White House in 1991, the night that the Gulf War began.

"Billy Graham has been an inspiration in my life," said President Bush. "It is my firm belief that no one can be president without understanding the power of prayer, without faith. And Billy Graham helped me understand that."

Billy Graham made a deep impression on William J. Clinton when he was a young boy. President Clinton recalled, "When I was a small boy, about 12 years old, Billy Graham came to Little Rock, Ark., to preach a crusade." President Clinton was impressed by Billy Graham's refusal to segregate the audience racially.

When he was governor of Arkansas, Bill Clinton joined Billy Graham at a Little Rock crusade. Billy also visited Clinton in the Oval Office when he was president.

President Clinton said, "Billy and Ruth Graham have practiced the ministry of being friends with presidents of both parties, always completely private, always completely genuine."

Billy Graham has long understood that God loves people—regardless of any divisions or walls we may create between us. God wants all people to know Him—to focus on the common ground, not the dividing lines.

LORD OF ALL, *while there are certainly boundaries I should respect, help me to see people as You see them and treat all with that respect and care.*

# SACRIFICE OF SERVICE

*Anxiety weighs down the human heart, but a good word cheers it up.*
—PROVERBS 12:25

Lori Hollingsworth always wanted to be a paramedic.

As a child, she often told her parents that she was going to work on an ambulance one day.

After a divorce left her with full custody of her two children, Lori finally realized her dream when she gave up the comfortable life of a paralegal and enrolled in the University of Mississippi School of Health-Related Professions EMS program. She earned an associate's degree in para-medicine and, as a newly registered paramedic, began work for a private ambulance company in the Jackson area.

"I love my job and I like helping people," Lori said. As a single mom of two children with no other financial assistance, the pay of a paramedic can be a challenge. She works over 80 hours every two weeks, earning an annual salary of just over $30,000. She pays $400 a month for her part of her health insurance benefits program. She has no retirement and no vacation pay, but can earn paid time off. She depends on garage sales and hand-me-down clothes from family members to keep her and her children clothed.

What drives a single mom with two children and the burden of a household to stay at a job, when she could make more money elsewhere? It's her heart and spirit to serve and make a difference with her life. But serving often equates with sacrifice.

Anytime you have an opportunity, encourage your fellow first responders and military personnel. Words of thanks and affirmation help keep spirits high.

SUSTAINER, *bless all those on the front lines of service today—on our streets and over the seas. Take care of them with protection and provision.*

# ALL THEIR OWN

*If a brother or sister is naked and lacks daily food, and one of you said to them,*
*"Go in peace; keep warm and eat your fill," and yet you do not supply their bodily*
*needs, what is the good of that?* —JAMES 2:15-16

In the United States, 300,000 children per year are removed or rescued from their homes where abuse, abandonment, neglect, or endangerment is taking place. Many of these children will go to a government agency or a shelter with nothing except the clothes on their backs. This is where "My Stuff Bags" comes in.

This organization provides children with their own bags filled with a stuffed animal, blanket, coloring books/crayons, small toys, school supplies, toiletries, clothing, and games.

"Not long ago this agency worked with a brother and sister whose father has sexually assaulted them over a period of several years. Because of the nature of the investigation they were not allowed to remove anything from their home before being immediately placed in foster care. They were thrilled when we gave each of them a bag of their own," said the executive director of the Mercer County Family Crisis Center.

"Many children whom we serve come to us with very few belongings or nothing at all. These bags give them the ability to go into their new foster home with their own toothbrush, toothpaste, soap, crayons, toys, a special blanket, and stuffed animal of their own," stated the development liaison of the South Carolina Youth Advocate Program.

For most Americans, moving takes weeks and an 18-wheeler. For children like these, it takes only minutes to leave with just a few items in a bag. Simple solutions like My Stuff Bags not only provide a practical solution, but help children know that someone cares. In such a dire situation, so little can go such a long way.

MIGHTY GOD, *remind me when I desire more stuff that these kids have everything they own in just a small bag. You see each one of those 300,000 children, God, so please bless and protect them.*

# HOOK, HELP, HEAL

*The cords of death encompassed me; the torrents of perdition assailed me; the cords of Sheol entangled me; the snares of death confronted me. In my distress I called upon the Lord; to my God I cried for help. From his temple he heard my voice, and my cry to him reached his ears.* —PSALM 18:4-6

In 2003, after a drug overdose, Annie Lobert began a journey of healing and recovery to emotional, physical, and spiritual wholeness. She is a survivor of more than a decade of sex trafficking, working as an exotic dancer and a high-class escort prostitute in Hawaii, Minneapolis, and Las Vegas.

Today, Annie is an internationally recognized expert and minister to men and women in the commercial sex industry. She understands the traumatic psychological, emotional, and physical effects of choosing the sex industry as a job, only later to be trapped, beaten, and sold to the trafficker's highest bidders.

She is also a survivor of post-traumatic stress disorder, domestic violence, sexual abuse, cancer, drug addiction, abortions, miscarriages, pornography, anorexia, and bulimia.

Annie decided to go back and reach those she left behind who were still working in Las Vegas as prostitutes. What started as a grass roots outreach to sex workers soon became a non-profit ministry called Hookers for Jesus. Their mission is the 3 H's— to Hook (outreach), Help (housing), and Heal (restoration).

She reaches out to abused women while she educates leaders, organizations, and churches to minister to sex workers and sex trafficking victims.

No one is better suited to minister in any area than one who has been there and found the way out. No one can tell Annie, "Yeah, but you don't understand," because she does. God can use anyone who will place his/her life in His hands. To Him, it's not about where you've been, but where you're going.

RESCUER & REDEEMER, *bless those like Annie who escape Hell, but run right back in to rescue the perishing. Thank You for providing salvation, redemption, and healing for all those who call on Your Name.*

# I BELIEVE IN MYSELF

*For you, O Lord, are my hope, my trust, O Lord, from my youth. Upon you I have leaned from my birth; it was you who took me from my mother's womb. My praise is continually of you.* —PSALM 71:5-6

Drew Mitchell, founder and president of Fathom Design in Washington, D.C., interviewed former infantry platoon leader Scott Quilty for a job for which he had little training. Scott quipped, "Jumping out of airplanes and raiding houses doesn't come in handy when you're doing business development at a design firm. They don't need people who can kick down doors."

Scott has a titanium right leg and a prosthetic right hand from being wounded in Iraq when he stepped on an IED. Now, he sits across the desk from Drew.

The president is impressed by the quiet confidence that Scott expresses when he says, "I believe in myself and I don't fail."

Drew decides that the expertise that Scott utilized in planning missions and leading others in life-threatening situations will translate well into the workplace.

Two years in, Drew is proven right.

Seventeen percent of the men and women returning from military service over the past decade remain unemployed.

It takes men with foresight like Drew to change that statistic. It should be easy as there are many intelligent, honorable men like Scott ready to contribute.

If you are a veteran, look for ways to encourage those who come home in your community. If you aren't a veteran, look into programs that help returning soldiers in your area. If you are currently in service, do all you can to plan for life after your discharge, and pray for the right opportunity.

REDEEMER, thank *You for life, health, and another chance to breathe air and touch lives today. May I make a difference with all You give me and bring my way today.*

# GOING DOWN THE CHIMNEY

*Even to your old age I am he, even when you turn grey I will carry you. I have made, and I will bear; I will carry and will save.* —ISAIAH 46:4

The USS Miami is a nuclear submarine that cost almost a billion dollars. It was docked at the Portsmouth, N.H., Naval Shipyard when a vacuum cleaner ignited a blaze onboard that spread quickly. Firefighters described the effort as "fighting a fire in a fireplace by going down the chimney."

Eric Hardy, a 13-year veteran firefighter and his team were called to the sub fire. The firefighters described the scene: "Complete darkness, heavy black smoke, and extreme heat; tunneled space, having to crawl on our bellies; suited in full bunker gear, including breathing apparatus and air tanks; following a hose line and relying on a thermal imager, because you can't see two feet in front of you, can't hear well, moving on to attack the fire."

Suddenly, the order came to evacuate.

As Eric went topside, he noticed the last firefighter seemed to be suffering from heat exhaustion, Eric heard his teammate scream, call out his name, and let go of the ladder.

Eric dropped headfirst into the hatch and grabbed the strap of the man's breathing pack to stop him from falling down the hatch. Yelling for help from those topside to assist him, he was able to get his teammate to grab the ladder and pull himself out of the hatch, where other firefighters took over. Both men made full recoveries.

A sense of teamwork, loyalty, and sacrifice are necessities in many areas of service—few more so than firefighting.

HOLY TRINITY, *we see the perfect Union in the Father, Son, and Holy Spirit. We also see the spiritual battle You wage together throughout Scripture to save the souls of people. Thank You that I get to be on Your team.*

# MERRY CHRISTMAS!

*When they had finished everything required by the law of the Lord, they returned to Galilee, to their own town of Nazareth. The child grew and became strong, filled with wisdom; and the favour of God was upon him.* — LUKE 2:39-40

Imagine for a moment being chosen by God to parent His Son and the paradoxes that would certainly come. The pride, yet humility. The fear, yet faith. The responsibility, yet rest. The promised Messiah has indeed come!

Joseph and Mary served the world in a manner few have. They served God and humankind—past, present, and future—through their unfaltering obedience.

Mary's response to the angel telling her she would carry and give birth to God's Son was: 'Here am I, the servant of the Lord; let it be with me according to your word.'

Joseph believed Mary and continued on in their relationship, when he could have left, believing she must have betrayed him. This was an obvious sign of Joseph's deep love for Mary and trust in God.

After they traveled to Bethlehem and Jesus was born, imagine the confirmation and security that came when the shepherds arrived and told them about the angels' appearance, announcing the birth of their child—God's child.

Luke 2:19 said, "But Mary treasured all these words and pondered them in her heart."

On the eighth day when they went to present Jesus in the Temple, yet another confirmation—both Simeon and Anna approached them, knowing that the child was Jesus. So many miracles surrounded this amazing couple. (Luke 2:21-38)

Today, no matter where you are, no matter if you're with family or haven't been able to be with family in months, know that the presence of Christ is available to you. Salvation has come. Join the shepherds of old and the angels today who celebrate the birth of our Savior. Merry Christmas!

LORD JESUS, *thank You for coming to earth. Thank You for showing us how to live. Thank You for being obedient to the Father, even to death on a cross. Thank You for rising again to make salvation available to me. I celebrate You today.*

# A HIGHER COURAGE

*Though an army encamp against me, my heart shall not fear; though war rise up against me, yet I will be confident.* —PSALM 27:3

General Robert E. Lee issued this proclamation from the headquarters of the Army of Northern Virginia, August 13, 1863:

> "The president of the Confederate States has, in the name of the people, appointed August 21st as a day of fasting, humiliation, and prayer. A strict observance of the day is enjoined upon the officers and soldiers of this army. All military duties, except such as are absolutely necessary, will be suspended. The commanding officers of brigades and regiments are requested to cause divine services, suitable to the occasion, to be performed in their respective commands. Soldiers, we have sinned against Almighty God. We have forgotten His mercies, and have cultivated a revengeful, haughty, and boastful spirit. We have not remembered that the defenders of a just cause should be pure in His eyes; that 'our times are in His hands,' and we have relied too much on our own arms for the achievement of our independence. God is our only refuge and our strength. Let us humble ourselves before Him. Let us confess our many sins, and beseech Him to give us a higher courage, a purer patriotism, and more determined will; that He will hasten the time when war, with its sorrows and sufferings, shall cease, and that He will give us a name and place among the nations of the earth."

Note that Lee prayed for the war to end; he did not pray to win. Let the fact that great warriors of our nation's history relied upon God and His leadership, inspire you to rely on Him as you lead.

PRINCE OF PEACE, *remind me to pray. When things are good, bad, peaceful, or chaotic, remind me to pray.*

# UNLIKELY ALLIANCE

*Therefore we ought to support such people, so that we may become co-workers with the truth.* —3 JOHN 1:8

At the Arizona-Mexico border, U.S. Border Patrol agents and Mexican federal police officers are training together, sharing intelligence, and coordinating patrols for the first time. This historic partnership is designed to impact the northbound flow of drugs and migrants and the southbound shipments of guns and cash. The crackdown involves hundreds of U.S. and Mexican officers in the border's busiest smuggling corridor.

"We are planting a seed of bi-national cooperation that interests all of us," Commander Armando Treviño, who leads the Mexican federal police contingent in the state of Sonora, said. "We are fighting a common enemy. We are going to work together like friends, like comrades, like brothers."

But the unprecedented effort faces many tough obstacles: violent drug cartels, reluctance to interfere with illegal immigration, and a legacy of corruption.

U.S. and Mexican officers both admit the alliance would have been hard to imagine a few years ago. "It's historic," Captain Eduardo Peña said. "15 years ago, there were bad feuds between the federal police and the border patrol. There was a bad image, the old ugly image of the border patrol. But now there is a new partnership. Good citizens won't dislike this collaboration. Criminals will dislike it."

To get things done in the world, addition and multiplication have always been better than subtraction and division. In your area of service, are there alliances you could form to improve your reach and effectiveness? Is there a line that could be crossed to expand how the public is served? Some boundaries are for protection, while others are just limiting; wisdom is deciding which is which.

LORD OF ALL, *strengthen me to add to any situation I can and stay away from division. Give me courage to respect healthy boundaries, but to cross unnecessary lines.*

# SEEKING SERVICE

*For God did not give us a spirit of cowardice, but rather a spirit of power and of love and of self-discipline.* —2 TIMOTHY 1:7

*"How can we expect our children to know and experience the joy of giving unless we teach them that the greater pleasure in life lies in the art of giving rather than receiving."*

—JAMES CASH PENNEY

*"I don't know what your destiny will be, but one thing I do know: the only ones among you who will be really happy are those who have sought and found how to serve."*

—ALBERT SCHWEITZER

*"Never doubt that a small group of committed people can change the world. Indeed, it is the only thing that ever has."*

—MARGARET MEAD

*"You make a living by what you get. You make a life by what you give."*

—WINSTON CHURCHILL

*"It was character that got us out of bed, commitment that moved us into action, and discipline that enabled us to follow through."*

—ZIG ZIGLAR

Let character, commitment, and discipline be not only qualities of your service, but of your life. Life is not compartmentalized. When we improve in one area, it affects all others. Your service is an extension of you and you of your service.

MIGHTY GOD, *I know that every ounce of character costs me something to gain, so grow me as You see I can handle the next challenge. I commit to You.*

# MILITARY MIRACLES

*Preserve my life, for I am devoted to you; save your servant who trusts in you.*
*You are my God.* —Psalm 86:2

Ripley's Believe It or Not has been around since 1918 and has amassed 20,000 photographs, 30,000 artifacts, and more than 100,000 cartoon panels. Their 80 attractions have attendance of 12 million annually. Ripley has collected many unique U.S. military stories over the years. Here are a few examples: —Lieutenant Commander Robert W. Goehring, aboard the Coast Guard Cutter U.S.S. Duane, was swept off his ship by a mountainous wave during a storm. The ship was turned around to rescue Goehring, when suddenly another giant wave tossed him back on board to safety. —Returning from his 22nd mission over Germany in a Fortress, Joe Frank Jones of the Eighth Army Air Force, had a mid-air collision and fell 13,000 feet in the severed tail section of his plane—without serious injury and no broken bones. —During the Korean War, Lieutenant Fred J. Fees, Jr. continued to direct air strikes after he had been shot through the head. —U.S. Infantryman Donald Morehouse was shot through the chest while fighting in the Korean War. Still, he walked 35 miles to safety, discovering later that the bullet had gone through his heart. —Private William Parker, a U.S. Army soldier fighting in Vietnam, survived after a shot to his head was deflected by the Bible he kept underneath his helmet.

PROTECTOR, *these stories suggest that it is not our time to go until You ordain it. My eternity is in Your hands, but I want today to be in Your hands as well. Lead me.*

# NOT ON MY WATCH

*Incline your ear to me; rescue me speedily. Be a rock of refuge for me, a strong fortress to save me. —PSALM 31:2*

Chicago fire department Lieutenant Steve O'Malley was working on his boat at the 31st Street Harbor on Lake Michigan. He had noticed a couple pushing a stroller with a toddler in it, just before they walked onto the pier.

"It was just a freak thing," said witness Maynard Welch. "The wind was high and the wheels of the carriage were turned toward the lake. The wind just whipped it right in." In moments, the wind blew the stroller and it fell sideways into the water with the 18-month-old still strapped inside, face down.

"I was determined that the baby was not going to go down on my watch," O'Malley said. As the baby's mother screamed for help, the child's father jumped in to rescue his son. O'Malley, who has two adult daughters of his own, followed. "I saw the yellow t-shirt the baby had on and grabbed and pulled the baby up in the stroller," O'Malley said.

The frightened toddler began to cry, but was unhurt. "It gave me goose bumps," said witness Alexandria Hall. "It was a happy ending, but it's an eye opening for everybody with children." O'Malley downplayed his actions, crediting his years of fire department training, "Glad I was here," he said. "Right place and the right time." The grateful parents invited fireman O'Malley to a cookout on their boat.

As we all know, first responders are never off-duty. The natural instinct to save and protect, kicks in when a crisis arises. All over our nation, on any given day, lives are saved, people are protected, and disasters are averted, because God puts the right people at the right place at the right time, just like O'Malley said.

EVER PRESENT GOD, *You have my days planned for me. Help me to walk with You and listen for Your voice, so I can be at Your place in Your time, to serve.*

# AULD LANG SYNE

*As you therefore have received Christ Jesus the Lord, continue to live your lives in him, rooted and built up in him and established in the faith, just as you were taught, abounding in thanksgiving.* —COLOSSIANS 2:6-7

Congratulations! If you're reading this today, it likely means you have completed one full year of daily devotional messages. You have read several hundred Bible verses, some amazing stories of your fellow servants and inspiring people, as well as personal and spiritual challenges and applications.

It is interesting how an infinite God with no beginning or end gave us all stopping and starting points, allowing for new places in life.

If today you have old patterns, unhealthy ways, or excess emotional or spiritual baggage that you are tired of carrying, what a great day to tell it all goodbye and turn over a new chapter in life. You can reflect back over the blessings and beauties of this past year, be grateful for the victories, then let go of the failures and begin anew. God is in the business of new beginnings and fresh starts.

You are ending a year today and about to begin a new one. Take the daily habit of reading God's Word, praying, and taking in spiritual encouragement into the new year. God is ready to speak to You, listen to you, and bless You as You follow Him.

May this next year be your best ever!

ALPHA & OMEGA, *thank You for every blessing this past year. Thank You for the ways You took care of me and provided for me. I commit this new year to You. Keep me close as I follow You.* .